TONY & CHERIE

PAUL SCOTT is a freelance journalist and author. He is a former senior national newspaper executive and has worked in Fleet Street for twenty years. He has contributed to a variety of newspapers and magazines and writes regularly for the *Daily Mail*. This is his second book. His first, *Robbie Williams: Angels and Demons*, was a *Sunday Times* bestseller.

PAUL SCOTT

TONY & CHERIE

Behind the Scenes in Downing Street

PAN BOOKS

First published 2005 by Sidgwick & Jackson

First published in paperback with a new epilogue 2006 by Pan Books
an imprint of Pan Macmillan Ltd
Pan Macmillan, 20 New Wharf Road, London N1 9RR
Basingstoke and Oxford
Associated companies throughout the world
www.panmacmillan.com

ISBN-13: 978-0-330-44006-6
ISBN-10: 0-330-44006-3

1 3 5 7 9 8 6 4 2

A CIP catalogue record for this book is available from
the British Library.

Typeset by SetSystems Ltd, Saffron Walden, Essex
Printed and bound in Great Britain by
Mackays of Chatham plc, Chatham, Kent

Acknowledgements

I would like to thank those people who
made it possible for me to write this book
– you know who you are

I would also like to thank my agent Dorie Simmonds
and the team at Pan Macmillan,
particularly my editor Ingrid Connell,
for their commitment and support

Contents

Prologue

RITUALS

The places change, the rituals remain the same. Amid the striped soft furnishings of a hotel's grand and spacious presidential suite, the prime minister and his wife are deep in conversation. Sitting facing each other, knees touching, his head is bowed forward, but she is fixing him with a steady gaze while she speaks reassuringly in the manner of a boxer's trainer delivering an inter-round pep talk. It is an intimate scene, but not a private one. Around the room swarm the many bit-part players in this expensive production. Downing Street staff, press officers, political advisers and assistants, all have become used to invading the personal space of their bosses. They are no longer embarrassed about marching into the Blairs' bedroom, stepping over Cherie's underwear, which, more often than not, she has unselfconsciously left strewn over the carpet. Prime ministers and their families get used to trading in their privacy when they enter Number Ten.

Before Tony Blair gives a speech or meets another leader the two will sit in a tight huddle. Often it is Cherie who speaks; advising, counselling, briefing. Her words, make no mistake, are not the standard wifely platitudes, nor a spouse's usual straightening of a tie or banal good wishes. This, it is important to remember, is a political marriage unprecedented in British politics. Its bedrock is shared ambition and beliefs. However, the extent of Cherie Blair's influence has long been an issue that New Labour image-makers have sought to downplay.

Before Bill Clinton became president of the United States in 1993 he announced that his wife Hillary, whose political motivation and ambition matched his own, would play an active and significant part in his administration. He described his vision of spousal governance as 'two for the price of one'. Once in the White House, in an unprecedented move, Hillary set up an office in the West Wing and assembled her own staff. She was appointed to head the Task Force on National Health Care, the centrepiece of her husband's legislative agenda. But Congress rebelled over her unelected position. The backlash wrecked the bill and played a vital part in the Republicans recapturing Congress in the 1994 elections. After the debacle Hillary was forced to make a humiliating retreat from the political front line. Given a succession of makeovers in an attempt to soften her image as the Lady Macbeth of the White House, she resorted to giving out her favourite cookie recipes, but the impression that she was pulling the strings behind the scenes remained. In Washington's Beltway the couple will forever scornfully be remembered as 'Billary'.

Watching from the other side of the Atlantic, the architects of New Labour vowed not to make the same mistake. In 1994 Tony Blair, newly anointed leader of the party, and his savvy band of spinners led by former tabloid journalist Alastair Campbell, were only too aware of the unavoidable comparisons between Hillary Rodham Clinton and Cherie Booth. Both were highly intelligent women, successful lawyers and feminists; they were also pivotal influences on their husbands' political thinking. Fresh in their memory, too, was the damage done to Blair's predecessor as party leader, Neil Kinnock, by the speculation that his intelligent wife Glenys exerted considerable influence over him.

The potential for Cherie to provide ammunition to the Blairs' political enemies could not be underestimated. She had, after all, joined the Labour Party before her husband and had stood as a parliamentary candidate. She was known also for the strident and often hectoring expression of her beliefs in private. Above all, she was credited with fashioning the dilettante Blair's thinking from her own political credo. As New Labour set about the task of making itself electable, a strategy was formulated to neutralize the threat. It was decided that, publicly at least, Cherie would become mute. She would do no interviews, never be heard to speak save for her legal submissions at the Bar. The appearances of this woman, whose influence over her husband cannot be overstated, would be confined to spontaneous displays of affection for the cameras: Cherie clinging on to Tony for dear life, arms clasped around his chest, eyes gazing upwards into his in suitably supine adoration.

It is a role that both accepted, although it has not always sat well with the fiercely ambitious Cherie. Long ago, however, she acknowledged that her childhood dream of leading the nation would have to be lived out vicariously through her husband. Early on the Blairs made an agreement that the first to win a seat in the Commons would pursue a political career while the other supported the family financially, and Mrs Blair became the first ever wife of a British prime minister to carry on a high-profile career. Although latterly her attempts at filling the Blair coffers have proved a minefield, for Cherie it has been the price worth paying for power. Soon after her husband took office she quietly began chairing a regular series of meetings inside Number Ten and ministers of the Crown have become used to sitting like spare parts while she holds court. For a premiership continually dogged by accusations of overt cronyism and scorn over its presidential style, Mrs Blair's involvement in the government has been particularly controversial. But while Blair remains in power Cherie's influence over all aspects of policy, even after an unprecedented three Labour victories, endures, not least because as well as valuing her counsel above all others, he continues to be in his wife's debt for the sacrifices she has made on his behalf. While the focus of attention since his accession has remained on the much speculated upon treaty between Blair and Gordon Brown over the leadership, his deal with his wife remains to this day the critical and primary New Labour pact.

*

Surrounded by a phalanx of clipboard-toting staff, the prime minister leaves the suite and emerges into the harshly strip-lit corridor. He gets only a few step before he turns, puts his right hand to his chest and performs a neat 360-degree turn and disappears silently back into the suite, leaving his retinue unsure of whether to follow or remain in the hallway. As they mill about distractedly, he heads into his bedroom, makes for his bedside table and picks up a small grey velvet pouch which he places inside his breast pocket before rejoining them outside. Very few even within his entourage are aware of the existence of this pouch. Certainly, until now, none of his cabinet colleagues have known of it or its significance to him. Inside the pouch are a small piece of red ribbon and a tiny rolled up piece of ragged paper. The ribbon is now so old and threadbare that in places it is barely holding together, but Blair will never venture out without the pouch tucked inside his jacket. Its origin and that of its contents can only be speculated on: some treasured heirlooms from childhood, or keepsakes of his dead mother, perhaps? But the symbolism of these small items is such that no meeting can be held, no decision made without them resting next to his heart. Many frantic dashes have been occasioned from Blair or his wife when he has realized he has inadvertently left them behind.

Of equal significance to the PM is the battered and well-thumbed Bible placed next to his bed wherever he sleeps. He will not travel without it and will read from it at almost any time of the day or night. No hotel Bible will do, no corporate Gideon's dished out from the housekeeping trolley with the yours-to-keep pen and the mini shampoos. According to those close to the prime minister it has, in times of enormous stress during his premiership, when faced with war in Iraq, the Hutton Inquiry or disturbing family problems, provided an emotional and spiritual crutch that has seen him through. Constants in his life are important to Mr Blair. To insulate and protect himself from the travails and chaos of the outside world, he has sought to create his own regimented order on the inside. On trips abroad he will play the same Belinda Carlisle CD over and over again.

Mrs Blair, too, has sought out ways of dealing with the pressures of her position. Secreted in her luggage she keeps a piece of A4 paper on which are drawn strange-looking symbols. Before she and her husband conduct any meeting she will unfold the paper and lay it on a flat surface. She then places a glass of water in the middle of the paper. It is a ritual she repeats faithfully wherever she goes. What she is doing is a tradition, well known to the practitioners of white witchcraft, called casting a circle. The symbols on the paper depict the elements air, fire and earth, with the glass holding the fourth element, water. It is also traditional for the person casting the circle to declare out loud, 'I cast this circle, my circle of power, to be a shield of protection and a boundary between the worlds of men and the realms of the Mighty Ones. I bless thee and consecrate thee, in the names of the Lady and Lord. The circle is cast. So mote it be.'

Casting a circle is a deeply symbolic act in magic. It is said to create 'sacred space' which enables the believer to focus on his or her work by adding 'spiritual vibrations to their spiritual setting'. It is also believed to give a 'protective shield to keep out unwanted influences, allowing only positive energies in'. Those casting a circle are advised to visualize it as 'an iridescent dome of positive, protective energy that extends a few feet above your head, a clear bubble that holds in the energy of your spell'.

Energy is the buzzword for the prime minister's wife and her inner circle, which notably includes her infamous lifestyle guru Carole Caplin. Mrs Blair has a seemingly unquenchable thirst for therapies, regimes and diets of all types, New Age or otherwise. Her approach, say friends, is strictly nondenominational. But while in themselves harmless enough, these fads are at odds with the image that their PR advisers, and it should be said the Blairs themselves, have sought to create. The notion of Britain's first family being like any other hard-working household has been exploited to considerable success; it has formed the core of the strategy to sell Brand Blair to the electorate. Crucial to the vision has been the perception of Mrs Blair as a working mum, juggling her hectic work life with bringing up four children. The fact that she has the time and the money to indulge in unusual treatments is at odds with the carefully crafted picture. Those inside New Labour who have the task of creating and sustaining this Everyman image for Blair have long been concerned to minimize any accusations of crackpotism levelled at his wife. Together with their fervent belief that she should not fall victim to the mistakes made by Mrs Clinton in highlighting the extent of her influence, this is the reason Mrs Blair has submitted herself to a virtual Trappist vow for many years, except for the most highly controlled and vetted situations. Even during her more recent forays into the foreign lecture circuit she has steadfastly continued to draw a veil over the central role she has played in the Blair phenomenon.

The idiosyncrasies of the powerful have been legend throughout history. Like her husband, Mrs Blair has in private sought to fortify herself against the stresses of her very unusual position with the help of a set of superstitions and sacraments. As we shall discover, they are, indeed, very odd. But on such quirks and foibles has many a Camelot been built . . .

1

1994–7: DOUBLE ACT

There is, of course, no room for sentimentality in politics. Moments after hearing the news of the death of John Smith on the morning of 12 May 1994, Cherie Blair was hastily collecting her things at her central London law chambers and preparing to take a cab to Heathrow to meet her husband. Tony, who had heard the news in a car on the way from Aberdeen's Dyce Airport to make a speech in the city, was already planning an early return to Westminster. Cherie was determined that no time must be wasted.

Both were shocked by the sudden death of the Labour leader from a heart attack, but Mrs Blair recognized that it presented her husband with an earlier than planned opportunity to become his successor. As Blair cut short his trip, he gave a television interview outside the Labour Party offices in Aberdeen. 'He had the extraordinary combination of strength and authority, humour and humanity,' he said of his late leader. 'I think the whole country will feel his loss.' It was a classic Blair performance. Though undoubtedly deeply saddened by the news, he had for some time been highly and often openly critical of his boss. Later with admirable candour Blair admitted, 'It was a cataclysmic event because I was in a state of shock and grief over John, who I was very close to and to whom I owed a lot. And then – I mean, you know, whatever anyone says – within moments of these things happening, the world just moves on.' Having spoken to her husband briefly on the phone, Cherie 'appeared dangerously close to hyperventilation', says a friend. 'It was a combination of the real shock over John's death and the realization that they needed to move quickly if they were to engineer a head start for Tony in the obvious battle for the vacant job between him and Gordon Brown.'

Blair, the consummate politician, the assured front man in this spousal double act, was instinctively aware of how his campaign should be pitched publicly. There must be no unseemly overt jostling for the crown while the body of Smith was still warm. Cherie, encumbered by no such public proto-col, was privately fired with vicarious ambition. 'I don't think I have ever seen her so animated,' says one who saw her that day. 'She was nervous and excited at the same time. She was acutely aware, perhaps even more than Tony, that Gordon must not be allowed to steal a march on him. Was it unseemly? Let's be honest, they all – Tony, Cherie and Gordon – felt for John's wife Elizabeth and his three daughters, we all did, but this was about the future not what had gone before.' However, Brown's supporters would later claim that the Blair bandwagon was already rolling as his rival observed a respectful period of mourning.

Indeed, in the car on the way back from Heathrow, the Blairs were busy drawing up their battle plan. As Tony arrived back at Westminster he was already telling those close to him that he would be standing in the election to choose a new Labour leader. For the next three weeks in every major poll Blair was ahead of his rival in the fight for the succession. Cherie was convinced that Blair's family credentials – wife and three young children – was a major asset while Brown was then still single and the subject of speculation about his sexu-ality. 'Both she and Tony were fully aware that the image of Tony as a family man would play well with a wider audience and the Labour Party would have more than an eye to that when choosing their new leader,' says a friend. It was an advantage which was subtly, and at times not so subtly, employed in the following weeks as Blair sought to garner support. But using his family as political capital was to let the genie out of the bottle. Later, as the Blairs' attempts to protect their children from the press became increasingly draconian, it was to leave them open to accusations of double standards.

An early example of how the Blair children unwittingly became political capital to be traded and bartered over came in the spring of 1994 as Blair launched his bid for the party leadership. In his quest for favourable publicity he invited Michael Brunson, then ITN's political editor, to the family's north London home at 1 Richmond Crescent, Islington. The idea was to project Tony Blair as the devoted family man and the piece included shots of him playing football in the local park with his two boys, Euan, then ten, and eight-year-old Nicky. There was also a rare interview with Cherie which contained a gaffe that might go some way to explaining Mrs Blair's enforced silence in the coming years.

'Cherie became sufficiently relaxed to admit quite openly that she was indeed looking forward to the prospect of life at Number Ten Downing Street, should it ever happen,' Brunson revealed in his autobiography, *A Ringside Seat*. 'Even as she was uttering the words I could sense Tony Blair's considerable unease that his wife appeared to be mentally measuring up the curtains for the prime ministerial flat before he had even been elected leader of the Labour Party.' Brunson asked for one last shot in the house and his cameraman filmed Euan playing the piano. But Blair was obviously bothered about his wife's faux pas. 'In the street outside, however, as we prepared to leave, he could no longer contain his anxieties about the whole operation and especially about the interview with Cherie,' said Brunson. 'He quietly suggested a deal – that we should use the pictures of Euan at the piano in return for not using Cherie's remarks about Number Ten.' Brunson agreed and Cherie's remarks were removed.

As Blair developed clear blue water between him and Brown in the polls, the two men met on 31 May for the now infamous dinner in the spartan but chic confines of the Granita restaurant in Islington. The much disputed deal to allow Blair a free run at the party leadership was done. Brown, who had been Blair's political mentor when they were first elected to the Commons in 1983, had, years earlier, tipped his one-time closest friend as a future Labour leader. But he had added two important words: 'after me'. Now he was forced to accept, for the present at least, that the inheritance he believed was his by right would be denied him. Relations between the two men had been strained for at least two years. Brown had been angered by Blair's plan to stand for the deputy leadership of the party when Neil Kinnock and his deputy Roy Hattersley resigned after the 1992 election defeat. His reaction to Blair's naked ambition persuaded Tony to ditch the idea but led Cherie, who had been pivotal in convincing her husband to put himself forward for the position, to harbour a grudge. The Granita deal remains the cause of continuing animosity in both camps. Brown's supporters insist Blair handed him control of domestic policy in a future Labour government and fixed a date in any second term when Blair would stand aside for his ex-ally. Blair's friends insist no date was agreed. But the fallout from the disputed details of the meeting would cast a long shadow over the relationship of the two men who were destined to become the most powerful in the New Labour revolution.

*

There is a common misconception that has the Blairs forever marked down as the Odd Couple. He, after all, is the thoroughly middle-class Oxford-educated public schoolboy from a resolutely respectable family whose career trajectory was mapped out by a father who transferred his own huge political ambitions to his son. By contrast, she is the working-class Scouse girl raised in unusual, straitened circumstances by her paternal grandparents and her mother but without a father. Neat though the theory is, it misses the common threads that run through Tony and Cherie's lives. Both have been shaped by strong women: in Tony's case his mother Hazel, in Cherie's her mother Gale and, perhaps more importantly, her indomitable grandmother Vera, who was responsible for her granddaughter's fervent Catholicism. But their lives have also been defined by men. His, by taking over the mantle of his beloved father Leo's political ambitions when a stroke at the age of forty wrecked his dreams of entering politics and becoming a Tory prime minister; hers by her father, the actor Tony Booth, whose parenting skills trailed a distant last to his prowess as a serial adulterer, feckless husband, alcoholic and unreconstructed hellraiser.

Tony Blair, born on 6 May 1953 in Edinburgh, the middle of three children, was eleven when his father fell ill. Leo, the illegitimate son of theatre performers, had been fostered as a baby and brought up in the Glasgow slums, but after the war he had gone to night school to study law and become a successful barrister and lecturer. After the stroke, which left him unable to walk or speak for three months, he looked to his son to fulfil his dreams of public life. Blair would later say of Leo, 'After his illness my father transferred his ambitions on to his kids. It imposed a certain discipline. I felt I couldn't let him down.' It was, Tony said, 'one of the formative events of my life'. Cherie's ambitions were shaped, in part at least, by more negative emotions. Via her early academic brilliance and subsequent high-flying career as a barrister, she was sending two simultaneous and equally potent messages to her errant father. One was a plea for his attention – a wretched longing to be loved and noticed through her achievements. The other was a metaphorical two fingers, a contemptuous 'Who needs you?' from a child who refused, point blank, to be bowed by his rejection of her. For very different reasons, and despite their different social backgrounds, the Blairs have a shared ambition.

*

Unfair as it might seem, a simple law applies to political spouses: for all their intelligence and success in their own field, they will inevitably remain, in the eyes of the general public, mere appendages. If, as she stepped out at 8.30 on the morning of 21 July 1994, Cherie Blair was relishing her place in the partnership at the head of the party she had been a member of since the age of sixteen, she was blissfully unaware of the comment her stroll in the park near their home with her husband, the newly elected Labour leader, would unleash. What followed would, according to one friend, 'absolutely shatter her'. 'It is no exaggeration to say she was shocked to the core by it. She was suddenly playing a new game, but had no clue as to what the rules were.' In the ensuing days, in column inch after column inch, her hair, make-up, outfit, smile and body language were stripped down, put back together, analysed and thrown open to public debate. Never, it seemed, had a powder-blue ankle-length skirt, boxy jacket and iridescent slippers provoked such a flurry of comment and debate. But the simple sum of those thousands upon thousands of words in the pages of the national press was that Cherie looked a mess. She was clearly not naturally suited to her new role as high-profile political consort. Those who know her well attest that she never had so much as a passing interest in clothes or style.

Mrs Blair's look at the time was typical of many women in those parts of north London which had undergone recent gentrification. They wore the uniform of a moneyed post-hippy set who, while they had acquired by early middle age enviable lifestyles, had seemingly never come by the barest understanding of the visual. The result was an expensive and messy metropolitan melange. And then there was Cherie's hair, an unflattering spiky fringe at the front and what can most accurately be described as a mullet at the back, plus bushy eyebrows, a lack of make-up and a gawky self-consciousness before the cameras. Of those arbiters of style who were wheeled out that week, Mary Spillane, founder of CMB Image Consultants, spoke for the majority. Cherie, she concluded needed an image makeover. And fast. 'She could not even walk properly in the clothes she was wearing,' Spillane told the *Sunday Times.* 'She looked dazed, frozen and ill at ease. They both need to work on the face because their smile looks as though it is glued on. Cherie's smile is almost chilling.' Cherie faced crueller treatment from other commentators. She was ridiculed for her 'letterbox smile', and Ann Leslie of the *Daily Mail* described her as having 'gob-stopper eyes'.

For the team of media spin doctors whose job it was to sell New Labour and more particularly the Blairs, Cherie was a problem. Alastair Campbell, who took over as Blair's spokesman in September, had a background in tabloid journalism that told him she could quickly become a liability. There were already fears that Cherie's political influence over her husband might become damaging in PR terms if the rumours of behind-the-scenes string-pulling were to gain wider exposure. However, both Blairs were aware of the dangers and also knew that Cherie would, after years of concentrating purely on her career and family, have to smarten up her act.

Step forward Carole Caplin. The two women had known each other since the late 1980s, when Cherie, thanks to her burgeoning interest in New Age therapies and homeopathic remedies, had come across Holistix, the company Carole ran for a time with her mother Sylvia. Cherie also knew several fellow barristers who had gone to Carole for fitness training. Caplin, slim, pretty and well groomed, was everything that Cherie was not. She was the girl all the boys at school had wanted to date. Confident about her looks and effortlessly cool, she was the antithesis of the bookworm Cherie had been. Cherie knew she needed help; Carole, she decided, would be ideal for the role of her 'style adviser'. Their friendship, however, and Carole's influence over Cherie and later her husband, would become one of the most bizarre and intriguing aspects of his premiership.

Three months later Blair addressed his first Labour conference as leader amid an atmosphere of expectancy unprecedented in recent times. As the conference opened on 2 October 1994, the slogan 'New Labour, New Britain', devised by Blair's strategist and pollster Philip Gould, adorned the green backdrop of the Blackpool conference hall. Blair would use the speech to announce the rewriting of Clause IV of the party constitution, which bound the party, in name at least, to a belief in public ownership of the means of production. Though Clause IV had long since been an irrelevance as far as Labour Party policy was concerned, Blair's announcement was a signal to the party, and more importantly to the country at large, that he intended to throw off the shackles of socialist dogma and reach out to an electorate with dark memories of Militant and Scargill still relatively fresh in its mind.

It was a speech that immediately went down in political history as the moment Labour again became electable. Blair told his Winter Gardens audience, 'Some of you, I hear, support me because you think I can win. Actually, that's not a bad reason for supporting me. But it isn't enough. I want more.' The faithful loved it. As far as the press was concerned, though, a moment of equal importance had occurred on the north-west coast of England. Even the *Guardian* was moved to push Tony's bravura display aside in favour of concentrating on the change in his wife. 'Have you seen Cherie Blair this week?' wrote Jan Moir. 'What has happened to her? The greatest revelation to emerge from this Labour Party conference in Blackpool has not been the new tax plans for the undeserving rich, but how Tony Blair's wife has transformed herself from an uncomfortable appendage, wearing awkward clothes in the Norma Major tradition, to a svelte political wife like Hillary Clinton. This month's Cherie is wearing tailored miniskirts and sexy leather boots. She looks fabulous; her hair shines like glass . . . we all knew that Cherie was going to have to shape up. None of us expected an executive superbabe and none of us expected quite so much of the Cherie amour routine.'

Cherie came to Blackpool armed with a new and expensive wardrobe: a chic cream silk dress for church on Sunday and a stylish power suit for the conference hall on Monday. She had lost weight thanks to twice-weekly gym sessions at Albany Fitness in London's Regent's Park, where Carole was a fitness trainer. Carole, happy to show off her own figure in public by wearing a leotard under a long coat, also introduced her to hairdresser André Suard. He was a friend of Caplin's who worked at the exclusive Michaeljohn salon in Mayfair. Suard encouraged Cherie to grow her hair longer, gave her a softer look, and dispensed with her weird spiky fringe. With the fresh look came a newfound confidence and the first signs that if she was not exactly easy in her new role, she was easing into it with considerably less stress than had been so painfully evident that summer. Tony and Cherie displayed as well a physical intimacy that was to become a feature of their public appearances: she, like a smitten newly-wed rather than a wife of fourteen years, clutching her husband's jacket, holding his hand and linking her fingers around his chest. It was, observers decided, the body language of a woman intimidated by her environment and the pressures of her new role, attaching herself limpet-like for security to her man. Looking at those pictures again today, there is also something deeply proprietorial about her displays in and around that conference hall. It was as if, rather than displaying her weakness, she was, albeit subconsciously, exhibiting their oneness emotionally, politically and physically; as though not even a chink of light would be allowed to come between them.

If Cherie was feeling pleased with herself, it was a feeling that was not destined to last. On Wednesday that week Alastair

Campbell, at the first major event of his tenure as Blair's spokesman, received a phone call from Stuart Higgins, editor of the *Sun* and an old friend. Higgins wanted to know if a story his paper had been given that Caplin was a former topless model and dancer had any truth to it. Campbell, sensing immediately a PR disaster in the making, said he did not know but would speak to Carole and come back to him. Campbell summoned Carole and put the story to her. She flatly denied it. Campbell rang Higgins back fervently hoping he was about to kill the story stone dead. 'I've spoken to her and she denies it completely,' he told the editor. 'Then why am I sitting here looking at a picture of her with her tits out?' Higgins replied.

The following day's *Sun* front page proclaimed SECRETS OF BLAIRS' GIRL FRIDAY, and featured a nude picture of Caplin in a pose for the cover of soft-porn magazine *Men Only*. Mrs Blair's interest in the more unusual approaches to health care was also aired. Caplin, it was said, had told Cherie to rub Tony's body with scented oils and drink infusions of celery leaves. Carole, who had in the past also posed topless for the *Daily Star*, was said by the *Sun* to be occupying the room next to the Blairs' suite at Blackpool's Imperial Hotel. As Labour Party spinners tried to play down the relationship, the next day it was revealed that she had also been a guest at Cherie's fortieth-birthday celebrations. Both women, it transpired, had been reticent even then about their relationship. It was reported that while Cherie had helped a newspaper's caption writer by supplying names for the photographs of her family and friends at the party, she had clammed up when asked to identify the striking brunette helping her celebrate the occasion.

Caplin's colourful past included being the ex-girlfriend of pop star Adam Ant and membership of Shock, a raunchy 1980s dance group which had toured with Gary Numan. Carole, say friends, is a wannabe who was determined as a teenager to become famous by any means necessary. Other

than her naked poses for photographers, the closest she had
come to celebrity before her trip to the Lancashire seaside was
a fleeting appearance as a courtesan alongside Diana Dors in
the Adam and the Ants video for their number-one single,
'Prince Charming'. Later she worked as a dance instructor with
her mother at Covent Garden dance studio Pineapple and set
up Holistix in 1986 only to see the firm go under in 1992.
Since then she had been providing her own brand of health
and fitness treatments to clients who included actress Felicity
Kendall and the singer Sinitta from the studio of a Kensington
Mews house.

As Blair was spelling out his new vision for Britain the
news that he was linked, albeit through his wife, to a nude
pin-up with a taste for New Age fads was causing red faces
all round. It is reported that so desperate was Campbell to
distance the new leader from Carole, he decreed that a statement should be put out by the party which insisted Miss Caplin
was there as 'Cherie Booth's personal assistant'. It was an
early classic in the tactic of obfuscation that would become
a feature of the New Labour spin machine. The deliberate use
of Cherie's maiden name, which she retained for her legal
work, was designed specifically to shift the focus away from
Blair himself. In a foretaste of the ferocity with which Campbell
would go about his job, a newspaper vendor selling copies of
the *Sun* with its exclusive story about Carole was unceremoniously bundled out of the hotel.

This, surely, was the moment for Campbell to step in and
insist to Cherie that the colourful Carole was a risk to the
carefully constructed Blair image and should be quietly shown
the door. But perhaps Campbell's own rather saucy history as
the one-time 'Riviera Gigolo', his nom de plume while writing
for porn magazine *Forum*, meant he was inclined to be indul-
gent of the youthful excesses of others. Further newspaper
revelations about Carole were to emerge later that month,
including claims she had been a trainer in a 'mind-bending

cult' called Exegesis. This group, which attracted scores of impressionable recruits in the late 1980s with its self-help programme, had been condemned in Parliament as 'puerile, dangerous and profoundly wrong'. Former cult members who had paid £500 for weekend courses came forward to claim that Caplin had been trained to use psychological methods by the group. It was reported that she subjected members to humiliating verbal abuse. One said he had been forced to act like a dog while Caplin shouted at him, 'You're useless. You're a bloody failure. You're not trying.' A female former member also revealed how Carole had encouraged her to write down her sexual fantasises. Despite all this, however, Caplin would be allowed to remain within the Blairs' circle. It was to be a decision that would later rebound on Tony and Cherie with stunning effect.

*

The image of Blair as a man in tune with the real concerns of those with young families was a potent one. In 1994 both he and Cherie believed that being married with three children gave him a distinct advantage over his rival Gordon Brown. Blair would continue to play on this down the years, but the use of his family for political purposes was to become a vexed issue for both Tony and Cherie as well as their detractors. The consequences of the couple's use of their children first emerged five months after Blair's elevation to the leadership of the party when the press reported their decision to send their eldest child Euan to the London Oratory school in Fulham, west London, eight miles from their home. This Roman Catholic school, though officially part of the state sector, had been accused of operating a interview policy for would-be pupils. The Blairs, who have brought their children up as Catholics, chose the school, which had an enviable academic reputation, over up to fifty local schools, including a RC comprehensive close to their home. The news brought a storm of protest from the left of the party and inevitably laid the Blairs open to claims they were selecting their children's education. It left the *Observer* spluttering, 'It is difficult to be precise as to when the comprehensive ideal took hold of the Labour Party, but much easier to date the day it died – 1 December 1994.' Blair, it said, had 'voted with his feet, or, more accurately, those of ten-year-old Euan, and raised a metaphorical two fingers at Labour members who believe the comprehensive system has provided opportunities for working-class children previously denied them, and that it ranks alongside the National Health Service as the most important Labour reform.'

Blair was angry at his son's education being used as a political football while Cherie was of the opinion that they should go on the attack and demand privacy for their son in the face of the newspaper coverage. But ever the politician, Blair was aware that the bridge-building he had been pursuing assiduously with a press previously hostile to Labour could be damaged. On the back foot, he set out his dilemma in a way that many left-leaning parents could identify with. 'I am not going to make a choice for my child on the basis of what is the politically correct thing to do,' he said. 'The Labour Party,' he added, 'is in favour of choice for people and decent schools for people.' He did not add what many of his poorer Islington neighbours might have been thinking: that the high-achieving Oratory, with its record number of Oxbridge entrants, might have been their choice too if they could afford to send their children halfway across London.

But if Blair's decision over Euan's school played out badly with the left, it did him no harm with those he sought to seduce on the right. Through Alastair Campbell he had begun making overtures to Rupert Murdoch's News International group, which includes *The Times*, the *News of the World* and, crucially, Britain's biggest-selling daily paper, the *Sun*. Murdoch, who was becoming increasingly disenchanted with John Major's Tory government, had been impressed with Blair when the two met in the galleried splendour of the Belfry, Anton Mosimann's private dining club in Belgravia. Stuart Higgins of the *Sun* was also susceptible to Blair's charm and sympathetic to his modernizing approach to the party. Blair knew that neutralizing the *Sun* would be key to winning an election, and in the event the *Sun* came out for Blair in an historic switch from the Tories, but his schmoozing was almost scuppered by his wife's tactlessness when, in December 1995, she blurted out to Anne Robinson, herself a former *Sun* columnist, that she wouldn't have the paper in the house.

*

When Cherie was made a QC in April 1995 her workload increased considerably and left precious little time for the family. Tony, one of only a handful of Labour MPs who had taken advantage of concessions to allow parents to leave the Commons earlier, found combining care of the children with his role as party leader hard work. Later he would admit, 'With my older children, if I was looking after them Friday, Saturday and Sunday because Cherie was away doing something, I'd go back to the House of Commons on the Monday and be completely wiped out. It was the toughest thing I ever did.' Life had changed dramatically for the Blairs with Tony's new job. While he still tried to take Euan on the tube to school every morning, he got home a lot later than when he'd been merely a member of the shadow cabinet.

Another unwelcome development in his new role was the press interest in his wife. She was accused of undermining the party by acting as counsel in a series of court cases which, in the past, would have gone under Fleet Street's radar but were now considered legitimate stories. In 1995 she represented a Tory council pursuing poll-tax defaulters. She also acted for Conservative-controlled Brent Council over accusations of racial and sexual discrimination against union members. Fellow barristers sprang to her defence by pointing out that she was subject to the 'cab-rank' rule which means barristers must take on cases regardless of their personal opinion of the client.

More potentially damaging to Blair was the suggestion that his wife was meddling in party politics. Early in 1996 she raised eyebrows by pledging during a speech at a book launch that New Labour would give unprecedented legal rights to gays and the disabled, and she left herself open to comparisons with Hillary Clinton when she publicly nominated Derry Irvine, the friend and legal mentor of both Blairs, for the post of lord chancellor in a New Labour government. The press sensed there was mileage in what was seen as her covert influence. The Tories, too, hoped she might prove Blair's Achilles heel. In June 1996 the Tory chairman Dr Brian Mawhinney put out a press statement entitled 'Cherie Blair in the Dock' which highlighted what were claimed to be political comments by her in the *Times Educational Supplement*. New Labour stuck to the rehearsed tack that Cherie was not a public or political figure but the Conservatives were scoring points and a riled Blair was forced to deny she was his backseat driver. 'Cherie is a successful career woman in her own right and wants to get on and do that,' he said. 'She has no desire to do my job. People should just accept the position for what it is. I think it is a shame that people always have to look for this sort of stereotype – someone is either living in the shadows of their husband or alternatively is trying to run the country through them.'

New Labour set out to improve Cherie's image. In her first major newspaper interview Cherie had talked to the now-defunct *Today* newspaper's Fiona Millar about her style and taste in clothes. Millar could be relied on to toe the party line; she just happened to be the partner of Alastair Campbell and the mother of his children. Cherie, Millar and Campbell decided, must appear less political and more the wife and mother. The strategy culminated with Cherie editing one edition of the women's magazine *Prima*. So, in September 1996, its readers were treated to the eminent QC's interest in knitting and the pressing question, 'How do you produce a meal that's nutritious and interesting in 30 minutes?' The plan might have been to soften Mrs Blair's profile, but the *Prima* episode inadvertently opened up a new set of questions about the exact nature of her role. Simply put, if Cherie Booth was a lawyer who just happened to be the wife of the Labour leader, as Blair himself had argued, what on earth was she doing editing magazines?

2

1997: FIRST FAMILY

If evidence were needed that life would never be the same for Tony Blair and his family, it did not come on that short flight from his constituency in the north-east to Stansted after it had become clear that he was about to lead the first Labour Government in eighteen long years. It did not come with the stage-managed euphoria of that night's celebrations at London's Royal Festival Hall, or even during that first famous appearance on the steps of Number Ten when the new leader and his wife presented a perfect family to an expectant nation. It came instead a day later, on 3 May 1997, after a few snatched hours of sleep had left all concerned wondering if they had, indeed, dreamt the momentous events of the previous day. The family had not, of course, yet moved into Downing Street; they would have to wait until their new home was cleared of the last possessions of the outgoing premier John Major. They were awoken on that Saturday morning at their Richmond Crescent home by the prolonged sound of banging on the front door. Mrs Blair, still half-asleep, padded downstairs to see who it was. Opening the large black front door, she was blinded briefly by the spring light flooding into the rather gloomy hallway of the Blairs' Victorian end-of-terrace home. On the doorstep was a policeman with a florist who had arrived to deliver two congratulatory bowls of mixed blooms to the new first family.

It was the sudden, simultaneous whirring of a hundred camera motor drives that sparked a sharp and unpleasant return to the land of the living. Assembled outside the garden gate was a horde of photographers, TV news crews and reporters. Their pictures were to become one of the defining images of the election and its immediate aftermath. They did not, however, make happy viewing for Mrs Blair over the cornflakes the following morning. Her hair, still caked in yesterday's styling mousse, had contrived during the night to rearrange itself in the manner of a cartoon character which has found itself the victim of a prolonged and particularly high-voltage electric shock. Meanwhile, her eyes, rimmed black by the make-up she had failed to remove before falling exhausted between the sheets, gave her the look of someone auditioning for the role of Siouxsie Sioux in a tribute to 1980s Gothic rockers Siouxsie and the Banshees. Clutching desperately at the front of the short and flimsy blue-grey nightie she had slept in, Cherie beat a horrified and hasty retreat behind the door. But it was too late. The off-guard moment, so adored by Fleet Street picture editors, had been caught for posterity. It was a scene echoed two years later to comic effect in the Hugh Grant film *Notting Hill* and for Mrs Blair it was a moment that will forever be remembered with a shiver of mortification. But it was a salutary lesson that from here on in the private life the Blairs had enjoyed would be opened up evermore to public scrutiny.

*

Three days earlier, victory had been in sight. With twenty-four hours of campaigning left, all polls were indicating a substantial Labour majority but Tony Blair remained nervous and strangely downbeat. His mood throughout that 1997 campaign had been resolutely pessimistic. Each new opinion poll or focus group, with its ever-increasing evidence that a landslide could be expected, seemed to have the reverse of the expected effect on the party leader. It was as if the nearer the prize came, the greater he would feel its loss if it was denied him. In truth, the atmosphere at Labour's Millbank HQ was of a group of people seemingly unable to accept that victory would soon be theirs. They had been gripped as one by a fear of hubris: that even allowing themselves the thought of victory might cause fate to step in and remove it at the last second. This feeling was evident in no one more than Blair himself. The spectre of four successive defeats by the Tories loomed large. Particularly fresh in the memory was Neil Kinnock's humiliation in 1992, when a series of rogue opinion polls led to the premature triumphalism of his party's pre-election 'victory parade' in Sheffield a week before the vote which saw John Major returned to office.

On the last day of campaigning, when Tony Blair's battle bus left Millbank and edged into Whitehall offering him a view of the gates to Downing Street, Blair could not bring himself even to look. Later that day, he attended a primary school in Middlesbrough with his wife. As the children belted out the hymn 'Jerusalem', accompanied by Mrs Blair, she shot him a meaningful look as they sang about not ceasing from mental fight and the sword not sleeping in the hand. He refused to meet her eye. On 1 May as the country began voting the Blairs flew up to Myrobella, their rather ugly Victorian house in his Durham constituency of Sedgefield. Blair, according to one who spent the day at the house, was 'a complete mess'. 'He was a nervous wreck, obsessed that something would go wrong. At this point there was no denying the pressure had got to him.' Once more the Blair children were called into action. Euan, Nicky and Kathryn, who spent most of the day apparently nerve-free, were herded together in the middle of the morning to traipse across the field at the side of the house and accompany their father as he went to cast his vote. This was a prime photo opportunity for the Blairs and Cherie was quick to bark an instruction to 'smile for the cameras' to her brood.

When they arrived back at the house even the children began to pick up on their father's nervousness. Cherie, who had arranged for a chef to come to the house to cook for those who would spend the day with them, could think of nothing more exciting than cheese and pickle sandwiches when asked what she wanted to eat. Tony's father Leo and his second wife

Olwen, who had been invited for the day, attempted to ease the tension by playing with the children. Tony, having spent much of the morning discussing with his chief of staff Jonathan Powell and Alastair Campbell how the reins of power would be handed over to New Labour, went for a lie-down in the garden, hoping that the warm sunshine would calm his nerves. It was a call that afternoon from Philip Gould that finally convinced him his worst fears would not be realized. Gould told him that a BBC exit poll was giving Labour a ten-point lead over the Tories. By 10 p.m., as the polls closed, Tony told Cherie that he thought Euan and Kathryn, who were still up and watching the television coverage, should go to bed like their brother Nicky. Cherie told him, 'I think it's a night they'd like to remember.' Blair's reply, 'Fair enough, it looks as though we're going to make it,' was the first time that day he had allowed himself to voice his hopes. It was a sign, perhaps, of the pessimism that Blair had been responsible for during the whole campaign that thirteen-year-old Euan felt compelled to chide his father with, 'You can't take anything for granted, Dad.'

In the car on the way to the count Tony was quiet, almost tearful. As it dawned on him that he was, at forty-three, about to become his nation's youngest prime minster for 180 years, he thought of his mother Hazel, who had died of throat cancer as he finished university. Accepting the applause following his re-election as local MP he told the audience, 'All that could make this complete was that my mother was still here.' Within the hour, John Major had phoned him to concede defeat and Blair told his supporters, 'You know me; I am never complacent, but it's looking very good.' It was only after they had boarded the private plane, hired by the party, to head back south that the full extent of the landslide began to emerge. As Tony worked on the speech he would give to the party once back in London, Cherie took his hand and told him, 'Now be strong and realize what a great opportunity this is for you. Make the most of it.' But, despite the success, his mood remained strangely flat. Later he would admit, 'Although it may sound absolutely ridiculous, all I could feel was a great sense of anticlimax. I felt that it was such an extraordinary thing to happen to me. While others did the celebrating I really felt the need to tell myself how very fortunate I was, and "Don't you damn well blow it." ' Later that day, it took nearly ten minutes for the Blairs to walk the hundred yards from the security gates at Whitehall to Number Ten. More than 1,000 supporters hand-picked by Millbank lined the pavements in the sunshine to welcome the new prime minister to his new home. As Tony plunged his arms into the mass of the ecstatic party faithful to grasp their outstretched hands, Carole Caplin and her mother Sylvia followed a few paces behind. They had travelled in the Blairs' motorcade and would enter Downing Street before any cabinet minister in the new government.

*

It is natural to suppose that those who lead the nation are used to a grander and more comfortable existence than the rest of us. To the public Number Ten Downing Street is that big black shiny door; we imagine that beyond it must be a world equally as splendid as that imposing entrance. Tony and Cherie had little idea of what to expect when they became the latest tenants of the historic address on 2 May 1997. Tony had been in Number Ten only once before, when he was invited to an official dinner with Bill Clinton the previous November. Stepping inside for the first time as leader, he could still hear the crowds which had greeted them as the family arrived and stood on the steps in that memorable image that came to sum up the nation's hopes for a new era. Tony and Cherie had already decided that the small flat above Number Ten would be impossible for a family of five. Gordon Brown, who as the new chancellor would have expected to take up residence in the five-bedroom Number Eleven flat, had generously agreed he would do a swap with the Blairs and take the smaller one.

So, it was with a real sense of excitement that Tony, Cherie and the three children, having passed through the interconnecting doors between Numbers Ten and Eleven, climbed the stairs to view their new home. It was not, however, a pleasant surprise. 'It was an absolute dump', says a source. 'There was a certain amount of jaw-dropping when they went inside the Number Eleven flat.' To begin with the family was hit by the smell of stale cigar smoke – a house-warming present from former occupant Kenneth Clarke. But that was just the first in a succession of unpleasant surprises as they surveyed their new abode. 'I have to say,' the source adds, 'that it was a thoroughly nasty experience for them. You could see the huge grins, that were on the faces of the whole party when they entered, gradually slip to be replaced by expressions of complete incredulity. The place was quite large, but totally shabby. The carpets were filthy and old. The kitchen consisted of an ancient cooker, a grill and no more than three cupboards which were made of plastic and Formica. But worse was the main bathroom, which I can only describe as horrific.'

Tony did his best to put a brave face on things but, says a friend who saw the family that day, 'It put something of a dampener on it for them. I think in their naivety that they were expecting something quite lavish.' It should be pointed out, however, that while many of the acquaintances the Blairs had made during Tony Blair's rise to the political summit lived impressively – their friends at the time, the millionaire novelist Ken Follett and his wife Barbara, regularly treated the Blairs to dinner in the palatial surroundings of their mansion in Cheyne Walk, Chelsea – their own home in Islington was not exactly a candidate for a *Homes and Gardens* feature. A tall Victorian house on four levels, it was narrow and dark inside with only two rooms per floor. Furnished taste-free with ornate swag curtains, it too had seen better days. 'The bathroom was falling apart and they'd let things slide,' says a regular visitor at the time. 'They were both working hard and couldn't spare the time to keep on top of things.' Cherie, snowed under as she was with work and her young family, did, however, come up with a novel, if flawed, approach to time-saving.

One friend reports how Cherie has been known at Christmas and birthdays to recycle unwanted presents by simply rewrapping them in the same paper in which they were delivered. She has not always been careful, however, to remember who sent the items in the first place. One friend delights in telling how she was presented with the present she had given to Cherie the previous year, complete with the same wrapping paper and bow. Having impeccable manners, she not only accepted graciously, but even wrote a card to Cherie thanking her for her 'touching generosity and good taste'.

Housework often came well down the list of priorities for the Blairs. Another visitor to their Islington home says:

It was a nice enough house, but it was always such a tip. For all her talents, Cherie is a total slattern. The house was in a constant mess: kids' toys abandoned everywhere, her legal briefs strewn on the floor. It was a bomb site. She has the capacity to live in a state of total disarray. She is forever searching frantically for things she has lost amongst the clutter. Everything about Cherie is messy, even her handwriting is a scrawl. Tony is slightly better, but with Cherie around keeping the place tidy is a losing battle. But even they were amazed at just how decrepit Downing Street was. The state rooms are fabulous, but the living quarters were awful when they moved in.

One pleasant surprise as they toured Number Ten for the first time was the discovery of a bottle of champagne left by the outgoing John Major with a note: 'It's a great job – enjoy it.'

Despite the state of the Number Eleven flat, they could clearly no longer stay at Richmond Crescent. For one thing, the Blairs were aware that the constant coming and going of TV news crews, radio cars and Fleet Street journalists had already become an inconvenience to their neighbours; now there would be a substantially increased police presence too. But, crucially, they had been told by Special Branch officers that the house represented a major security risk because it was easily approached from the street and had only a tiny backyard which adjoined those of other houses. In a interview she had given days before the election Cherie said, 'As far as I'm concerned we are a family. Wherever Tony goes we all go. If that means Downing Street then so be it.' It was to be one of the very few thoughts she would share with the country during the campaign. Only American viewers were allowed to witness an interview recorded in February for the CBS programme *Sixty Minutes*.

It had not been a performance, Labour spin chiefs concluded, likely to enthuse a British audience. Seated on the sofa at Richmond Crescent, Cherie looked ill at ease and came across as suspicious and even slightly resentful of her husband's success. The last joint interview the Blairs had done was with Barbara Amiel of the *Sunday Times* when Tony was shadow home secretary. This had not been an unqualified success either. While Amiel had described Blair as 'the shape of Tory worries to come', interviewing Cherie, she declared, was 'like pulling teeth'. Bubble-wrapping Mrs Blair for the election was a priority for Campbell and Blair himself, although those close to Tony say that he had to 'tap dance very carefully around her' to persuade his wife that her gagging was for the good of the party. 'The Tories were on the attack over her and Alastair was very definite about it,' says one. 'He knew Cherie could be used as a battering ram. He is very blunt about most people, but I never heard him criticize Cherie at that point. He was very loyal to them both. He respected Cherie and, even though it ran against every instinct she has to play the silent wife hanging on to her husband's arm, she knew it was essentially a sensible plan.'

But in the *Sixty Minutes* interview Cherie let slip the real competitiveness she feels towards her husband. It dates back to when they found themselves pupils to London-based barrister Derry Irvine QC in 1976. Cherie, who came top in the country in that year's Bar examinations, was angry when Irvine later took on a second trainee barrister. The new boy was not as academically gifted as his rival, but he was charming, witty and sharp. His name was Tony Blair. 'It didn't please me at all because I was assured I would be the only one,' Cherie told her TV interviewer. While she worked through her lunch hours in the library, Tony would go to the pub with his colleagues. But when, after a year, Irvine decided he was going to keep only one of his pupils on, Cherie was furious to be told it was Blair. The rivalry between the two had not, however, stood in the way of romance. Cherie was gradually charmed by her affable fellow junior. A rapier legal mind is one thing; the ability successfully to hold a balloon between the legs is quite another. It was the latter that ignited the passion between the two when they had to pass a balloon from one to the other using only their knees during a game at the Christmas party of a legal friend. The next day Irvine took his two students to lunch at an Italian restaurant called Luigi's. Blair later reminisced, 'I can still remember it. It was the longest lunch I've ever had. Cherie and I were still there in the evening and ended up having dinner too. Derry tactfully made his excuses in the middle of the afternoon, but I can't say that I noticed him going.' Of Cherie, he remembered, 'I thought, and still think, she was one of the most unusual and interesting people I've met. I was attracted to her looks of course, but also she was so different. She's a one-off, unusual and totally her own person.'

Even so, Cherie would still take time to win over. 'She wasn't quite sure whether I was what she was looking for,'

Blair added. 'She felt I'd had it easy, which in a way I hadn't.' Notwithstanding her reservations, the relationship developed apace despite the strain of Irvine's decision only to keep on Blair. For an ambitious student whose academic results were beyond compare, it was a substantial kick in the teeth. Irvine, a formidable power broker in the chambers, would later imply that Cherie had been made an offer elsewhere but the truth was that he had decided that he would only need the services of the dynamic Blair. Cherie found a place in another set of chambers, but she was stung by the rejection. While it has gone into folklore that Blair was the lesser lawyer, the shrewd Irvine is convinced of his talents. 'Tony obviously enjoyed himself more at university,' said Irvine. 'But he was a lawyer of the highest intelligence. He has a remarkable ability to sift through a mass of material, define the issues and come up with answers.'

The couple's wedding in March 1980 was a simple quiet affair with the bride in a cream dress she bought at the Liberty's sale. She was, however, insistent on one rigid pre-nuptial condition: her husband, she decreed, would smoke his last ever cigarette before the service. Fittingly, at the reception Irvine made a speech in which he described himself as 'Cupid QC'. The couple moved in with Cherie's friend Maggie Rae in Hackney before finding their first home nearby and both became committed members of the Hackney South Labour Party.

Blair was undoubtedly hugely influenced by the lifelong socialism of his new wife, but it was his time at Oxford that can take the credit for the first dawning of his political and spiritual beliefs. Prominent in this process was Peter Thomson, an Australian priest and mature student who, like Blair, attended St John's College. Thomson introduced Blair to another Australian, Geoff Gallop, also at St John's, on a Rhodes scholarship. Gallop, who at the time was a committed revolutionary Marxist, went on to be premier of Western

Australia. While Gallop was a key player in student politics, Blair refused to become involved. He was, however, deeply influenced by his friendship with Thomson. The priest introduced Blair to the work of Scottish philosopher John Macmurray, who had been credited as an original thinker in the 1930s but had since fallen out of favour. Macmurray's theme was 'community' and the relationship between individuals and society. His teachings, which had troubled few librarians in the intervening years, found themselves dusted off when Blair cited him as a primary influence just before his election to the Labour leadership in 1994. Hand in hand with his conversion to the arguments of Macmurray came Blair's interest in religion. With Thomson the midwife to his spiritual birth, Blair began to attend the college chapel and was confirmed in the Church of England in 1973 during his second year at Oxford. Religion, said Blair, 'became less of a personal relationship with God. I began to see it in a much more social context'.

In Cherie he found a kindred spirit. Both newly-weds were politically ambitious and, encouraged by Irvine, who had unsuccessfully stood in Hendon North for Labour in 1970, started to look for parliamentary seats to fight. In 1983 Cherie was chosen by Labour to contest the safe Tory constituency of Thanet North in Kent. She came a poor third behind the Conservatives and the SDP, while Tony, who a year earlier had fought and lost a by-election in true-blue Beaconsfield, won the traditionally Labour seat of Sedgefield. Years later Cherie is still prickly about their differing election fortunes. It was 'pure chance', she would later insist, that Tony got into Parliament before her. She clearly resented her position in the shadows. It was with clear regret that she was quoted as saying, 'I started out as the daughter of someone, now I am the wife of someone. I will probably end up being the mother of someone.'

*

If Downing Street was not the lap of luxury the Blairs had expected, their official country residence Chequers was little better. While the official rooms of the grand mansion in the Chiltern Hills contain a beautiful art collection, those who have visited the Blairs there say the private quarters remain dated and shabby. 'The part of the house where the Blairs live is straight out of the 1970s: very tacky with ghastly wallpaper and avocado bathroom suites. Lifestyles of the rich and famous it ain't,' says one visitor. Despite the decor, Tony has loved the house since the first time he visited. Every Friday evening when he is in Britain he will be driven down the A40 from Downing Street to enjoy the country air and the privacy of the vast Buckinghamshire estate. Cherie, however, dislikes the place. 'I am afraid her critics from the hunting community are right about one thing,' says a friend. 'Cherie hates the countryside. She is a city girl. Whenever the countryside is mentioned, Cherie always says "Oh, give me concrete any time."'

There were, of course, perks to the new job. In June Blair chartered Concorde at a cost of £250,000 to fly him and Cherie to Denver for a meeting of the G7, the seven largest industrial nations. In a spot of horse-trading which owed something to Del Boy Trotter, it was reported that he offset much of the cost by flogging seats on the flight to journalists at £3,700 a time. But his wife was about to come close to causing an international incident. When they arrived in Colorado for the summit they were accompanied by Mrs Blair's hairdresser André Suard, who was reported to be getting paid £2,000 from Mrs Blair's own pocket for the trip. Suard, a flamboyant Parisian, was already a regular fixture at Number Ten, and to this day he can be seen arriving at Downing Street every morning without fail, even when Cherie has no official engagements. Indeed, Mrs Blair's insistence that she cannot be without the colourful Suard is the subject of a running joke among staff at Number Ten. One says, 'You'd think after watching the guy dry her hair a thousand times, that she might have picked up how to do it herself by now.'

But the prime minister's wife had quickly become used to having her retinue around her. She enjoyed the attention of Carole Caplin, Suard, Caplin's mother Sylvia and Fiona Millar, who had given up journalism to work for her. Those close to Mrs Blair noticed the change: 'It was subtle,' says one, 'but Cherie developed something close to regality. She came to expect more, was more demanding and aware of her position. She took very quickly to people doing things for her.' Two years earlier, as she struggled to come to terms with the demands of her new role as the wife of the Labour leader, she had buckled under the pressure. Self-conscious about her looks and her lack of dress sense, she had lost so much weight that rumours circulated that she had become anorexic. This was not true, but she was, say insiders, 'lost for a while', while her plight had come to the attention of Neil and Glenys Kinnock, who went out of their way to be supportive.

By the time she touched down in the US for the first time as Britain's unofficial first lady, Cherie was much more confident. Her new assertiveness stretched to throwing a tantrum in the couple's suite at Denver's Marriott hotel as the G7 leaders and their wives prepared for a gala dinner in a vast hall normally used for cattle shows and rodeos. The event, which had as its theme a celebration of all things American, featured performances by Chuck Berry and Kool and the Gang, as well as a meal including buffalo and rattlesnake. The sticking point for Mrs Blair, however, was the outfit her hosts had planned for the evening's merriment. Lying on her bed at the hotel she found a cowboy outfit and Stetson, both carefully chosen so they would be a perfect fit for the PM's wife. But one look at the denim shirt and ten-gallon hat and Cherie 'went ballistic'. 'She made it plain in no uncertain terms that there was as much chance of her slipping on the outfit as there was of her streaking through the White House,' says a source. 'Her hairdresser was saying, "There's no way she's wearing this. It's not happening."' Her husband, sensing a diplomatic emergency, tried in vain to talk his wife into agreeing to wear the fancy dress, but she was having none of it. Blair did, in fact, attend the party in the jeans and check shirt the Americans had chosen for him, but as the other politicians and their wives tucked into their prairie food at the hoedown, Cherie, her regal air intact, sashayed in wearing a long black evening gown and blue shawl.

It was sign of the already warm relationship with the Clintons that no offence was taken by their hosts. The couples had met the previous month in London and hit it off instantly. Both men were would-be musicians, Blair as an adequate guitar player and Clinton a keen saxophonist. They had also both attended Oxford in the 1970s. As lawyers and significant influences on their respective husbands Cherie and Hillary had much in common too, but it was most of all a meeting of minds for the two first ladies over the sea bass, salad, lemon tart and berries supplied by chef Anton Mosimann at the Number Eleven flat. Another dinner, at the Pont de la Tour restaurant next to Tower Bridge, went on so long that Clinton's staff had to delay the president's plane.

A Blair court insider says of those first meetings,

It wasn't just a matter of them being *simpatico* politically, they genuinely warmed to the Clintons from day one. I remember that everyone was very excited because we had been in office less than a month and there was an element that we were all, the Blairs included, a little bit star-struck by them. But Clinton is a master at putting you at your ease. In person he has a slow effortless charm that is completely seductive. What was, and is, amazing about the guy is that he was just as adept at being charming to the waiters as he is to his fellow leaders. The next time we saw him in London, I was amazed that not only did he come over to say hello, he had also remembered my name. Yes, there was an large element of the showman about him, but he did it all so incredibly well.

The Blairs, still coming to terms with the new levels of security surrounding them since coming to office, were 'flabbergasted' at the entourage of secret service men that arrived with Clinton. 'It was unbelievable,' says a New Labour source. 'Tony joked that there was no room in Number Ten for anyone else once Clinton's guards had all filed in. The contrast between our Special Branch and the US Secret Service is amazing. Their guys are all huge, well over six foot and built like linebackers. They wear dark suits, talk into little radios in their sleeves and actually wear those wraparound shades indoors.' The source adds,

In Florence once at a heads of government conference Tony sat in the airport and watched all the planes take off: Gerhard Schroeder's, the French contingent's. Then Clinton's plane appeared: not one, but two Air Force Ones. He had two 747s so one can be used as a decoy. There were hundreds of people with him, twenty-three limos and two helicopters that take off on either side of the plane. A helicopter flew him the few yards from the airport building to his plane. But you never know which plane he is on because he has a lookalike who walks out of the terminal building at the same time and you only ever see the backs of their heads. The whole thing is so impressive. Tony was open-mouthed the first time he saw the whole production. Frankly, it sticks in his craw. I remember we chartered a little plane for Tony and it had this old sort of seat that turned into a bed, a bit like the sort of thing you find in an ancient old caravan. But when the press got to hear about it he was slaughtered for wasting taxpayers' cash. We really are the poor relation.

The Clintons might have been honoured guests, but other unfortunates were not so welcome inside the portals of Downing Street. Within months of taking office Blair was engulfed in a scandal that would have brought down an older and less popular government. The question was not that of the £1 million the Labour Party had taken from Formula 1 boss Bernie Ecclestone as he negotiated to have motor racing exempted from the government's proposed ban on tobacco advertising; rather it was the case of the missing person. Disappeared presumed dead.

Humphrey the Downing Street cat had vanished from Number Ten suspiciously soon after Labour came to power. There were dark rumours that the moggy had been killed off as an unwanted legacy of eighteen years of Tory rule. Conservative MP Alan Clark, a former minister who had grown fond of Humphrey at cabinet meetings, threatened to table a Commons question demanding that the government confirm whether he was dead or alive. Morning lobby briefings were dominated by questions about him and, when the story made the national TV news, Downing Street went into panic mode. Their insistences that Humphrey was alive and well were met with demands for evidence from a sceptical press. Alastair Campbell's press office went on the offensive. He arranged for a television news crew and a Press Association photographer who knew Humphrey and could therefore verify his identity to be escorted to a secret address in south London to where Humphrey had been retired. Cue happy pictures of said cat licking his paws providing the perfect 'And Finally' for Sir Trevor MacDonald on that night's *News At Ten*.

'The whole family was sorry that Humphrey's failing health meant he had to retire from the hectic pace of life in Downing Street,' said a spokesman. 'We are delighted that he has settled so well in his new home.' But was that the full story? Claims of a plot against poor Humphrey have circulated inside Number Ten ever since, but who could have demanded his departure in that first reshuffle? Papers released in early 2005 failed to shed light on the mystery. But for the first time the truth can be told! In fact Humphrey's exit visa was signed the day Mrs Blair posed for pictures with him after moving into Number Ten. The reason? 'She is completely allergic to animal fur. She came out in blotches, her eyes were red and streaming and her nose began running straightaway,' says a source. And what of Blair's spokesman's claim that the family are animal lovers. 'Cherie can't stand animals,' says a friend. 'As soon as the pictures of her were taken with him, she said she wanted "that bloody thing" out.' So Humphrey was given his marching orders as Number Ten began the spinning. Far from the black and white long-haired moggy getting old and needing a quieter life, official Whitehall papers say that Humphrey, who arrived as a stray in the Cabinet Office in 1989, was only nine when the Blairs moved in, hardly old for a cat. And to add to the intrigue, as Blair began his 2005 election campaign, a spokesman said Humphrey's official minder had not seen him for seven years and could not say if he was alive or dead. In fact it was announced in March 2006 by Downing Street that the cat had recently passed away. Humphrey was, it seemed, just another long-forgotten political casualty.

*

Blair's 179-seat majority might have been the largest of any party since the war, but there remained a mood of scepticism about New Labour within large sections of the population. It said much for Blair's leadership in those first months of his premiership that the spirit of optimism came for many not with the announcement of the election result, but with the passing of the weeks afterwards. If every prime minister is remembered for one moment in history, Blair will be for his assured handling of events after the death of Diana, Princess of Wales, on 31 August, four months after his election victory. In the days that followed the tragedy he would demonstrate how he was able, in the early days of his office, to judge perfectly the mood of the nation. Not only would he become in the process the most popular peacetime leader in living memory, he would save the Queen from a crisis of her own making that threatened to divide her from her nation.

Blair was given the news of Diana's death at his constituency home Myrobella by Angus Lapsley, a private secretary on duty at Number Ten. He called Blair at 2 a.m., but the prime minister was sleeping and didn't answer the phone. Lapsley had been told that the Mercedes carrying Diana and her boyfriend Dodi Fayed had crashed in the Place de l'Alma in Paris. He decided the news was urgent enough to get his boss out of bed so contacted Blair's personal protection officer, who was stationed outside the house, and asked him to go in to wake up the PM. Lapsley told Blair that Diana was seriously injured and Fayed probably dead. Blair told Lapsley to find out as much as he could and keep him informed. An hour and a half later Lapsley was back on the phone. He had spoken to the British ambassador in Paris, Michael Jay, and been told the princess had died thirty minutes earlier in hospital. In London Alastair Campbell had received the same news and was on the line to Blair within minutes. Blair later told friends that the next few hours passed in a haze of shock and unreality.

Blair's every instinct told him that this would be a landmark event in the recent history of the nation and that there would be an outpouring of public grief on a scale barely seen before. But above all his antennae told him that whatever happened in the hours and days that were coming, he had to be at the centre of it. His words, later that morning outside St Mary Magdalene church in his constituency, both set and predicted the mood of grief that overtook the country. Wearing a borrowed black tie and cufflinks, a pale-looking Blair was asked by ITN's Michael Brunson, 'On this sad day, is there anything you would like to say, Prime Minister?' Blair's reply, crafted with the help of Campbell and memorized in the living room of Myrobella that morning, was masterly in its melding of real emotion, mawkish sentiment and pure political profiteering.

'I feel like everyone else in the country today, utterly devastated,' he replied solemnly.

> Our thoughts and prayers are with Princess Diana's family, in particular her two sons, her two boys. Our hearts go out to them. We are, today, a nation in shock, in mourning, a grief that is so painful. How many times shall we remember her in how many different ways, with the sick, the dying, with children, with the needy? With just a look or a gesture that spoke so much more than words, she would reveal to all of us the depth of her compassion and her humanity. She was the People's Princess and that is how she will remain in our hearts and our memories forever.

The phrase 'People's Princess', though used before about Diana, touched such a chord it was to become her epitaph. Watching Blair deliver those rehearsed lines now without the benefit of the zeitgeist is to lose the effect. This is, perhaps, a consequence of the passing of time or, more probably, a familiarity with the stock Blairisms: the overlong pauses, the theatrical hand gestures, the 'I feel your pain' haunted look. It is not possible to see that performance now, or the drama-student overplaying of his Corinthians reading at her funeral, as anything other than mildly absurd, but in a week that began with a nation gorging itself on grief and ended with a retread requiem, originally penned for a three-times-married alcoholic actress, and performed by a bewigged pop singer, Blair's eulogy was perfect in its prescience.

In comparison, new Tory leader William Hague's public response to Diana's death was dignified, restrained and proportionate – and an utter disaster. Hague might as well have called it a day there and then, saved himself the trouble and toddled off back into oblivion. Like the royals, Hague was guilty of seriously miscalculating the temperature of the nation. In those six tumultuous days between Diana's death and her funeral the House of Windsor was gripped by an inertia that at times looked set to destroy it. How ironic that into the void should move New Labour, populated as it was by key players like Campbell and Cherie Blair whose dislike of the monarchy was said to be so deep-seated. As hysteria overtook the country, the Queen, whose curt and cold original statement after the tragedy barely concealed her dislike of her former daughter-in-law, resolutely distanced herself from the febrile atmosphere by remaining on her Scottish estate at Balmoral. But by now the 'Princess's People', whipped up by the tabloids, were demanding that the monarch return to London, lower the flag at Buckingham Palace to half mast and submit herself to the displays of grief her subjects found came so much more easily to them. Her delay incensed the mob sufficiently for Blair to believe a wave of republican sentiment was in danger of being unleashed. At this point, and with the backing of Prince Charles who had more correctly judged the public mood, Blair made the Queen a gift of his own unique personal standing in the eyes of the nation and moved into the breach. For the rest of the week Downing Street took over from the Palace the strategy for retrieving the situation and limiting the damage already done to the Queen. In the game of brinkmanship with her people, Her Majesty blinked first and agreed to return to the capital. For the next week Campbell and Blair's advisers Hilary Coffman and Anji Hunter chaired meetings at the Palace. Under pressure from Number Ten it was agreed the flag would be lowered and plans for a private funeral scrapped. The Queen would also go on television on Friday evening to address her nation and pay tribute to Diana. Her eventual script, approved by Number Ten, included the line 'speaking as a grandmother', inserted by Campbell.

But why did Blair step in to save the Palace? Would there

not have been amusement at the plight of the monarchy even inside his own home? The answer, says one close to him, is threefold. Blair the pragmatist had no desire to see the established order of the country disrupted; that would be of no benefit to the nation or his government. Nor did he wish to see the Queen, whom he liked, damaged. Finally, says a senior source, it appealed to his ego. 'Bailing out the royals was an enormous power trip for all involved. How many prime ministers, how many governments can demonstrate themselves to be more popular than the monarch? It put him in a unique position.'

Given the obvious service New Labour had done the Crown, it might be supposed that the Blairs would be welcomed with open arms by the royal family on their subsequent annual visits to Balmoral.

*

All in all, it had not been the most comfortable of nights. The bedroom was cold and damp, the ancient plumbing in the bathroom clunked and groaned in irregular and alarming spasms and Cherie Blair had lain awake in terror of a large and ugly statue at the foot of her bed, which, in her sleep-deprived state, had taken on a ghoulish menace. Now, as she and her husband were enjoying at last the blissful slumber denied them for most of the previous long hours, they were awoken with a horrible start. Yards away in her suite of rooms at the royal family's Scottish estate, the Queen Mother was performing her daily Deeside ritual, instructing a lackey to fling open the windows of the castle so best to enjoy her 6 a.m. wake-up call. Outside stood her favourite bagpiper delivering his daily ear-piercing morning serenade with unbridled gusto. It was to be the first of many nasty surprises in a stay that Mrs Blair would later describe as 'too unbelievably horrible for words'. As those who know her well will attest, the prime minister's wife is most certainly not a morning person. Blair, on the other hand, is a natural early bird, but after such an unpleasant night at Balmoral, even he was ready for a lie-in. Cherie's reaction to her unexpected and unwelcome reveille was, according to one who was later told the story of her royal visit by Mrs Blair herself, 'unprintable'. Worse, much worse, was to come. For his part Tony's spirits on these trips have often been low as he has struggled to deal with his wife's obvious displeasure at being left alone for long periods while he holds talks with the monarch.

The royal clan had descended on the castle to join the Queen at her summer residence and to pose for their annual Christmas photograph. With Prince Charles were his sons William and Harry and also joining the Queen and Prince Philip were the Queen Mother and Princess Anne. The Blairs, though intrigued to see the Windsors in their natural habitat, were not relishing the trip. Mrs Blair is an ardent anti-monarchist. Though she has since submitted, after criticism in the press, to curtseying to the Queen in public, she steadfastly refuses to do so away from the cameras. It is a stand that is said to drive Prince Philip in particular 'hopping mad'. Rules are strict on the 50,000-acre estate. The royal men wear kilts – Balmoral hunting tartan during the day and Balmoral dress or Royal Stuart at night. At dinner the Queen always wears a full-length ball gown. Meal times are strictly adhered to and guests are asked not to move around the property without being escorted at all times by a footman. Those arriving are given instructions about how to approach the Queen: never initiate conversation, speak only when spoken to and under no circumstances turn your back on Her Majesty.

From the very beginning Cherie did not endear herself to the royal family. At a Sunday lunch shortly after Diana's death, the Queen Mother was said to be 'mortified' by the prime minister's wife's choice of trousers for the occasion. She was also upset by Cherie's refusal to dip her knee to the monarch. The Queen was annoyed by what she considered the hectoring legalistic tone of Mrs Blair when she engaged her in conversation. There was already barely concealed suspicion of the Blairs from senior royals and their courtiers. Not only were they by nature predisposed to be wary of any Labour government, there was also deep hostility among some senior members of the family about how, as they saw it, the Queen had been railroaded into giving way in the days after Diana's death by Blair and his 'henchmen'. In the face of such froideur during royal encounters, Blair has been keen to mend fences, aware as he was that his relationship with the royals was not merely a social one but constitutional as well. But while her husband was giving the royals his usual charm treatment, Cherie had appeared prickly and aloof. A source said: 'Tony is usually capable of putting on a good show of bonhomie on these occasions, but he has often found Cherie's unhappiness has rubbed off on him.'

Mrs Blair could be forgiven if her attitude was less than convivial. Soon after the Blairs arrived at the castle for their first stay, the Queen had introduced Cherie to her daughter Princess Anne. The Princess Royal, who is known for her occasional bouts of imperious and short-tempered behaviour, was not in the mood to indulge in chit-chat with the wife of a prime minister whose party manifesto promised to outlaw her favourite pastime, hunting to hounds. Shaking hands with the formidable Anne, Cherie, seeking to dispense with formality, invited the princess to call her Cherie. Anne, her face a picture of cool disdain replied, 'Actually, let's not go that way. Let's stick to Mrs Blair, shall we?' With that the princess turned on her heels and marched off to talk to someone else. A postscript to this unhappy meeting came several years later at the Buckingham Palace celebrations to mark Queen's fiftieth jubilee in 2002. This time there was ill-disguised contempt from some royals over the way they believed the Blairs had muscled in on the event by going on an impromptu walkabout among the crowds in the Palace grounds. Seeing the princess, Mrs Blair said hello, but Anne simply and silently turned her back on her. 'That bitch completely blanked me,' said an incredulous Mrs Blair.

The working-class-bred Mrs Blair has, say sources, precious little in common with her blue-blood hosts. Cherie, who rarely drinks, was quick to comment on the amount of alcohol consumed by the royals during their summer migration. 'The Queen, who is always friendly and welcoming, seems to think that her guests are not having a good time if their glasses are not filled up with alarming regularity,' says an insider. 'Cherie couldn't believe the amount of boozing that went on.' One such occasion was an afternoon tea party thrown by the Queen Mother in her rooms for a group of her aged women friends. It was not just tea but a steady supply of sherry that was on offer to the titled OAPs. Cherie was surprised to be told by a member of the Balmoral staff that the Queen Mother had requested she join the gathering. Reluctantly, she agreed. The party began in a genteel enough manner, but as the afternoon progressed it steadily descended into a raucous singalong with the Queen Mother leading from the front and insisting that a mortified Cherie join in every tune.

In future years Mrs Blair's loathing of their annual September visit to Balmoral was to become so complete that it was obvious even to royal courtiers. On their 1998 visit the usually amiable Tony was said to have been subdued as he tried in vain to placate his wife who was annoyed at being left alone for long periods in their freezing cold room while he talked privately with the monarch; the following year the Queen's private secretary Sir Robin Janvrin apparently decided to make an effort to make the Blairs' stay more pleasant. Cherie's aversion to Balmoral, however, is not only psychological but physical as well. Put simply, she is utterly allergic to the castle. She has, say friends, such an allergy to the fur and feathers of the stuffed animals and numerous hunting trophies that adorn its walls that every minute there is miserable. 'Every time she walks into the place her eyes bulge, go red and begin to water.

She comes out in red blotches and her nose runs constantly,' says a friend. 'By the time she leaves she has lost her voice completely. Quite honestly, it is pure torture for her. The whole castle is packed to the gunwhales with stag heads, stuffed foxes, rabbits; you name it.'

Mealtimes at Balmoral are a further cause of dread for the couple as Tony endeavours to deal with his wife's misery and irritation. She is said to hate the fact that the Queen's numerous corgis, to whose fur she is equally allergic, are allowed to mill around the dining table in the hope of being given titbits. 'She absolutely despises the creatures,' says a source. 'She thinks it is disgusting that they hang around her feet. She said it was bizarre that when they let out a yap a footman would have to escort them outside, wait with them while they went to the toilet, and scoop what they left behind.'

It has often been suggested that one of the reasons for the royals' antipathy to the Blairs was Cherie's allegedly close friendship with the late Princess of Wales, whose *Panorama* interview with Martin Bashir had made her a figure of undiluted hate in the royal household. In fact Cherie hardly knew Diana, and Blair, though keen to trade on her popularity, had only met her on a few occasions. Diana had visited Chequers with the royal princes after the election, but Cherie found she had very little in common with her and told friends she had found the princess 'an airhead'.

Prince Charles, who was initially warm to New Labour and remains on good terms with both Blairs, was however furious over what he saw as the government's ignorance of countryside issues, particularly its positive attitude to GM crops and its 1997 commitment to banning fox-hunting. This is a subject Blair and his wife have often found themselves buttonholed over when visiting the royals. It is a widely held misapprehension that Cherie Blair has been the force behind the drive to ban hunting with hounds which eventually came into force in February 2005; pro-hunt protestors even went so far as to block lanes around Chequers in September 2004 in an attempt to sabotage her fiftieth birthday party. But in truth neither of the Blairs shed any tears for the hunted fox. It is a policy, say sources, Blair inherited and both he and his wife feel it has distracted attention from more important issues. That is not to say however that during those miserable stays in Scotland Cherie has never indulged in a country sport of her own – arguing the case for the ban with her blue-blooded hosts.

*

It was partly in an attempt to find a natural remedy for her chronic allergies to all things furry that Cherie found herself being recommended by Carole Caplin's mother Sylvia to an octogenarian ex-market gardener called Jack Temple. Temple, who died in 2004, ran a 'healing centre' from a breeze-block barn next to his home in West Byfleet, Surrey. Mrs Blair was drawn to the OAP, who proposed a series of theories about health and well-being that owed little to the established laws of medicine or, for that matter, any convention of logic. By the time Blair came to power Cherie was already a regular client of Temple's. Sue Harris, a former business partner of Carole Caplin, has claimed she visited Temple with Carole, Cherie and the Blair's eldest son Euan, then aged thirteen, shortly after the 1997 election.

Harris told the *News of the World* that Temple told them he was able to read their DNA by consulting rocks he kept in a room at the centre and by swinging a pendulum over their bodies. One by one, the women and the prime minister's son were shown separately into a room while Temple performed his DNA ritual. Then, claims Harris, they were all ushered out onto the lawn of his home to stand in a circle Temple had mown in the grass while each drank a glass of 'blessed water'. This, they were told, was to make use of the 'positive energy levels' which had seeped into the water from the ground. 'It was a load of nonsense and could have come out of an episode of *Absolutely Fabulous*, but we must have been there for three hours,' says Harris, who also admits to being concerned about the teenaged Euan being exposed to the 'gobbledegook'.

Blair court insiders reveal that this was not the full extent of Mrs Blair's connection to the odd Mr Temple. Shortly after the election and at Temple's suggestion, Cherie gave him a selection of small jars each containing the hair and toenail clippings of not only herself, but her prime-minister husband as well. Temple claimed that by 'dowsing' the jars with his pendulum he was able to detect by proxy any signs of 'poisons and blockages' in the first couple. But there was an added benefit for the Blairs. 'Temple told Cherie that his pendulum could tell her when it was a good time or bad time to make major decisions,' says a source. In this way, during the years before Temple's death, the wife of the prime minister would seek his assistance over the timing of important events in her and her husband's life. It was not uncommon, say Downing Street insiders, for her to fax several A4 pages of questions at a time to Temple so he could advise her which decisions should be taken immediately and which should be put off until the 'vibes' he was receiving from their hair and nail clippings were more positive.

Another unconventional figure to receive the patronage of Mrs Blair was a New Age practitioner called Chloe Asprey. She advised Cherie to meditate with stones and crystals and used the cycles of the moon to tell the prime minister's wife about the optimum time to conduct various pieces of business. If the moon was in the wrong place she would tell Cherie to postpone important events or decisions. Mrs Blair was also advised by her to visualize animals in her head, such as bears, a deer or bats which would protect her. Perhaps, given Mrs Blair's views on hunting, and animals in general, they might not have felt inclined to bother.

*

Soon after moving into the Number Eleven flat, the Blairs made the decision to sell Richmond Crescent. It was to be a colossal financial mistake as in the years to come the house would be resold on several occasions, each time at a substantial profit for the owners. One of the reasons the couple decided to sell was political. Blair and Campbell were concerned about the potential for embarrassment should the property be rented out. Some years earlier Tory Chancellor Norman Lamont inadvertently became front-page news when the *News of the World* discovered the London home he had leased out was occupied by a 'sex therapist' known as Miss Whiplash. The Blairs sold Richmond Crescent for £615,000 in the summer of 1997. Mrs Blair, in particular, has, since then, watched unhappily as the house has rocketed in value. She views the decision to sell with a regret that has not eased but become more nagging with the passage of time. Out of this ruefulness has come a desire to mitigate their lost financial opportunity.

With the decision made to sell the family home. The Blairs set about improving the living conditions inside their run-down Downing Street flat. Although a £100,000 project to renovate parts of Number Ten and Number Eleven had got under way, much of the money was earmarked for the staterooms. Meanwhile the press was quick to point out that at least £20,000 was to be spent on a German-designed kitchen in the Blairs' flat. In fact, as Cherie never tires of telling friends, she and Tony were forced to finance much of the work out of their own pockets. Not only that, she is wont to complain, but they were also forced because of civil service and security protocols to use an authorized firm, whose bill, she claims, was substantially larger than she might have expected to pay if she had been able to put the job out to tender.

The living arrangements did nothing for the already strained relationship between the Blairs and their next-door neighbour. Gordon Brown, whose ambitions to take over the tenancy of Number Ten are well known, was initially thrilled to swap the Number Eleven flat for the one above Number Ten, home as it was to past prime ministers. But tensions began to mount as Brown complained to his aides about the constant noise coming from his neighbours' children, in particular Euan's piano. The truth is that neither Tony nor Cherie has ever found the discipline of their children a priority. Early visitors to the flat tell of children 'running wild'. Mrs Blair, in particular, appears to have developed the knack of shutting out the barrage of noise made by her brood. Says one regular Downing Street visitor, 'Neither of them ever seemed to make the vaguest attempt to control the children. They could be complete monsters, particularly when they were young. Cherie has employed nannies for as long as I can remember and she seemed happy to let whichever childminder she had at the time sort the kids out.'

Another friend, who went on holiday with the Blairs, reports the friction the bad behaviour of the children caused between the couple. Cherie was happy to let the nanny take care of her offspring and would sit by the pool topping up her tan and reading a book as they kept up an incessant wailing. 'She was able to tune them out no matter how much racket those bloody kids made,' says the friend. Meanwhile, Tony, whose pleading with his wife to attend to the children invariably fell on deaf ears, would be forced to abandon whatever he was doing in an attempt to restore order. 'It led to them bickering constantly about who should be responsible for them,' says the friend. Neither has his position as PM always meant he was able to hand over responsibility for the children to his wife. Another Downing Street visitor tells of watching in bemusement as Tony, who had popped up to the flat one evening before an important Commons vote, was about to leave in order to make the vote on time. 'Cherie was telling him she wanted him to attend to some pretty trivial thing to do with the kids,' says the friend. 'She wasn't shouting. She was basically telling him that she was too busy with the work she had brought home to take care of it. Tony was trying to explain that he needed to go, but she was determined that he should see to the kids, not her. I thought to myself, I know she has an important job and everything, but he's only the fucking prime minister.'

3

1998: PUBLIC PROPERTY

Tony Blair, it is fair to bet, is the only CEO in Britain who doesn't own a mobile phone; there is simply no need for him to carry one. Every hour of every day he is never alone. Wherever Blair travels in the world he is accompanied by a retinue of advisers, bodyguards, PAs and secretaries. At any time of the day the Downing Street switchboard has the number of someone no more that twenty feet away from the country's leader. If you want to get hold of Tony Blair somebody will always be on hand to pass him their mobile. It is the same when he is at home in the family flat at Number Eleven. Government duty officers as well as the ever present Special Branch are on hand throughout the night to wake him up if he is needed urgently.

The security presence has increased dramatically since the events of 11 September 2001, but even in Blair's first year in office he found the constant attention of his staff, their unending calls on his time and the incessant restrictions on his personal privacy draining. When the Blairs go on holiday, the prime minister's office goes with him; a team of key personnel travel with the first family and set up in a hotel room or some corner of a rented villa. There is absolutely no escape from his job. One of the first lessons a new prime minister learns on arriving at Number Ten is that the people who work there see the place purely as an office. Civil servants, policy advisers and press officers have no problem whatsoever in wandering unbidden into the flat above the shop that is the Blair family's home. Cherie Blair called her book about the life of prime ministerial spouses *The Goldfish Bowl*. In it she recounts the story of the wife of a former PM waking to find one of the Number Ten PAs sitting on the end of the bed in conversation with her husband. She could so easily have been talking about her own life. Cherie writes of life in Number 10: 'It is, of course, an enormous privilege but it can also impose unique stresses on family life . . . It can in no way be described as a normal family home but our children have found the staff here like a large extended family.'

The couple and their three children had to adapt quickly to the new demands on Tony's time and attention. They became used to a morning routine that starts the same way whenever he is in Downing Street. The working day begins at 7.45 a.m. when his staff arrive. In the early days it would be Alastair Campbell and Jonathan Powell, his chief of staff. As Blair fought the 2005 election, Powell was joined by Campbell's replacement Dave Hill, plus senior Downing Street staff members Hilary Coffman and Dame Sally Morgan. His staff march into the flat as Blair is having his usual breakfast of toast, marmalade and herbal tea. The PM, still in his pyjamas and slippers, is talked through the important events of the day, told of the major stories in the press that relate to the government and briefed about upcoming meetings.

Breakfast over, Blair enters the en suite bathroom next to his bedroom followed closely by his team and has his bath while Powell and Hill talk on. There is simply no time for modesty. Coffman and Morgan, though, at this point stand half out of the room, being careful to avert their eyes from the naked prime minister while he performs his ablutions. The two women, however, are happy to carry on briefing Blair as he puts on his clothes ready for another long day leading the country. All the while life goes on with the children and Cherie getting ready for school and work; they have become used to the daily intrusion. Blair returns to the flat at around 7 p.m. to see his family and, in recent years, to spend some much-needed time with his fourth child Leo, but the meetings continue in the yellow-painted living room of the flat which doubles as an office for the PM. Then, invariably, it is back downstairs for some official function or other, accompanied at every turn by his team.

Blair has a huge appetite for work. Cherie Blair's diary is also full. Most nights are booked up months in advance with dinners for visiting heads of state, newspaper editors and industry leaders which she is expected to attend. On the occasional evening the couple spend together they will generally not find time to eat before 10 p.m. Surprisingly, there is no team of domestic staff at Number Ten ready to take care of the every whim of the most powerful man in the country. Once inside their flat the Blairs are expected to fend for themselves although they have always had a nanny to take care of the children. On the rare occasions Cherie and Tony sit down to dinner together upstairs Cherie will most likely have rustled up a quick bowl of pasta or they will have made use of the regular food parcels sent over by Martha Greene, a long-standing friend and the owner of Villandry, the trendy London restaurant and deli popular with politicos and BBC executives from the nearby Broadcasting House.

Eating out at a restaurant, always difficult for such a high-profile couple, has become a virtual impossibility since 9/11. Now, if the Blairs want to go out for dinner, the restaurant has to be closed and checked by sniffer dogs trained to find bombs. Special Branch officers have to perform risk assessment on the building and devise escape routes should the prime minister be attacked. A team of armed guards needs to be posted to watch their fellow diners. It makes popping out for a Chinese difficult. Consequently Blair almost never goes out to dinner anymore. The same security considerations apply if he wants to go shopping; as a result he never does. Christmas presents for his wife are bought for him by a member of his staff. For their twenty-fifth wedding anniversary in 2005 Mrs Blair bought the gift from her husband herself. The prime minister has, because of his circumstances, effectively been cut off from the people he is elected to lead.

The adjustment to their lives has taken its toll on the Blairs' children. Aged thirteen, eleven and nine when their father entered office, Euan, Nicky and Kathryn had quickly to get used to seeing little of their father even if he was working in the same building. Blair had been a hands-on dad to the children when he was in the shadow cabinet and even as Labour leader spent a considerable amount of time with his family. Now he had precious little time to devote to them. The sudden change was difficult for all three of them. Like her husband, Cherie was also finding life in Downing Street an enormous drain on her time. She was called on to act as Britain's unofficial first lady as well as concentrating on her flourishing legal career and taking care of the family. Added to this, she not only continued to act as Blair's closest political adviser, but in his first year in office, ratcheted up her role to the point where she was regularly writing a steady stream of briefing documents and memos advising her husband on a broad spectrum of policy. In private she was, and remains, a pivotal part of the Blair regime. In public she continued to act the role of silent partner, noticed for her outfits and hair rather than the considerable work she did for her husband's administration.

As the early gloss of their new position wore off Cherie became increasingly exercised about the strain her husband's new job was putting on the family finances. Already preoccupied by regret over the ill-judged decision to sell their home after moving into Downing Street, she was now increasingly having to make time available for the unpaid work of supporting her husband on official visits. Essentially a freelance barrister, she was expected to pay a fee to the chambers she belonged to while the chambers would pass legal work her way. If she was not working, though, she was not earning, and she was now expected to act as an ambassador for her country and her husband. This meant, she believed, that she must look her best at all times. Following the negative press coverage of her appearance at Blair's accession as party leader four years earlier, she had begun to spend increasingly large amounts of money on clothes, hair and make-up. At one party conference her outfit alone was said to be worth £3,900. Cherie's stylist Carole Caplin began touring the fashion houses of London and Paris to find new clothes for her. Top designers like Paddy Campbell, Ally Capellino and Louise Kennedy regularly delivered their creations to Number Ten for Mrs Blair. A year after Blair came to power, Cherie also spent several thousand pounds on a new wardrobe from couturier Paco Rabanne. Now, wherever she travelled she insisted on taking André Suard, whose clients at his London salon were even then used to spending more than seventy pounds for a cut, as well as Caplin, to whom she was reportedly paying up to £5,000 a month. The Blairs' financial position had not been helped by her husband's decision on taking office to impose a pay freeze on the new government. This decision, which infuriated his colleagues and particularly his deputy John Prescott, cost him £41,000 annually and meant he drew £102,000 in his first year as prime minister.

What is undeniable is that having spent the first forty years of her life untouched by the world of fashion and style, Cherie had undergone a road to Damascus conversion. It is widely reported that on an official trip with Blair to China in October 1998 she insisted on taking no less than four outfits just for the first day. She arrived wearing a blue trouser suit and before the day was over had given outings to a skirt slashed to the thigh, a gold and white mandarin-style trouser suit and ankle boots and, for the evening, trousers and embroidered jacket. So keen was she to show off as many outfits as possible her staff even commandeered a private house for one of her quick changes. The more than twenty outfits she took on the visit came with a hefty price tag and were at odds with Cherie's

continued assertion that she was not a clothes horse. It also
gave the lie to her husband's claim that he was an average Joe
bringing up an average family. In fact, in almost every respect
the Blairs were different. They wanted more for their children,
they wanted more themselves.

Cherie's obsession with her look and her clothes had led to
accusations that she was trying to replace Princess Diana as a
style icon. Unfortunately for Cherie there was no royal bank
balance available to foot the bill. Nor, as someone with no
official role, does she receive the allowances for clothes that
her husband gets from the state. The effect was to leave the
Blair family coffers severely dented and the cost of her life at
Number Ten was to be the source of a long-running series of
disputes between Cherie and civil servants.

Mrs Blair was also earning substantially less than the
£250,000 per year regularly quoted in the press. This was one
of the reasons she insisted to her husband that she should
continue to draw the £1,562-a-year child benefit to which she
was entitled. She became increasingly frustrated at what she
saw as the penny-pinching of the pen-pushers. The family was
issued with a Ford Galaxy people carrier when they arrived at
Number Ten, but if Tony was not actually travelling in the car
Cherie would be given a bill for its use. Likewise today she has
to pay the London congestion charge like anyone else. And if
the Blairs want to entertain someone, like, say, a newspaper
proprietor, it is considered non-government business and they
must pay the costs themselves. It is a situation that, perhaps
understandably, provokes regular outbursts of fury from Mrs
Blair, particularly when she compares, as she is in the habit of
doing, her own circumstances with those of British ambassa-
dors abroad or the US first lady, who draws on a lavish expense
account. One civil servant who had the temerity to question
Mrs Blair over a minor payment for use of the Blairs' official
car was subjected to a 'full-tilt bollocking' from Cherie. In
Blair's first year in office money was a recurring theme, with

an animated Cherie telling a friend who idly mentioned her many outfits, 'I can't win. If I buy nice clothes, I'm accused of profligacy; if I don't, Lynda Fucking Lee-Potter will crucify me in the *Daily Mail*.'

Few, one suspects, would shed a tear for a woman, the wife of a Labour prime minister at that, who can afford to spend annually on clothes what many of those who voted for Blair earn. Those who know Cherie point out that she developed nothing short of an obsession with her appearance after her husband rose to leader of his party. One says,

> She began to believe that it was really necessary to spend such huge amounts on clothes and that she needed the assistance of style advisers and hairdressers. Yes, she needed to do something about her look, but there seemed to be no middle ground. I always knew Cherie as a serious woman with a serious agenda, but she started scouring the tabloids for references to her clothes. She would become alternately furious or overly hurt if there was any negative comment. The whole thing was doing her no favours and I think it has affected her credibility as the great brain she was said to be.

An example of her prickliness over comments about her looks comes in a bizarre story told by former *Daily Mirror* editor Piers Morgan, whose paper had traditionally been a loyal friend to Labour. Morgan fell out with the Blairs over a series of personal and petty squabbles that saw his paper withdraw support for the government and turn into its bitter and damaging enemy over British involvement in the Iraq war. Part of the bitterness Morgan felt towards the Blairs can be traced back to his claim that Cherie tried to persuade Philip Graf, Morgan's boss at the *Mirror*, to have him sacked. Morgan's antipathy to the Blairs was eventually to contribute to his downfall when in 2004 his paper published a series of faked pictures of abuse by British servicemen against Iraqis. Morgan was dismissed, but kept a long-standing commitment to have dinner with the Blairs, who belatedly wanted to let bygones be bygones. In *The Insider* he revealed how, as the evening at their Number Eleven flat wore on, he became emboldened by the drink served by his hosts and bluntly asked Mrs Blair why she had hated him so much. Cherie replied that in the early days of her husband's first term the *Mirror* had described her as having bad skin. She was, she told him, very proud of her clear complexion.

Mrs Blair's fixation on the frivolous has been a source of vexation for the many women juggling career and family, who had held up Cherie Booth QC as a role model. Part of the problem was, say friends, a self-consciousness about her looks that stretched back to her childhood. Another was a tendency to self-obsession that had not been helped by her projection into the public eye. Moreover, both the Blairs and Cherie in particular had become increasingly seduced by money. The affliction was a side effect of the court of celebrities that had become a feature of New Labour and of Downing Street in Blair's first term. There had been the parties where rock stars like Noel Gallagher of Oasis and DJ Chris Evans sipped champagne at Number Ten. Mrs Blair had struck up friendships with her musical heroes Cliff Richard and fellow Scouser Cilla Black. Not only that, Tony and Cherie found themselves being offered hospitality by these rich new friends. It gave the Blairs, whose first marital home was in humble Hackney, a peek into the pampered world of the super-rich that was to prove dangerously seductive. Tony and Cherie, who despite their proximity to wealth during their years in office continue to be impressed by it, wanted a piece of the action. Cherie, in her displays of sartorial gluttony, was doing nothing more than acting like the moneyed women to whose set she aspired.

From 1997 to 2001 the Blairs hosted a succession of dinner parties at Chequers for the great, the good and the merely famous. In the past prime ministers had usually used their weekend residence to play host to cabinet colleagues; now the

300-strong roster of guests contained a wealth of A-list show business names like Sting, David Bowie, Elton John and Bono. Both Blairs but particularly Tony, say insiders, remain almost childlike in the awe with which they hold stars. Added to their musical heroes and the all-important loyal journalists was the best that Britain had to offer from the world of stage and screen with Judy Dench, Helen Mirren, Emma Thompson, Jeremy Irons and Lord Attenborough all receiving the call to break bread with the leader and his wife. In later years, when the luvvies had flown the New Labour nest, Tony and Cherie were reduced to mining deeper into the celebrity strata with invites to Des O'Connor and Geri Halliwell. The consolation for the Blairs is that because Chequers is run as a charity for prime ministers and is manned by servants from the Royal Navy, they do not have to put their hands into their own pockets as they do at Downing Street. Another plus is the Chequers swimming pool, which the Blairs insisted should be heated all year round so the children can swim.

*

Cherie's preoccupation with money can be traced back to a disadvantaged childhood in Liverpool. Struggling to bring up Cherie and her younger sister Lyndsey as a single parent, their mother Gale took on a series of jobs, including working in a chip shop, to make ends meet. The girls' father Tony Booth, famed for his role as the left-wing 'Scouse git' in the TV comedy *Till Death Us Do Part*, effectively walked out on the lives of his daughters before they had the chance to get to know him. He was and remains a committed socialist, but while his sympathies have always lain with the common man, they have not always extended to those closest to him. In the first of his autobiographies, *Stroll On*, published in 1989, he makes no mention of his marriage to Gale and includes not one reference to the eight daughters he fathered from a variety of relationships except for a request for forgiveness from the women in his life in the dedication. Instead he concentrates on his many sexual adventures, described charmlessly as 'crumpeteering'.

Booth met Gale Smith when she was an aspiring actress. She was already three months pregnant with Cherie by the time they were married at London's Marylebone register office in the spring of 1954. When Cherie was born on 23 September at Fairfield General Hospital, Bury in Lancashire, the announcement of her birth was made by her father from the stage of the town's Hippodrome Theatre, where he was dividing his time between acting and his job as stage manager. The couple and their newborn baby then began a nomadic existence around the theatres and repertory companies of the north of England. It was during this time that Booth began an affair with another actress, Pat Phoenix, who would later find national fame as *Coronation Street*'s Elsie Tanner. The couple subsequently renewed their relationship thirty years later and married before Miss Phoenix's death from cancer. The baggage of a wife and young baby was an annoying hindrance to the serious business of adding to Booth's already formidable list of sexual encounters. The solution, he decided, was to dump his wife and daughter on his parents Vera and George Booth. So Gale, now pregnant again with Lyndsey, was packed off to 15 Ferndale Road, Liverpool, a small three-bedroom yellow-brick back-to-back house in the less than affluent Waterloo district.

Over the next nine years the visits Booth made to see his wife and two daughters became increasingly irregular. They were short stays with a wife who was aware that he was already living in Putney, south-west London, with Julie Allan, an American-born sketch writer who would also go on to have two daughters by him. In the close-knit working-class community his absences did not go unnoticed. When Cherie was nine the relationship between her parents ended for good, though Gale refused to grant Booth the divorce he wanted and

Julie Allan was forced to take on his name by deed poll. The death knell for his relationship with Gale came with the notice cruelly placed in Gale's local paper the *Crosby Herald* which announced the birth of his first daughter, Jenia, by Miss Allan. Any pretence Gale and her daughters could continue to make about the state of the marriage was blown out of the water. Cherie, then a pupil at the local Roman Catholic primary school, was humiliated. A shy child, she was mortified by the nudge-nudge gossiping of her schoolmates. Her father's later television fame became the cause of even greater embarrassment as the tabloid press delighted in relating his colourful sexual and alcohol-fuelled exploits. This infamy by association she achieved at school would later drive her desire to protect her own children from unwanted public scrutiny.

Tony Booth was not a regular contributor to his family's coffers. Times were hard and Gale, who had given up acting to concentrate on bringing up her children, struggled. That financial insecurity has had a profound effect on Cherie's life ever since. She remains to this day irrationally preoccupied with the thought that she might again find herself poor. One thing her background did give her, however, was a desire to better herself. Encouraged by her grandmother Vera, she was an uncommonly bright and committed student. At school she achieved four A levels at grade A, followed by a first in law from the London School of Economics. But it was from her father that she inherited her socialism. At fourteen she told her classmates that she wanted to be the country's first female prime minister, and at sixteen she was already a member of the Labour Party. It is still her biggest regret that she never achieved public office in her own right.

Her political principles have gone hand in hand with her religion. A year after Tony came to office the Catholic charity Cafod described Mrs Blair as 'Britain's most prominent Catholic citizen'. There were also strong rumours that she was to receive a papal damehood, a mark of recognition usually reserved for those of unblemished virtue or unstinting generosity. Cherie's religion was and is fundamental to her life. She attends Mass every Sunday, her children were bought up in the faith and Tony, raised and confirmed in the Church of England, is now a de facto Catholic who is regularly to be spotted at Mass. Those who know Cherie describe her religion as the 'single most important influence on her life'. 'It is the foundation on which she has constructed everything else,' says one friend.

So, it remains a fundamental contradiction that running in tandem with her Catholicism has come a new faith, whose self-proclaimed prophets worship at the altar of New Age mysticism, whose cross is the crystal pendant and whose cathedrals are the expensively furnished consulting rooms of alternative therapists and healers. Few techniques, it seems, have not been tried by our first lady; few new remedies are too weird, few fads too absurd. Her interest is made all the more noteworthy by the fact that Cherie is famous for juggling, not only her role as the prime minister's consort, but those of top lawyer and mother. Yet she still has found time to indulge in an array of treatments that are not only expensive, but time-consuming as well.

One such treatment came in the form of Flowtron leggings. In 1998 Cherie was in her mid-forties and, like millions of other women, had become aware that she was suffering the effects of cellulite and water retention. Mrs Blair had been a regular visitor to the Mayfair-based therapist Bharti Vyas since 1988. Now Mrs Vyas recommended to Cherie the leggings, which were originally designed to prevent thrombosis in patients undergoing surgery. So, once a month and helped by Mrs Vyas, Cherie would climb into the vibrating pants resembling a huge pair of inflatable wetsuit bottoms which are filled with compressed air then deflated at thirty-second intervals. The treatment lasts half an hour and the effect, says one who has tried this unorthodox procedure, is to leave the patient looking like 'a cross between someone from the Wallace and Gromit cartoon *The Wrong Trousers* and a semi-dressed Michelin man. I felt like a complete twerp in them.' The patient adds disappointedly that the treatment also made no impact on her fat ankles.

Another treatment Cherie received from Vyas was Chinese electrical ear acupuncture, which is meant to treat the symptoms of stress, and she also invested in a bioelectrical shield, a crystal pendant worn round the neck which, it is claimed, protects the wearer from harmful energy rays. Mrs Blair paid Bharti £239 in 1998 for her pendant which, according to its American inventor former pensions clerk Dr Charles Brown, contains a 'magical configuration' of quartz and other crystals which deflect electromagnetic radiation from modern office equipment and counter 'negative vibes'. Dr Brown says he invented the shield after hearing voices in his head which told him which combination of minerals to use. 'The shield puts a cocoon around you,' insists Brown. 'At the edge of the cocoon is a layer that spins. That spinning layer is like a gatekeeper.' Cherie was regularly to be seen, say insiders, hanging her pendant up at the Downing Street windows so as to recharge the shield using the power of sunlight. Vyas not only supplied her products to Cherie, but also to Mr Blair, who she proudly proclaimed was lost without her own-brand skin polisher which he used as an alternative to shaving cream. Mrs Blair, she declared, was a 'remarkable woman' whose spiritual growth she had observed since their first meeting. 'Every role she plays is so wonderful,' she enthused. 'I haven't seen anybody so together anywhere else and she very much holds her family together.' Cherie's good spiritual health, she said, was due to the fact that she had advised the first lady to drink water from copper jugs as well as Vyas's own-brand liquids containing minerals from around the world.

*

If his wife was finding the time to indulge her mystical whims, Blair himself had rather less time on his hands. He had personally secured the historic Good Friday Agreement on peace in Ireland in April 1998 and had made the decision to deploy paratroopers to restore order in Sierra Leone after the west African nation descended into civil war. Another foreign policy objective actively pursued by Blair was that of improving British relations with China. For some time the Chinese had been staking their claim to becoming the next superpower and the trade potential with such a huge nation was of course considerable. The only problem was that China had a record on human rights that did not bear the most cursory scrutiny. The massacre of pro-democracy demonstrators in 1989 was still fresh in the memory, but Blair was keen to build bridges with China's totalitarian leadership.

By way of advertising this new conciliatory approach, Britain, at the time holder of the presidency of the European Union, joined the US in agreeing not to sponsor a United Nations resolution condemning China's appalling human rights record. In the spring of 1998 Blair went further by hailing Zhu Rongji, the new Chinese prime minister, as 'a modernizer if ever I met one'. In October Blair and Cherie chartered a Boeing 747 for their trip to meet their new friends in Beijing. While the headlines at home were devoted to Cherie's numerous and expensive costume changes in a country where most workers earn less than forty dollars a month, Blair was setting about winning over his hosts with a long interview on the state-controlled television, while in a ham-fisted attempt to display its liberal sensibilities, the Chinese government, who had jailed a leading pro-democracy campaigner, promptly released him on Blair's arrival. His opposite number told Blair when he landed, 'You can feel at home in China. You are free to talk about everything. Nothing will offend us. I invite you to say anything that is on your mind.' In public at least Blair demurred. Downing Street spinners were quick to point out, however, that he had taken a tough line in private with his hosts on human rights. The Chinese themselves said these discussions had been 'brief'.

So how far did the spirit of friendship and openness go? Before leaving Britain Blair had been briefed by MI6 that every conversation he had in China would likely be bugged and the prime minister and his wife were warned not to have any sensitive political discussions during the week-long trip. The CIA carry bug-proof 'tents' that can be erected inside rooms to shield conversations from hidden microphones, but Britain could not afford such sophisticated equipment, although Blair was given a secure phone so he could communicate with London and other world leaders about the crisis that had erupted in Kosovo.

Had the ruthless Chinese leadership been charmed enough by Blair's warm words to dispense with its old shameful tactics? A Blair insider relates a previously untold story that suggests an answer. The Blairs were put up by the Chinese in the sumptuous state guest house, a huge and beautiful villa filled with Ming vases and priceless artefacts. One evening Cherie, exhausted after a day of glad-handing members of the Chinese government, decided to have a relaxing shower. As she took off her robe to step naked into the hot water, she noticed that the large mirror on the wall of the bathroom had steamed up, all except for a small section in the middle – through which her hosts could watch via a two-way mirror.

*

Families, it is safe to say, sometimes have the habit of causing not inconsiderable embarrassment. When your family is headed by Tony Booth, the chances of beating the odds aren't in your favour. Booth, though a distant figure in Cherie's childhood, had managed successfully, however, to be the cause of mortification from afar as she and her sister Lyndsey were growing up in Liverpool. Now, in October 1998, Booth married for the fourth time at the age of sixty-six. His new wife was a politics student called Stephanie Buckley, who, at twenty-three years younger than him, was herself marrying for the fifth time. Tony and Cherie stopped off on the way back from the Labour Party conference in Blackpool to attend the blessing in Merseyside. The barest appraisal of Booth's romantic history didn't give rise to hopes of a long and happy marriage.

The youngest of Booth's eight daughters, Joanne, was born in 1990 to another failed relationship. His two daughters from his affair with Julie Allan, Jenia and Bronwen, live in North America. Bronwen is a television actress in Montreal, while Jenia is a researcher in Los Angeles. Another daughter, Lucy Thomas, born after her mother's brief affair with Booth, was discovered living in Australia in 2002. Two other daughters, Sarah and Emma, were born during his 1970s relationship with a former model called Suzie Riley. It was in 1979 during the stormy affair with her that Booth almost died when, after a drunken row with his lover in which she locked him out of their home, he tried to break back in by climbing on some paraffin drums which then exploded. He was left with 42-per-cent burns and spent months in hospital. His brush with death did, however, allow him to renew his relationship with the twenty-five-year-old Cherie, who, after years of little contact, became a regular visitor to her father's bedside.

It was during this period as well that Cherie made contact with Sarah and Emma for the first time. Sarah changed her name to Lauren when she began training as an actress, but gave this up to launch a career as a newspaper and magazine columnist on the back of her brother-in-law's political success. She has gone on to become a perennial embarrassment to the Blairs with her increasingly bitter attacks on his government. As a result she has all but been cut out of their lives. Tony Booth has been described publicly and only half-jokingly by Blair as 'the father-in-law from hell'. Although now a reformed drinker, his steady stream of off-message remarks about the

Labour government, including his claim that he smoked cannabis while a guest of the Blairs in their home, has led to much tugging of the hair inside Number Ten. In 2004 Booth moved to Ireland claiming he was being forced out of Britain because of its poor treatment of pensioners. Nobody in Blair's private office was sorry to see the back of him.

4

1999: WE THE GOVERNMENT

It cannot be easy being the son or daughter of the prime minister. Perks there may be, with introductions to royal princes, celebrity premieres and holiday invitations from Daddy's rich and famous friends, but, given the opportunity, wouldn't most kids be happier to melt into the background at school rather than taking the flak that invariably comes from being different? This issue presented a problem for the Blairs that would have long-term implications not only for their children, but also for their credibility as parents. When the Fleet Street feeding frenzy that was Cheriegate erupted in the dying days of 2002 over her disastrous scheme to cash in on the property boom, its subplot was about the political capital the Blairs had accrued from their children. The Faustian pact they had made over their young family had come back to bite them.

The most memorable image of Tony Blair will always be him posing in the spring sunshine with his wife and children on the steps of Number Ten on 2 May 1997. That picture did not happen by accident. It was not stumbled on by a lone photographer hiding in the undergrowth with a telephoto lens; it was choreographed and stage-managed by Blair's wily team of press handlers. The boys, dressed in their chinos, sweatshirts and trainers and Kathryn in her baseball cap looked like they could have been yours or mine. The message was a potent one: this was a new dawn and a new era, fresh and pure. Our new leader was a family man, a man of the people whose hopes and aspirations were the same as every other father out there.

Blair, as evinced by his use of Euan in the horse-trading

he conducted with Michael Brunson over Cherie's early PR gaffe, was well aware of the unique selling point his children offered him. As the election drew closer in early 1997, he had given a major interview to *Woman* magazine. In the exclusive article entitled 'The three women in my life' Mr Blair played the family card to the max. He was quoted as saying, 'My daughter Kathryn has my mother's red hair and her second name is Hazel after my mum. She's a gorgeous girl with a great personality, sweet and strong willed. We've always tried to treat her the same as the boys, but she's so different and has always been completely uninterested in their passion for football. She went straight for dolls. I think all fathers dote on their daughters and it's lovely to have a girl in the house.' The article came complete with six family photographs including one of Tony with Kathryn as a toddler, a portrait of the Blairs with their children and a specially commissioned photograph of nine-year-old Kathryn with mother Cherie and grandmother Gale Booth. It would not, by any means, be the last time Blair would use his children in his efforts to win round electors.

The couple's attitude to the exposure of their children to the prying eyes of the media can be illustrated by comparisons with their political contemporaries. How many people, for example, could have picked out Stephen or Rachel Kinnock, the children of Blair's predecessor as Labour leader Neil Kinnock, from a line-up? Would anyone have been able to recognize the young family of Iain and Betsy Duncan Smith? Of course, the Blairs were of far more interest to the media and the public, but Tony and Cherie's children were an important ingredient in the image of a new Camelot that Blair, his wife and his advisers were keen to sell to a willing nation.

With Blair's appointment as prime minister in 1997, however, came a significant change in policy regarding his children. On 5 May, four days after polling, Alastair Campbell wrote to editors to demand that the Blair children be given the opportunity to go about their lives and education without the attention of the media. This was a situation the press was happy to accept; for some years it had observed a no-go area around the young princes, William and Harry. The death of their mother Princess Diana four months later also encouraged an atmosphere of self-reflection in Fleet Street that ushered in a new code of conduct giving children unprecedented rights to privacy. The press was therefore willing to cooperate. The issue was clearly an important one to the Blairs; as caring parents, they were naturally concerned for their children. But why had they waited until after the election to make their plea for their children's privacy; why not at the beginning of the campaign? The timing, then, did nothing to quell the suspicion that invading the privacy of the Blairs' children was acceptable as long as it was Blair himself doing the invading – and if there were votes in it. Cynicism was increased by the fact that the request came only after the Blair children had been photographed happily helping to move possessions, including Dad's guitar, out of Richmond Crescent into a series of cars and vans to be taken to Downing Street. When the Blairs could so easily have afforded to employ removal men for the task, the children's involvement was widely seen as a publicity stunt aimed to show the new first family's ordinariness.

The prime mover in the battle to ensure the children's privacy was Cherie. Through her own childhood experiences she was well aware of the pitfalls that come with having a famous father and she was adamant she did not want her children to suffer as well. Another factor was the criticism they had received over sending Euan to the Oratory, which still rankled. Her opportunity for revenge came in January 1999 when the *Mail on Sunday* ran a front-page story headlined SNUBBED PARENTS ATTACK BLAIRS' SCHOOL. The allegation this time was that the couple's ten-year-old-daughter Kathryn had received special treatment by being given a place at the Sacred Heart High School, a much sought after Roman Catholic girls' school in Hammersmith, west London, which operated a vetting policy for new applicants. The parents of other girls trying to secure entry to the school were quoted by the paper as accusing the Blairs of 'stealing' their daughters' places. The Blairs, it should be said, had done nothing wrong, but the story again raised the question of why they considered it necessary to choose a school so far from their home. There were, after all, plenty of schools in Westminster. It also high-lighted the issue of non opt-out schools which nevertheless operate interview procedures before allocating places, and how high-achieving parents are able to cherry-pick the schools they want for their children.

This time Cherie was in no mood to take lying down what she considered to be another invasion of her children's privacy. Cherie contacted Alastair Campbell in a fury and demanded that the *Mail on Sunday* be reported to the Press Complaints Commission for its story about Kathryn. Campbell's own support of the comprehensive system was at odds with the Blair's decision over the schooling of their children, but he dutifully did the bidding of his master and his master's wife.

Campbell's letter when it arrived at the PCC was a milestone in the relationship between prime minister and press. No PM had ever made a formal complaint about a newspaper to the body responsible for their regulation. The *Mail on Sunday*, for its part, was convinced the article raised questions of public interest in the debate over the quality of inner-city schooling; newspapers, it said, 'must be free to report these issues'. It did, however, offer to publish a correction in order to avoid censure from the commission. The PCC too was keen to resolve the issue without the need for a judgement, but Downing Street turned down the offer of a correction and Guy Black, the then PCC director, quickly became aware that Number Ten required blood. Concerned he was not finding it possible to broker a deal, he concluded that it was Mrs Blair and not Alastair Campbell who was the instigator of Number Ten's hard-line approach. Later Black would say, 'It looked to me that Alastair

himself was having difficulty handling Cherie. He made it very
clear to me that he must have a win against Associated Newspapers [the publishers of the *Mail on Sunday* and the *Daily
Mail*, which had been critical of the government]. He told me
that it was essential they had one on them.' The commission
duly obliged and upheld the complaint, saying that the article
had breached the PCC's new code which allowed children to be
free to complete their education without unnecessary intrusion.

Downing Street was jubilant and described the ruling as
a 'landmark judgement'. Cherie was cock-a-hoop, but battle
lines had been drawn. Her motherly concern was natural and
understandable, but there was a widespread feeling in sections
of the media that the Blairs' actions had been bullying and
were designed to stifle legitimate debate over an issue that
was inextricably linked to the government's education policy.
After all, the press had largely kept to its side of the bargain
on keeping the Blair children out of the pages of the papers.
Meanwhile Blair had been happy to employ the famous 'Euan
Test' when describing his vision for the Millennium Dome –
the test of the Dome's success or failure, said the PM, would
be its ability to stimulate and entertain his eldest son.

Neither was Cherie happy with her own treatment by the
media. Her thin skin had been badly bruised by the publication
in the press of unflattering pictures of her with her husband
on holiday in the Seychelles. The snaps suggested Cherie
had gained weight and proved conclusively the woeful under-
performance of the 'Flowtron leggings' in treating what the
newspapers described as her 'orange-peel thighs'. A year later
the *Mail on Sunday* would again fall foul of the Blairs. On that
occasion Cherie won an injunction to stop the paper publishing
extracts from the manuscript of a book by Ros Mark, a former
nanny to the Blairs' children. In the weeks and months that
followed, Mrs Blair used the law assiduously to go after Ms
Mark and her family to prevent them from revealing secrets
about life inside Downing Street.

While she pulled strings behind the scenes, Mrs Blair was maintaining her Trappist vow in public, but by the mid-term of Blair's first period in government there was growing evidence that the policy might be a double-edged sword. The less Cherie had to say the more suspicions grew that she might be hiding something. Was she really controlling the reins of power from the shadows? Was she kept quiet because her views were significantly to the left of her husband's? It did not help that Fiona Millar, erroneously described as Mrs Blair's 'social secretary', had a tendency to zealous enjoyment of her real job as Cherie's gatekeeper. Where others might have viewed their role as Cherie's media representative as a position which required tact and conciliation, Millar's approach was combative. In the process she made herself and her boss few friends. Old friends who tried to make contact with Mrs Blair often found themselves, much to their annoyance, being interrogated by Millar. Unknown to Cherie, her overprotective assistant succeeded in alienating a large number of her former acquaintances. Their predicament is neatly illustrated by one who had been at the Blairs' wedding and who had made many attempts to contact Cherie but never received a reply. After several unproductive conversations with a taciturn Millar, he told her he was an old friend of Mrs Blair. That was the problem, he was told; he was an old friend and not a new one. Millar has since admitted that she may have been overprotective of her charge. One friend of Cherie says, 'Fiona is a bright woman, but she was completely over the top, especially at the beginning. She was far too uptight and as a result nobody could get anywhere near Cherie. It led to Cherie being alienated.'

This overbearing approach was illustrated by a farcical attempt at public relations masterminded by Millar in the autumn of 1999. A journalist from the pro-Blair *Times*, Ann Treneman, was authorized to spend four days with Mrs Blair as she attended the Labour conference in Bournemouth, the only stipulation being that the writer was under no circumstances actually to speak to Cherie. What emerged was a tragicomedy with the mute writer following an equally mute Mrs Blair round the stalls outside the conference hall, visiting a children's cancer ward in Southampton and a community scheme run by Dorset police, with Millar filling the gaps left by the prime minister's wife's silence. 'She does speak, she just doesn't speak to the press,' Millar was quoted as saying. 'I know what journalists want her to do. They want her to fall on her face by attacking the government. They'd love to paint her as Lady Macbeth, wouldn't they? But she is not. She has her intellectual stimulation from her work. The press want her to talk about "My Life with Tony" and tell her inner secrets. Now why would she want to do that?' The result was a stunning own goal with Millar in the role of ventriloquist.

Neither were Millar's comments strictly accurate. If Mrs Blair was finding all the stimulation she needed in her work as a barrister, why would she have felt the need to chair a series of meetings on policy behind the doors of Number Ten and directly at the heart of government? These Millennium Summits flew in the face of the oft-repeated Downing Street line that Mrs Blair played no active part in her husband's administration and provided an illuminating insight into the pecking order that existed within the Blair court. Two years into her husband's first term Cherie was more confident about flexing her political muscles. She had, say those close to her, felt increasingly stifled by the gag she had agreed to when her husband began his tilt for Number Ten. Those years in the shadows had fuelled her enthusiasm for taking a more hands-on role in policymaking. Blair remained unconvinced; he had no desire to undo their success in keeping her input at the highest level hidden from public view. But Cherie's restlessness was obvious and, more than anyone, Blair was aware of the debt he owed his wife in allowing her own considerable political ambitions to be sublimated in his favour. He was also not unduly concerned about members of his court taking over areas that were by rights the terrain of elected cabinet colleagues. He had long valued the opinions of his small unelected group of special advisers over those of his ministers, particularly in the field of foreign affairs.

Mrs Blair's eleven seminars, held amid the formal surroundings of Number Ten over the next two years, covered such diverse topics as crime, transport policy, Africa, science, wealth creation and art and culture. They consisted of approximately a hundred invited movers and shakers, with Cherie as organizer and chairwoman. If ever evidence was needed of Mrs Blair's elevated position at the heart of New Labour, it came at the seminar devoted to art and culture. Those attending the meeting were astonished to see the then culture secretary Chris Smith sitting meekly in the audience as Cherie ran the proceedings. Journalist David Lister, who attended the meeting, recalled, 'It seemed odd. It was a little odder,' he added, 'that Mrs Blair said that anyone with further points to raise about arts policy should make them known and "we" will take them on board.' It was a slip of the tongue repeated at least twice in the coming years by Mrs Blair which inadvertently allowed the veil to slip. So used had she become in private, even in front of selected political journalists, to dropping the facade about the true position she occupied at the very top table of government, that she often forgot to keep up the pretence in public. On another occasion it was the turn of the transport secretary at the time, Stephen Byers, and his junior minister John Spellar to sit as spectators as Mrs Blair held court.

When the seminars came under the spotlight after Blair had won a second election victory Downing Street mounted a hastily prepared rearguard action to counter the expected accusations of cronyism. 'We are totally unapologetic,' Campbell said. The meetings were no more than 'an intellectual kickabout' with Mrs Blair acting as moderator, he added, because 'she plays that role in her work life and therefore it is sensible for her to do it'. It did not, it seem, occur to Campbell that in their 'work life' Byers and Smith might have been expected to chair the odd meeting in their role as ministers of the Crown. The problem for Cherie, and more particularly for Blair himself, was that her behaviour raised questions about the government's attitude to the democratic convention, endowed as it is with important inbuilt checks and balances on those in power. If Mrs Blair had been a minister, her colleagues in Parliament would have been able to ask her to explain her actions to them in the chamber of the House. If she had been a paid civil servant, a parliamentary committee would have had the right to call her before it to question her over her role. As a public figure she would have had to submit herself to scrutiny and questions from the media. As it was, Cherie, the queen of the New Labour court, was, it seemed, utterly unaccountable to anyone but her husband. She refused to speak to the media and was under no obligation to explain what recommendations if any she would be making to the PM as a result of these forums on some of the most crucial issues relating to government. Also, if these meetings were, as the Downing Street spin machine tried to maintain, merely glorified talking shops, why was the precious time of ministers being wasted at what by implication were only sops to a spouse who wanted to know what playing with the train set was like? And if that was the case, why were these round tables permitted in Number Ten, the epicentre of British political decision-making? Few, particularly the ministers publicly humiliated by this illustration of their subservience to the prime minister's wife, were under any illusion as to where the power really lay. Even her Number Ten-headed notepaper was inscribed Cherie Booth, the name she used in her professional life and the one that had appeared on the ballot paper when she stood for Parliament.

*

If Cherie was the most powerful woman in government, Anji Hunter ran her a close second. Blair's special assistant in his first term had known him since she was fifteen and he two years older. They met, long before he knew Cherie, at a house party in the Scottish town of Forfar when Blair was a student at Fettes College, his private school in Edinburgh. The two had been overnight guests but nothing romantic had happened between them. More than twenty years later when Blair made a speech to his supporters and campaign team after his election as Labour leader, he praised Hunter's part in his success and with a wry grin said of that meeting, 'It was my first defeat.' Rebellious and free-thinking, Hunter, the daughter of a success-ful rubber planter, was expelled from her private girls' school at sixteen and later followed Tony to Oxford where she enrolled in a sixth-form college in the city.

She attended the Blairs' wedding in March 1980, but later she and her then husband, Blair lookalike landscape gardener Nick Cornwall, moved to Ireland and she lost contact. In 1986, however, she recontacted her old friend and asked if, for a polytechnic dissertation she was writing, she could work unpaid in his office two days a week. Blair, then establishing himself as a star of the future in the Labour Party, was so impressed with her he asked her to join his team permanently and run his office. As Blair stood first for the leadership of his party and then for prime minister, Hunter was by his side, efficiently running the whole of his political life. In 1995, when Jonathan Powell took over as Blair's chief of staff, Hunter was freed from her administrative duties to concentrate on the job of being his sounding board and media fixer, as well as her vital role as comfort blanket and moral support when he was under pressure. Hunter was attractive, intelligent, dynamic and reso-lutely upper middle class. She was also plainly invaluable to her boss. This was, perhaps not unnaturally, an incendiary combi-nation as far as Cherie Blair was concerned.

Cherie's dislike of Anji had not been instant; she is not, say friends, possessive of her husband or jealous by nature. But as Blair moved into Downing Street he began spending long hours in the company of his small team of close advisers of which Hunter was key. Hunter, too, is skilled in an art that Cherie has not been able to master – presentation. While Cherie is a perennial help to her husband on matters of dry policy, she has little instinct for the crucial job of selling those same policies to the public. Her approach, say her detractors inside Number Ten, is too often legalistic and academic. 'She has never really understood the human element,' says one Downing Street veteran. Anji Hunter on the other hand has a natural understanding of the importance of delivering the message. She was invaluable to Blair, not just arranging his visits but also networking with journalists to sell her master's vision. Her influence even extended to choosing his wardrobe, a job that might traditionally have been seen as the remit of his wife. Unlike Cherie, who has often found social situations uncomfortable, Anji also proved adept at schmoozing those who were of use to Blair. Her charm was legendary in the male-dominated Westminster village. She played a pivotal role in helping win over Rupert Murdoch and his News International executives by acting as an intermediary when Blair became Labour leader. She was also well liked by President Clinton and US ambassador William Farish and equally practised at working her magic on the show-business stars New Labour so assiduously courted in its early incarnation. She was popular with the Westminster press corps, although her matey one-of-the-boys persona disguised an astute and ruthless political operator who made herself indispensable once Blair was in government.

None of this endeared her to Mrs Blair. Cherie watched with a combination of awe and envy as Anji went about the job to which she was so suited. 'In many ways they are polar opposites,' says one who has known both women since the beginning of the New Labour project. 'Anji is a natural. She has incredible confidence and a very easy way with people. She is actually quite fearsome, but she has enormous charisma, which she can use to devastating effect on those she wants to influence. Cherie is a brilliant woman but she is racked with insecurities and that makes her come over as aloof and cold. It is not who she really is but, despite all her obvious intelligence, I think she remains sensitive about her humble roots.' Who could blame her, then, for eyeing jealously the social ease that came with Anji's breeding.

But it was, in the final analysis, her role as his confidante and emotional protector that did most to foster the deep antipathy that came to characterize Anji's relationship with the prime minister's wife. At one of his early Labour conferences as leader the close relationship led to a 'blazing mad' Cherie storming out of her bedroom dressed in nothing more than her nightgown to tell Hunter, who was deep in conversation with Blair, to 'piss off' out of their hotel suite. On another occasion Mrs Blair, in a state about having mislaid some papers, suddenly and inexplicably began 'ranting and raving about what a bloody bitch Anji was', reports a source. Consequently, when Blair was installed in Downing Street, Anji, though as important to Blair as any of his advisers, rarely went up to the flat with Campbell and Powell. 'Anji was very aware of the atmosphere and both she and Tony knew it was best if she kept her distance from Cherie,' the source adds. 'She would have to hang around downstairs waiting for Tony, while Alastair felt far more comfortable about just barging into the flat any time of the day or night.'

During the 1997 election campaign Hunter had been tireless. Where Blair went, she went, criss-crossing the country in a gruelling schedule. More than anyone, Cherie included, she had been the voice of encouragement at his shoulder urging him on to find new levels of determination as the physically and mentally exhausting campaign took its toll. On the night of the election she had stayed up all night with Blair and his campaign team and headed back to her Sussex home on the train as he and his wife entered Downing Street for the first time. She was surprised that despite the obvious importance Blair placed on her, she had not yet been offered a job in the new Number Ten office. Even later that day, when she spoke to Blair on the phone, no concrete offer was forthcoming. What she was unaware of was that for several months Mrs Blair had been canvassing her husband to sack Hunter once the election was won. Blair was unwilling to lose someone on whom he had so completely relied for ten years, but he was also loath to incur the formidable wrath of his wife. Unable to decide, he at first did nothing. It was only later that day that he decided to risk Cherie's ire by ringing Anji to tell her he wanted her to meet Jonathan Powell the following week to discuss her role in his new administration. It was a rare snub to his wife that Cherie would not forget in a hurry.

Mrs Blair was not without allies in her stated aim of dislodging her enemy. Sally Morgan, Blair's political secretary, and Cherie's press spokesman Fiona Millar were at one in their loathing of Hunter. Millar had for some time been plotting with her boss to undermine Anji, and Blair was well aware of the personal animosity between the two. Morgan and Hunter had been conducting a turf war within the Number Ten hierarchy and Morgan was jealous too of Blair's reliance on Anji and their close easy-going relationship. Millar, who in Blair's second term negotiated a wider role that included working for Blair as well as his wife, refused point blank to answer to Anji and insisted on reporting only to Jonathan Powell.

Cherie was also irked, say insiders, by the fact that Hunter had previously had no real attachment to the Labour Party; there were some inside Number Ten who speculated that the well-bred Anji was a closet Tory. Indeed, Hunter's concern was never primarily the party itself, but its leader. Cherie was open in her backing of Anji's rival Morgan, a former teacher steeped in the traditions of the party. The sniping reached fever pitch before the 2001 election and Hunter, wearied by the constant infighting and the poisonous atmosphere, told Blair she planned to quit. Cherie was 'beside herself with glee' says one Downing Street insider but Blair was mortified. With an election to face he was only too aware of how much he would need Anji in the coming weeks. Cherie counselled her husband that he should accept her resignation and give her job to Sally Morgan. Again he ignored his wife and begged Hunter to stay. He offered her a new job title, director of political and government relations, and a pay hike to £120,000 a year. Her new broader role would include handling relations with outside bodies and other nations. Much to the disgust of Cherie, Morgan and Millar, Anji accepted Blair's offer. Meanwhile, in a clear victory for Hunter, Morgan was given a peerage and shifted out of Number Ten into the job of minister for women. Hunter accompanied Blair on his gruelling missions around the world after 9/11, but her new role was not all she had been led to believe and in November 2001 she finally accepted an offer from BP to be its new £250,000-a-year head of communications. Morgan was brought back in from the cold and Cherie celebrated, but in the months and years ahead the prime minister would come to miss his ally.

There is a bizarre postscript to the Anji Hunter saga that says much about the deep personal antipathy she aroused in Mrs Blair. Two years after Hunter's departure from Downing Street she became embroiled in a bitter divorce battle with her husband after leaving him for Adam Boulton, the political editor of Sky News. In the dirty war that ensued over the sharing of their assets Nick Cornwall accused his wife of being a negligent spouse because of the long hours she had spent working for the prime minister.

So, given the public embarrassment caused by Cornwall, who was the public figure who wrote a letter to his lawyers with a glowing character reference lauding his skills as a husband and father? Step forward the prime minister's wife. Cherie, it seemed, was not the forgiving type.

*

In the battle for hearts and minds prime ministers are occasionally the beneficiaries of happy coincidences that can lift a
faltering administration. In June 1999 Labour took a drubbing
in the European elections. Four months later Blair brought
Peter Mandelson back into the cabinet less than ten months
after the former trade and industry secretary had been forced
to resign over an undeclared home loan of £373,000 he had
received from the paymaster general Geoffrey Robinson, who
had also resigned over the scandal. Mandelson came back to
howls of derision from the Tories and claims in the press
that the 'whiter than white' government Blair had promised
a little over two years earlier was now mired in the same
sleaze that had brought down the Tories. Amid all this, Cherie
Blair told her husband she was pregnant with their fourth
child.

When news of her pregnancy leaked out in November
agonized groans from Tory Central Office in Smith Square
could be heard all the way to Whitehall. In the days that
followed, Blair, who had seen his popularity lead over the
Conservatives slip to ten points the previous month, improved
it by 50 per cent. How the news leaked out would be a matter
of dispute for some time to come and would lead to a bitter
falling-out between Blair and his once-trusted rabble-rousers
on the *Daily Mirror*, but as Blair and more particularly his
wife were to discover too late, sixty years of unquestioning
tribal loyalty to the Labour cause count for nothing when
editors believe they have been stitched up over an exclusive.
When the person caught red-handed with the needle and thread
is none other than the glowing mother-to-be herself, the gloves
come off and no low blows are barred.

When, on 19 November, the *Mirror* ran the story it trailed
as THE SCOOP OF THE YEAR, it was still firmly in Blair's
corner. The prime minister and his wife were 'utterly and
completely gobsmacked, but ecstatic', the paper reported as it
revealed that Cherie was thirteen weeks pregnant. She had

taken a test the previous month and told her husband who was 'in a state of shock'. But the couple 'could not be happier with the situation. Tony is as proud as punch and has hardly stopped smiling for the last few weeks,' the *Mirror* quoted a source as saying. This was not, however, the recollection of one Blair court insider, who saw the prime minister shortly after he had been given the news by Cherie. 'He looked as though he had seen a ghost,' says the source. 'I will say that having Leo has been one of the most wonderful experiences for Tony, but when he first heard he was going to be a dad again, it took him quite some time to get used to the idea. They certainly had not been trying for a baby.'

The *Daily Mirror*'s 'scoop' was not a scoop anyway. In fact, its 'world exclusive' was actually shared with its biggest and deadliest rival the *Sun*, the nemesis of not only the *Mirror* but historically of Labour as well. But times had changed. When, in the run-up to the 1997 election, the *Sun* under the editorship of Stuart Higgins had come out in support of Blair, it was of monumental significance to the New Labour cause. Five years earlier the same paper had printed a picture of a light bulb on its front page on election day and invited the last person leaving the country to switch it off if Labour won. The move torpedoed Neil Kinnock, who had appeared to be heading for Number Ten, and led the paper to gloat, it was THE SUN WOT WON IT. Blair and Alastair Campbell had assiduously courted the paper and were only too aware that it would require payback for its support. The *Mirror* had come by the story of Cherie's pregnancy thanks to Max Clifford, the ubiquitous tabloid fixer and PR, but before running it editor Piers Morgan called Campbell to seek confirmation that what they were planning to publish was correct. Campbell told Morgan that Cherie was, indeed, pregnant, but the situation presented Campbell and the Blairs with a problem. The *Sun* would, of course, be furious to miss out on a story that was tabloid gold dust, but if Downing Street was to give the story to the *Mirror*'s rival it would risk alienating a previously loyal supporter. When the decision had to be made, Blair and his staff chose the *Sun*. Their reasoning was simple: the *Mirror*, historically the organ of the party, was not suddenly going to up sticks and pitch its tent in Smith Square; it could be relied on to remain faithful to the cause. The *Sun* on the other hand had always been a mildly reluctant bedfellow of New Labour and would need continual wooing to stay onside.

So the *Sun* was given the story too, but who was the source of this dynamite tip-off? Was it a shadowy Deep Throat in an underground Westminster car park or Alastair Campbell, perhaps, affecting the Scottish glottal-stop diction of a near neighbour of the Blairs in an anonymous call to the paper's Wapping news desk? Astonishingly, the whistle-blower was none other than Cherie herself, although the details of how her pregnancy was relayed to the *Sun* remain a matter of bitter dispute to this day. Morgan claims that Mrs Blair confirmed the news to the *Sun*'s then deputy editor Rebekah Wade, who is a friend of the Blairs, just as the *Mirror* presses were about to roll. Morgan, who was furious to find his 'scoop' also in the first editions of the *Sun*, smelled a rat. The following day he pulled an ancient tabloid trick on Fiona Millar, lying to her that he knew about how the story had found its way into the *Sun* and affecting an air of sanguinity about the matter. Millar, who as an ex-Fleet Street hack herself should have known better, took the bait and blabbed the lot, complete with Cherie's conversation with Wade. Morgan slammed down the phone and began plotting his revenge.

Internecine tabloid skirmishes aside, the Blairs were shell-shocked by the discovery they were to be parents again. Sources confirm that Cherie's pregnancy came at a time when she had submitted herself to a New Age technique which taught that inner harmony can be achieved through prolonged and regular bouts of sex. The approach, which became known in the amorphous world of spiritual healing as 'Karma Shagging', was central to the credo of two of Cherie's spiritual gurus. For some time Sylvia Caplin and Bharti Vyas had been preaching the same doctrine of sex as a therapy for a variety of psychological and physical problems. Both were convinced of the theory that many of life's ailments were brought on as a result of an underactive sex life. Cherie had sat intently through long lectures from both women on the subject. That was not all. The lectures had gone further than that; before her husband had become leader of his party Cherie had agreed to discuss in detail with Mrs Caplin the most private aspects of their sex life. Sylvia had long been a proponent of eliciting deeply intimate details from her clients. As shall be fully explored later, this was a tactic employed by the controversial Exegesis cult of which Mrs Caplin's daughter Carole was a former disciple.

Sylvia Caplin, a pensioner and former ballerina with no formal qualifications, was closely involved with her daughter's failed business venture Holistix. As well as diet and exercise tips, Sylvia preached a mantra of health through sex. Sources confirm what Sylvia herself admitted in an interview with the *Daily Telegraph*, that during her first two-hour consultation Cherie was shown a series of sexual exercises devised to make lovemaking more enjoyable and last longer. Carole also showed her a combination of massage techniques that she and Tony were supposed to use on each other before making love. One of the methods advocated by Sylvia was that of tantric sex, a Hindu form of prolonged and spiritual intercourse whose most famous proponent is the rock star Sting.

Bharti Vyas, who had made a fortune from her alternative health centre in London, was also an ardent advocate of sex as therapy. Mrs Vyas is a student of Ayurveda, the ancient Indian philosophy that divides people into three *doshas* or energy types. These three types are the dynamic *pitta*, *vatas*, who are full of nervous energy, and *kaphas*, laid-back individuals. By identifying which *dosha* a person is from, Vyas claims to be able devise appropriate diets for them based on their psychological make-up. She too is a promoter of mutual massage and gives regular lectures to her clients on her sex theories. One of her central theories concerns the use of sex as a means of relaxation. 'Men and women lead such stressful lives that they have forgotten the importance of touch, of hugging,' Mrs Vyas has said. Her course, she added, 'will teach people to understand each other's moods and stresses through touch and massage. If they can help each other relax, they may decide to take a bath together and then go to bed together.'

Two weeks before the birth of baby Leo, in an interview about her homeopathic approach to drug-free childbirth in a Sunday broadsheet newspaper, Mrs Vyas also offered in passing a flavour of the sexual teachings she handed down to her clients. After raising the spectre of her Flowtron leggings, which, she declared, were a vital tool in 'lymphatic drainage' and improving circulation, she went on to describe how sex during pregnancy would aid in toning the muscles used in childbirth. 'A woman should feel lots of love and enjoyment throughout her pregnancy,' she said. 'It's important for the woman to feel attractive. It's wonderful to experiment with new positions because you're pregnant. You can perform your own *Karma Sutra* in the bedroom.' In a further example of her forthright views on a full sex life, she added, 'I tell ladies that if their men turn to a younger woman it is their own fault. If they do not look good and have enough energy for sex, then their men will look to other women. A woman should tire her man so much that he does not have the energy to turn to another woman.' Tony, she had told Mrs Blair, should also massage her back, shoulders and calves daily. 'The lady of the house,' she added, 'is the pillar of the house and if she is well and has a lot of energy she will radiate that energy throughout the family.' Her comments were an embarrassment to Number Ten and, in an indication of its sensitivity to the issue, it made a bizarre move. Following publication of Mrs Vyas's remarks,

New Dawn: Tony and Cherie in July 1994 on the day he was appointed
leader of the Labour Party. Cherie's look was derided by the press.

Brief Encounter: Cherie's fierce ambition to succeed in her career at the Bar was driven in part by her father Tony's absence during her childhood.

(FIONA HANSON / PA / EMPICS)

Spun Out:
Alastair Campbell and his partner Fiona Millar were central to the creation of 'Brand Blair', but their relationship with the Prime Minister and his wife soured.

(RICHARD YOUNG / REX FEATURES)

Glamorous Guru:
Former model
Carole Caplin
became a fixture
of the Blairs' court,
but her influence was
to become hugely
controversial.
(REX FEATURES)

First Family: Tony, Cherie, Nicky, Kathryn and Euan (right) about to enter Downing Street for the first time on 2 May 1997. Once inside, however, they we shocked at the state of their new home. (ROOKE / JORGENSEN / REX FEATURES)

Election Fright: Cherie answers her door the morning after the night before, following Labour's 1997 victory, clearly not expecting to find the world's press camped outside.
(NICK CORNISH / REX FEATURES)

Special Relationship: The Blairs dine with US President Bill Clinton and his wife Hillary at London's Pont de la Tour restaurant in May 1997, shortly after New Labour came to power. It was a meeting of minds, particularly for the First Ladies.
(REX FEATURES)

Proud Parents:
Tony and Cherie pose with their fourth child, Leo, following his birth in May 2000. The couple chose Mary McCartney, the daughter of former Beatle Sir Paul, as official photographer.

(REUTERS / CORBIS)

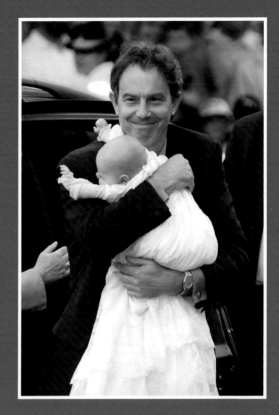

Blair Heir: Tony carries Leo to church for his christening in July 2000.
(ALBAN DONOHOE / REX FEATURES)

Under A Tuscan Sun: The Blairs enjoy a family holiday in Italy in 2000 with baby Leo, Euan, Kathryn and Nicky (far right) at the villa owned by Prince Girolamo Strozzi near San Gimignano. Their holidays have frequently led to accusations of freeloading.
(REUTERS / CORBIS)

We Are Not Amused: The Queen makes her displeasure known as she reluctantly joins the Blairs in singing 'Auld Lang Syne' at celebrations to mark the Millennium inside the Dome. (REX FEATURES)

Walking Tall: Blair gathers his family for a photo-shoot as he heads off to vote in his Sedgefield constituency in the 2001 General Election. A landslide victory for Labour had been predicted. (SEAN DEMPSEY / PA / EMPICS)

Campbell issued a Downing Street statement denying Mrs Vyas was helping in the birth of the Blairs' baby. But it was the second part of the denial that raised eyebrows: Mr Blair, Campbell claimed, had not massaged his wife. Campbell did his best to distance the Blairs from Mrs Vyas, but despite her unauthorized public comments she was, for the moment, to remain a firm fixture in the life of Mrs Blair.

Tony had clearly been the beneficiary of the combined wisdom of his wife's gurus, but the idea of being a parent again at the age of forty-six was a daunting one. Although a committed and devoted father, Blair remembered the many occasions when he had been left alone to take care of his three young children while his wife was away working. He was also well aware, say friends, that it would not be in his wife's nature to give up work once the baby was born. Despite his job running the country, Blair was under no illusion that he would be required to do his fair share of nights trying to get a screaming newborn back to sleep. He was by nature a modern father more than willing to play his part when it came to child-rearing duties, but the prospect of doing it all again in middle age was bitter–sweet. In public at least he admitted, 'We are quite old to have a baby. I admit I am just a wee bit apprehensive.' It would be the first time a baby had been born to a prime minister in Downing Street for more than 150 years and, more importantly, would do much to boost the image of the Blairs as the new Kennedys, but the news came as a surprise to Tony Booth, who had not yet been told about the imminent arrival of another grandchild.

Things are rarely as they seem in politics. In the days after the announcement that their fourth child would be born in May, the press began a quest to discover the story of the conception of Britain's most famous unborn. The smart money appeared to be on Tuscany, where the Blairs had spent a holiday the previous summer, but when national pride is at stake why, to borrow from the famous Fleet Street maxim, let the facts get in the way of a good story? As speculation mounted about where the baby had been conceived, Blair, at a meeting of centre-left political leaders in Florence, was asked by Italian journalists if indeed his new baby would be a bambino. Blair was quick to crush Italian hopes. 'I think it's probably British,' he said. So, as rumour had it, was the baby the result of a marital meeting under the Queen's roof while the Blairs were staying at Balmoral the previous September? No one was saying, but it was enough that the nation knew their new son or daughter would be a true Brit. In fact, Blair court insiders insist that Leo was the result of a European union.

By a happy coincidence the pregnancy coincided with changes to the Employment Relations Act which would allow fathers to take up to three months unpaid leave. But would the prime minister be handing over the reins to his deputy John Prescott to spend time off with his wife and new baby? The answer was yes, but Blair just didn't know it yet. The PM was reluctant to take time off after the birth. He and his advisers reasoned that while the electorate might be happy to know their leader was a modern man, content to do his bit in the first weeks of his new child's life, they would in all honesty prefer it if he was doing the job they were paying him to do and get on with running the country. The feeling was only intensified by the fact Blair knew that while he was away he would have to watch from Chequers while the gaffe-prone Prescott was let loose. But in the end the decision was taken out of his hands. 'Cherie made her mind up that Tony was going to take paternity leave and that, frankly, was the end of it,' says a source. Cherie had begun her campaign with a speech in March to law students. She told them she wanted her husband to follow the lead of the Finnish prime minister Paavo Lipponen, who took six days off when his first child was born in 1998. 'He's done it again recently and I for one am promoting the widespread adoption of this fine example,' she said.

Cherie, who had by now learnt a thing or two about political manoeuvring, had caught her husband in a pincer movement. In the weeks that followed he would also have to agree to Cherie's demand that he scale down foreign trips once the baby was born.

It was a sign, however, of Blair's reluctance that his wife felt it necessary to conduct a public crusade to win him round. Her stance led to Downing Street being questioned on the issue three days later with Alastair Campbell defending Blair's seeming prevarication. 'Cherie has made her position very clear,' he snapped. But Blair was still stalling. The same day, when asked if there were strong arguments for temporarily handing over power to spend more time with his family, he told ITN, 'Of course there are, but I have to make sure the country is properly run too. To be completely honest, I haven't thought it through properly yet. I haven't decided what to do. I know I should have and I'm sure I will. I'll decide in the next few weeks.' Later he broke off from a EU summit in Lisbon to say, 'I am going to have to sit down and discuss it with the family first. That's the right place to start.'

Cherie, however, was not in the mood for discussion. A source says, 'She is a feminist and her principles about these issues are incredibly strong. She could not go on making these arguments about women demanding more for themselves if she did not live by her own philosophy. She was very firm about that. It wasn't a subject that was up for discussion. He didn't want to do it, but she made him.'

5

2000: A ROYAL DUTY

It is an easy mistake to make. Without doubt, many of us fall into the trap of seeing our politicians in less than human terms. We rarely consider that once our leaders have made some major decision of national or international significance, once they have endured the bear pit of Prime Minister's Questions in the Commons or braved an inquisition from Paxman or Humphrys, they go home to the same domestic pressures we all face. In the weeks before his fourth child Leo was born on 20 May 2000 Tony Blair had made the difficult decision to send British soldiers into the former British colony of Sierra Leone to quell the civil war, while earlier that month he and Labour had been humiliated by the election of Ken Livingstone as London mayor. Livingstone had previously resigned as one of Blair's MPs to stand as an independent against Labour candidate Frank Dobson. And the month before that, forty-one of the prime minister's own MPs had given him a bloody nose when they rebelled in a vote on the paltry 75p-a-week rise in the state old age pension.

In the midst of all this Cherie was entering the final days of her pregnancy. Two days before Leo's arrival she had been taken to the Chelsea and Westminster Hospital after feeling what she thought were the first signs of contractions; Tony had had to break off from a Number Ten meeting to go with her. But within hours they were back at home as the doctors told them it had been a false alarm. If he was feeling more nervous than he had been for the births of his previous three children, it was understandable. Not only was Cherie, at forty-five, at considerably more risk, she was also determined to have if possible a natural birth. Kathryn, their last child, had been born by Caesarean section and it was unusual for mothers who have had a previous section to have natural births because of the danger of reopening the wound. When four months earlier the fertility expert Lord Winston, a friend of the Blairs, had let slip that Cherie would most likely have a Caesarean at the Chelsea and Westminster, he paid for his indiscretion by being shut out of their inner circle. But her NHS doctors were happy she was not presenting a risk to herself or the baby by opting for a natural delivery.

It was typical of the committed Cherie that she worked right up to the final days before the birth. Ironically, given the battle she had won inside Downing Street, she was appearing in the High Court just three days before going into labour, representing the TUC in an action against her own husband's government's plans on parental leave. On her feet for three hours as she made a lengthy legal submission, she refused an offer to sit down while she made her address and showed no sign of the tiredness Tony had earlier revealed she was feeling. She even managed a joke with Lord Chief Justice Woolf to the effect that she hoped he wouldn't mind if she was unavailable for his summing-up.

The PM himself had agreed to go into 'holiday mode' and substantially cut down his workload once the baby was born. At 10.30 on Friday morning Cherie felt her first contractions and by 11 a.m. she was arriving with Fiona Millar at the Chelsea and Westminster. Tony arrived at noon, but was soon heading back to Number Ten as his wife began a long and painful labour. By 8 p.m. her worried-looking husband was back at the hospital. For much of the next four and a half hours Cherie, in complete agony, screamed down the Josephine Barnes Ward of the hospital's maternity unit. Mrs Blair had turned down the chance of a pain-relieving epidural or labour-inducing hormones because of her belief in natural remedies, and as the excruciating pain kicked in had to make do with the gas and oxygen offered to her by the midwives. Tony, says a source, was ashen-faced throughout. 'He was terrified, poor bloke,' says an insider. 'Cherie was screaming her lungs out and I think Tony felt helpless. You have to remember that because she wanted a natural birth they both knew there was a risk of rupture because she had been given a section when she had Kathryn. He was pretty terrified that something was going wrong. It didn't help that Cherie was in so much pain and making such a racket.'

Finally, at 12.25 in the early hours of Saturday morning, Leo, named after Tony's father, was born weighing six pounds twelve ounces. Two hours later in a bid to avoid the press the first family's new member was spirited out of a back entrance with his parents to a people carrier with blankets draped over the windows. Cherie rested at Downing Street and issued a statement that hinted at the horrors of the previous hours: 'It is so long since we had our other three children that I had forgotten quite what an ordeal those few hours of labour can be.' Later that day Mr Blair emerged clutching a mug with a picture of his children on it to say, 'It wasn't a quiet night.' In the privacy of Number Ten he was more forthcoming. 'It was a complete bloody nightmare,' he told an aide. 'I never want to have to go through that again.' Two days later Blair announced he would, after all, be taking two weeks paternity leave, spending the Whitsun break with his family at Chequers. In the meantime the new parents posed for official pictures at Downing Street with Leo for Mary McCartney, the photographer daughter of former Beatle Sir Paul. The informal pictures were released to the media with proceeds from their sale going to Breast Cancer Care and Sargent Cancer Care for Children, charities of which Mrs Blair is patron.

As with the announcement of Cherie's pregnancy, the prime minister enjoyed a polls boost with the arrival of his new son, halting a slide in government fortunes over funding of the health service and rising crime. Mrs Blair had previously also been receiving negative publicity with accusations of 'empire building' over revelations that the taxpayer was funding a 'social office' of four people for her. The birth of her fourth child had, for a while at least, subdued the criticism.

Alas, the goodwill was short-lived. They soon found themselves embroiled in another row with the press, this time over christening pictures of baby Leo. Once again the Blairs reported the media to the PCC after photographs of them arriving with their baby at the tiny St John Fisher Roman Catholic church in the prime minister's constituency appeared in the papers despite instructions from Number Ten that the event was private. Their complaint left the couple open to claims of seeking preferential treatment, particularly as 300 well-wishers watched the event and some members of the public were allowed to cuddle and take photographs of the baby. Significantly, and in a sign of the bad blood that had been caused over the announcement of Cherie's pregnancy, it was the *Mirror* which was first out of the blocks, accusing the prime minister and his wife of heavy-handedness. The event, it said, was a public one. 'If they had wanted it to be entirely private, it could have been held away from the public gaze at Chequers.' In fact, the Blairs had been offered a private service at Downing Street or at the country house and had turned down the offer. The PCC agreed that the press could not be banned from taking photographs on a public road. Given that the Blairs had previously been happy to pose with Leo for pictures taken by Cherie's friend Mary McCartney and had given photos of their family to the press before, what had changed? What could have hardened their attitude?

*

It is not, let's face it, an uncommon scene to most Londoners or, for that matter, residents of any provincial town or city in the country. As forty-year-old Lindsay Maggs dodged the crowds as she headed home on a Wednesday evening through

Leicester Square, she found a teenage boy lying flat out in a pool of vomit. He merited barely more than a glance from the users of this particular capital landmark, who have become immune to the nocturnal overindulgence of those drawn there. But for Ms Maggs there was a reason to stop. This kid, barely conscious and slumped on the pavement, looked different. He appeared middle class, she thought. His mother would be worried about him.

'He had been sick,' recalled Ms Maggs. 'He was barely conscious and clearly in a terrible state. There was vomit on his trouser legs. What worried me was that he was on his own. He had no friends with him. I kept thinking they must have gone off when he got into difficulties.' As the crowds stepped over and around him, Lindsay stopped and stroked the boy's hair until police arrived. She told them he seemed out of place. An ambulance was called and the paramedics checked his breathing and tried to question the boy to discover what was wrong with him. He mumbled that he had been out drinking with friends who had left him to take the tube home. They had been celebrating the end of their GCSE exams. By now several police had arrived and they told the teenager he was being arrested. Thirty minutes later at Charing Cross police station the boy was lined up with the other drunks, prostitutes and petty crooks who had found themselves attracting the attention of the overstretched Metropolitan Police that night. Eventually a custody sergeant called him forward, asked him his name, age and address and warned him again that he was being formally arrested. The boy gave the name Euan John and an old family address. The sergeant told the arresting officers to search his pockets and they found a cashpoint card bearing the name E. Blair. The custody sergeant asked him if this was his real name. Then it clicked. 'Hold on a minute,' he said. 'Aren't you Tony Blair's son?'

In the Downing Street flat, working on a speech for a conference the following day entitled 'Faith in the Future',

Tony Blair was beginning to worry about Euan's late arrival home. The first he knew of his son's arrest was when he was called by the Number Ten switchboard. In the meantime, the custody sergeant at Charing Cross, realizing he was involved in something major, had contacted Special Branch to tell them of his famous client. By the time Blair got the call at around 1 a.m., his son, nursing a sore head and a severe case of shame, was heading back to Downing Street in a Special Branch car. It did not, of course, take long for word to get out. Fifteen minutes later the news desk at the *Sun* received word from a police source that the sixteen-year-old Euan had been arrested. *The Times* also received the same information. Both papers rang Scotland Yard for information and within moments of their calls Dick Fedorcio, head of corporate affairs at the Yard, was relaying the events of the evening to the then Metropolitan Commissioner Sir John Stevens. Scotland Yard liaised with Downing Street to discuss handling of the episode. The following day plain-clothes officers seized video footage of the square taken by CCTV cameras of local businesses.

Blair's first two words were the same as those of nearly every member of his staff when told of the arrest. 'He said simply, "Oh fuck",' says a Downing Street staffer. 'His next thought, after imagining the field day the press would have with it, was to cringe at the prospect of what Cherie was going to say when she found out,' adds the insider. Cherie was out of the country, taking a well-earned rest after the birth of Leo, with the new baby, her mother and Carole Caplin in Portugal. Tony was supposed to be taking care of their eldest children.

With Cherie away and Blair unwilling to react publicly until he could talk through the options with his wife, there was, say some inside Number Ten, an initial inertia as Blair and his staff argued about how best to handle the embarrassment. The timing could not have been worse, coming as it did just days after Blair had made his much-ridiculed and seemingly off-the-cuff proposals for the police to drag badly behaved youngsters to cashpoints to extract on-the-spot fines from them. He had quickly been forced to withdraw the idea after leading police officers described the plans as unworkable. Cherie, contacted on holiday by her husband, was furious. As Blair had expected, she went 'absolutely ballistic', says a source, but not over the actions of her son. She, like many parents, is aware that underage drunken excesses are a rite of passage for many British teenagers. This, too, is essentially Blair's view. Cherie's real anger was aimed at the media, which her husband told her was already gearing up to go to town on the story. Cherie, naively, given that the story was already out and Euan had been formally arrested, told her husband he must get tough and demand their son's right to privacy. She was also, it has to be said, angry with him for allowing their son to get himself into a position where he would become the focus of unwanted attention.

The episode would illustrate how a government policy has the potential to be thrown into chaos by events in the life of the leader. If Blair had had his way a week before, the young Euan would have been marched to an ATM and ordered to cough up cash to one of London's finest. Blair for his part was annoyed with his son for the embarrassment he had caused the government and also, say friends, angry with himself for not adequately explaining to Euan how much his father's position placed the whole family under the microscope. Is it too much also to suggest that the feelings of anger shared by the Blairs, were, in part at least, underpinned by a sense of guilt, the guilt that many in public life feel about exposing their children to scrutiny? In the end Blair and his advisers sensibly decided to throw themselves on the mercy of a public who, they rightly believed, would see the incident as little more than youthful high jinks. The following morning Alastair Campbell set the tone by asking for understanding for the teenage Euan. While being careful not to suggest that the Blairs were taking his behaviour anything other than seriously, he said, 'Euan will not be the only teenager out last night celebrating his exams, he won't be the only one worse for wear, but he will be the only one splashed over all the papers and television.' The PCC, however, was quick to point out that it would not be possible for the Blairs to demand privacy in this case as Euan had not been at school at the time of the incident.

As well as the unwelcome prospect of possible criminal charges against his son, Blair was faced with two more pressing and equally unpleasant events. First, he was committed to appearing the night after Euan's arrest on the BBC1 programme *Question Time*. Second, he was about to face his unhappy wife as she returned from her holiday abroad. The family were well used to what they call her 'courtroom voice' when she was displeased. As Cherie, 'looking like thunder', arrived in Downing Street just after 11 p.m. Tony's performance on the *Question Time* panel was being aired to a fascinated public. It was clearly an unpleasant experience for him. Acknowledging the strain he had been put under by the events of the previous twenty-four hours, he told the audience, 'It's not been the greatest day, let's put it like that, but my son is basically a good kid and we will get through this. We are a strong family and we will see him right the other side of it.' But he remained adamant, he said, that he was determined to tackle the problems caused by drunken yobs. 'I think it is important that we take action against violent, aggressive or disorderly conduct and I'm afraid that applies to my family as much as it applies to anyone else's,' added a drawn-looking prime minister. Euan, he insisted, like anyone else if they break the law, 'should suffer the penalty'. Asked by the programme host David Dimbleby if he thought his son should be prosecuted, Blair replied, 'Well, that is a matter for the police, but if he has done something wrong, he has to pay the penalty of the law. I don't ask for any special preferences for my kid.' The worst aspect of the episode had perhaps been his son's attempts to give a false identity to the police, but Blair remained convinced Euan had merely been trying to protect his father from any embarrassment. 'As a politician,' said the PM, 'I can't say that my family is always going to obey the very highest standards. But the fact that my kid has done something wrong doesn't mean I shouldn't get up as prime minister and say I think we should deal with this type of conduct in our society.'

Earlier that day Blair had appeared close to tears as he departed from the text of his speech to the Brighton conference of a church group. 'Being a prime minister is a tough job,' he said. 'But I always think being a parent is probably tougher. Sometimes you don't always succeed, but the family to me is more important than anything else.' He couldn't resist a dramatic flourish, reading from a poem by Longfellow: '"For thine own purpose, thou hast sent the strife and the discouragement. We need the strength when the strife and discouragement is there."' The Brighton flock gave him a standing ovation. That night, heading back from Brighton, Blair asked the driver of his official Jaguar to make an unscheduled stop at the Duke of York pub in the West Sussex village of Sayers Common. There he drank a pint and a half of Harvey's bitter before heading back to Downing Street for his first meeting with his wife since the episode exploded. Euan's drinking was a celebration that his exams were over. His father's Dutch courage was in preparation for the even trickier cross-examination to come.

The following day the Blairs and their son were spirited out of Downing Street giving waiting journalists the slip. The press pack had been staking out Charing Cross police station believing that when Euan was called back in to discover his fate, it would be at the station he was taken to after his arrest. Fearing a media circus, Number Ten however had cannily requested that they be allowed to attend at a different location. So when Tony, Cherie and Euan arrived at Kennington station in southeast London they were relieved to find their movements had remained secret. They were also thankful to learn that the teenager would receive only a police reprimand, the least severe of the three options open to the police. Perhaps surprisingly for Blair, the episode actually served to enhance his reputation in the eyes of the press and the wider public. Even his detractors at the *Daily Mail* were supportive. 'Today, there will be many families,' it reported, 'who will be uttering the mantra, "There but for the grace of God go I." ' It does no harm, it seems, for the public to be reminded that prime ministers are beset by the same domestic and family issues we all face. It would not damage Blair, often seen as an overly-polished political performer, to appear human and more like the real family man he has tried so hard to convince us he is.

*

Until her sunshine idyll was so unpleasantly interrupted, Cherie had been enjoying the privileges afforded to the powerful by their rich friends. She had been spending long days in the well-appointed surroundings of a beautiful villa near Faro, loaned to her by its owner Sir Cliff Richard. It would not be the first time, or by any means the last, that she and her husband would avail themselves of the holiday homes offered to them by their moneyed admirers. So used to the practice have the couple become that they invented the term 'house banditry' to describe their partiality to holiday freeloading.

Sir Cliff, whose Christian beliefs are much approved of by Cherie, is a regular benefactor to the Blairs, proud owner as he is of not only his sumptuous Portuguese property but also a vast estate in Barbados which has become a home from home for the high-living couple. Among others who have queued up to offer their holiday homes to the Blairs are the former Labour minister and multimillionaire Geoffrey Robinson and Sir David Keane, whose house in Saint-Martin d'Oydes near Toulouse has been a perennial favourite. Generosity has usually been rewarded with invites to Chequers.

This practice was eventually to inspire such widespread criticism that the Blairs have been forced to agree to pay sums to charity in lieu of the freebies they receive from their friends. Insiders however cast doubt on the idea that the amounts they hand over adequately reflect the true value of the lavish vacations to which they have become so used. Even this concession, Downing Street sources claim, was resisted by Mrs Blair for some considerable time after her holiday arrangements began to encourage negative headlines in the press. Her reluctance, say some, is due to two aspects of her character. First, she is often disposed to stubborn defiance in the face of what she sees as ultimatums, particularly if they come from a media she despises. Second, she possesses a natural cupidity, which would continue to leave her open to claims of serious errors of judgement.

This acquisitiveness can be traced back to the straitened circumstances she endured as the child of a one-parent family. Unlike many of her peers in her profession and to a large extent her husband as well, she has been far too familiar for her liking with the reality of severely limited finances. She remains to this day, say friends, very aware of the value of money. It has become a standing joke too among her staff that she has taken, rather in the manner of minor royalty, to sending them signed photos of herself at Christmas time. One complained, 'I've got more pictures of Cherie than I have of my own family, but still they keep coming.'

It was an arrangement used, it was reported, in 2004 when the Blairs were on holiday at the Red Sea resort of Sharm el Sheik. The family discovered that the swimming pool at their hotel was not heated and contacted the neighbouring Hyatt Regency to ask if they might be allowed to use its pool so Leo could swim. An aide told the hotel manager of the luxury resort that Mrs Blair, Tony and their son would be coming. The hotel opened up its £2,000-a-night presidential villa to ensure their privacy and security, but in the event Mr Blair did not arrive. Instead Mrs Blair showed up with a sixteen-strong entourage of assistants, her mother, her daughter Kathryn and some friends. The hotel laid on a lavish buffet and barbecue of chicken, salmon and prawns, but it was the luxury spa that proved the biggest draw for Mrs Blair and ten of her friends. They indulged freely in Swedish, Thai and Indonesian massages as well as facials, manicures and algae wraps. Cherie enjoyed the experience so much that she and her party returned two days later to repeat the exercise. But it was only when a hotel worker was dispatched to enquire how Mrs Blair planned to settle the bill that they realized she had not apparently envisaged having to pay at all. Instead, she produced from her beach bag a selection of signed photographs of herself and her family by way of thanks. And when, in 2004, Mrs Blair celebrated her fiftieth birthday, her friends were told in a tone one described as 'rather too like an old headmistress of mine' that she would rather they did not choose presents for her, but instead bought her eye-wateringly expensive Burberry luggage.

A constant refrain of Cherie's, to much eye-rolling from her friends, is her insistence that she and Tony have missed out on earning large amounts of money because of his 'service' to the country. She maintains, rightly, that they would, in all likelihood, be millionaires by now if they had both continued to practise at the Bar. She was described by a friend as 'nothing short of devastated' when their old home in Richmond Crescent was sold in 2000 by the people who had bought the house from them. The prime minister and his wife had sold the house for £615,000 but just three years later it changed hands for £1.5 million. It was against this background that Cherie decided that they must surely be entitled to some perks for holding the highest office in the land. 'There is a definite feeling of resentment,' says a friend. 'And it's certainly true that Tony would almost certainly be a QC by now and earning a lot of money. Because of his job Cherie has also had to scale down her workload and she feels they have had to make sacrifices. She sees how much money their friends have got and she can't help feeling jealous.'

*

The feeling that they have missed out is not confined to the prime minister's wife. In an interview in March 2001 Blair himself revealed more than a touch of the green eye when describing how many of his contemporaries are now million-aires. 'It is amazing,' he said, 'how many of my friends I was in school and university with ended up being so rich. There's a mate I ran into the other day. We used to run discos together ... Now he's worth millions.' The 'mate' was actually old friend Alan Collenette, whom a long-haired Blair met when he arrived in London in the autumn of 1971. Blair, who was taking a gap year in the capital before heading up to Oxford, had vague plans of getting involved in the music scene. So vague were the plans that the eighteen-year-old had not even got round to finding somewhere to stay in a city he barely knew. Of such teenage oversights are headlines made. More than thirty years later Cherie Blair let slip to guests at a Downing Street reception for the homeless charity Centrepoint that her husband had slept rough on a park bench near Euston station after being unable to locate the school friends he thought would give him a bed.

It was an inauspicious start, but the teenage Blair had long possessed the desire to make his mark. He was driven, in part at least, by a wish to make the most of the opportunities denied his father because of illness. Despite his humble upbringing in a Glasgow tenement, Leo Blair had, through hard work and determination, forged a successful legal career and made for himself a comfortable lifestyle. Charismatic and deeply ambitious, he had also set his sights on a career in politics having become chairman of his local Conservative association, and harboured dreams of one day becoming prime minister. But as he prepared to find himself a parliamentary seat to fight, at the age of just forty he fell victim to a catastrophic stroke in the summer of 1964 at the family home in Durham. Tony, then eleven years old, was woken by his mother Hazel to be told the news and spent the day not knowing if his father would survive. Leo lived, but at a terrible cost. For three years he could not speak and had to be taught slowly and patiently by his wife to communicate again. His father's illness was undoubtedly to cast a shadow over Tony's young life, but it also gave focus to a boy not yet in his teens but already shouldering the dreams of a father cut down as he was about to enter public life.

Throughout his father's convalescence, Hazel remained resolute in the face of the family's travails. Caring for a disabled husband, within months she was informed that her daughter Sarah, then aged just eight, was suffering with Still's disease, a form of childhood arthritis. For two years Sarah remained in hospital, treated with an array of drugs as doctors sought to control her illness. Tony would later say of his mother, 'She was an absolute rock. I didn't see her break down, never once. When you think what she must have gone through. But she never exhibited any signs of it, so I owe her a very great debt.'

Despite the financial strain caused by Leo's illness Tony followed his elder brother Bill to Fettes College, the prestigious Edinburgh school known as the 'Eton of Scotland'. For the thirteen-year-old Tony it was a rude awakening. Coupled with the strict discipline demanded by the masters was the ancient humiliation of fagging. This involved acting as dogsbody for an older boy: cleaning his kit, laying out his sports gear and making him snacks; Blair hated the experience. A talented student and sportsman, Blair's unease with his institutional surroundings was palpable. Though essentially popular with his fellow students and teachers, there grew during his time at Fettes a resentment against the place, a slow-burning rebellion that had him marked down as a dissident, a well-mannered insurrectionist who disguised his insolence under the cloak of the grinning leg-puller.

Rules were there to be tested to the limit. Even his favourite master Eric Anderson, who went on to be headmaster at Eton, was used to clashing with his young charge over having his hair too long or not wearing his tie properly; the argumentative Blair was more than willing to state his case. It was with the encouragement of Anderson that Tony found an outlet in drama, a skill employed, perhaps over-employed, in later years. Even so, as he neared his A levels in the summer of 1971 Blair's increasing disruptiveness, including his habit of jumping over the wall to chat up girls at the local fish and chip shop, was threatening his future. His father had been called in by the school's headmaster Dr Ian McIntosh and warned over his son's conduct. In the event, he escaped expulsion by the skin of his teeth when school governor Lord Mackenzie Stuart, father of Amanda Mackenzie Stuart, Blair's teenage girlfriend and the first female pupil at Fettes, spoke on his behalf to the headmaster. Tony was allowed to finish his time at Fettes with the proviso that he lived outside school at his lordship's Edinburgh home.

The relative ignominy of his departure from Fettes, though concerning for his parents, had no lasting effect on his prospects, and he was offered a place to read law at St John's College, Oxford. In the meantime, however, he decided he would take a year out in London. So, armed with a home-made guitar called Clarence and a fair imitation of the Mick Jagger walk and pout, Blair arrived on the Kensington doorstep of former St Paul's public schoolboy Collenette, who, he had been told, was a would-be rock promoter. The two decided they would go into business together, discovering unsigned bands and putting them on in small halls around west London. Blair stumped up fifty pounds for a dilapidated Ford Thames van, which was used to take the bands to the shows. Not content with running the disco or manning the spotlight at these small-scale gigs, the budding showman, perhaps displaying his theatrical heritage, was only too keen to get up on stage to belt out passable versions of his favourite Rolling Stones hits, 'Honky Tonk Woman' and 'Brown Sugar', as well as Elvis Presley's 'Blue Suede Shoes'.

The entrepreneurs generated interest by cycling around local schools distributing flyers to the students. The arrangements were distinctly free market with Blair and Collenette collecting up to 80 per cent of the takings, but then not every event was a success. Blair was left counting the cost after a concert staged on his nineteenth birthday at the 2,000-seat Queen Alexandra Hall in Kensington failed to attract more than a handful of fans. Later he would comment, 'It was a very good period for me because I was very anxious not to have to depend on my dad for money. I just wanted to demonstrate a bit of independence.' Collenette clearly learnt from their early moneymaking endeavours; during that chance meeting thirty years later, Blair discovered that his old friend had made a multi-million-dollar fortune running a real-estate business in San Francisco. Another contemporary who had gone on to become hugely rich was the comedian Rowan Atkinson, who was at Fettes College with Blair. The Mr Bean star is said to have made £40 million from his show-business career.

After leaving London Blair did not give up his dream of a career in entertainment. While studying at Oxford he was the lead singer in a student band called Ugly Rumours. Blair, who was known for his purple loon pants and shoulder-length hair, quickly developed an act that owed much to the strutting and preening of his hero Mick Jagger. However, despite Blair's hopes of making it big, Ugly Rumours managed just a handful of gigs, including one in the cloistered environs of the sixteenth-century oak-panelled hall of Corpus Christi that was notable only for the sudden and spontaneous collapse of the drummer's hastily assembled kit. Ugly Rumours went on to suffer a mercifully swift demise.

*

Despite the envy Tony feels over the fortunes made by his old friends, it has to be said that the Blairs are hardly poor, but by the standards of many of their friends and acquaintances they certainly feel it. Cherie's ex-boss Michael Beloff QC was known to be one of the few barristers to earn more than £1 million a year, and she became convinced she needed a fresh start if she was not going to lag behind her colleagues' earnings. Her opportunity came in October 2000 with the incorporation of the European Convention on Human Rights into UK law. Seeing the increased opportunities the new legislation created for her profession, she became one of twenty-two lawyers to set up a new chambers called Matrix. Quickly dubbed 'a collection of superegos' by their detractors in the legal world, Matrix was perfectly placed to exploit the plethora of litigation that resulted from the government's controversial new legislation.

But Mrs Blair's change of emphasis from employment law to human rights cases brought with it claims that she was set to benefit from her husband's government's changes in the law. The clamour was not silenced by an article she co-wrote with a partner in the new venture, Rabinder Singh, about the new act. In the piece for the *Daily Telegraph* in which she spoke out in praise of the legislation, she began, 'The Human Rights Act forms an integral part of the Government's constitutional reform, which has the aim of modernising Britain to make it strong and confident in the twenty-first century.' She added, 'The Human Rights Act represents the third way.'

While it was perfectly proper for an eminent barrister to comment on changes to the law, Mrs Blair, or in this context Cherie Booth, seemed to be acting as spokesperson and cheer-leader for the government. Not just that, but was it too cynical to see the *Telegraph* article as an exercise in free advertising for a firm that stood to profit substantially from an act which Scottish judge Lord McCluskey described as presenting 'a field day for crackpots, a pain in the neck for judges and a gold mine for lawyers'? Indeed in Scotland, where the Convention had already come into force, 600 new cases had already been brought under the act. The article produced catcalls from the *Daily Mail*, which argued that judges were wresting political power from those at Westminster. 'Our constitution is being reshaped and the Prime Minister's wife tells us not to worry. She has no time for our antiquated arrangements, one of which is called Parliament,' it thundered.

The Tories, too, smelled blood, with Cherie accused by Conservative Chairman Michael Ancram of being an apologist for her husband's government. His fellow Tory MP John Bercow went further, describing Mrs Blair as 'an unaccountable cross between a First Lady and Lady Macbeth'. The Conservatives even compiled a thick dossier on Cherie, listing her political comments and close links to Hillary Clinton. Bercow was unapologetic over the campaign. He said, 'We have experienced regular "noises off" from Cherie Blair over a period on controversial issues of public policy – parental leave, trade-union rights, job-share schemes, racial and sexual discrimination and now the highly charged issue of incorporation of the European Convention on Human Rights into British law.' Leaving aside the rhetoric, Mrs Blair's decision to come out so openly in support of an act which she clearly hoped would play a big part in the success of her new chambers laid her and her husband open to claims of nepotism and profiteering. But Cherie remained defiant: 'If the *Daily Mail* are taking shots at me I must be doing something right,' she told a colleague who offered his support over her stance.

Cherie's antipathy to the *Mail* was ingrained, spokesman as it is for Tory middle England. Blair had no such antagonism and had courted the Associated Newspaper stable in 1997, persuading the *Mail*'s sister title the London *Evening Standard* to join the New Labour corner. By the autumn of 2000, however, relations were certainly strained, but not enough to prevent *Daily Mail* editor Paul Dacre and Lord Rothermere, owner of the group, being invited to dinner at Downing Street. It is said that during the evening Cherie left the room and returned with the Blairs' new baby. Then, it is alleged, she embarrassed her guests by unbuttoning her blouse to breastfeed Leo openly at the dinner table. However, those close to Cherie say they have never seen her breastfeed Leo in company; she has always, they insist, made a point of leaving the room to feed him.

As Cherie devoted her energies to setting up her new chambers, there occurred the first major dip in the fortunes of her husband's administration. Since the birth of Leo he had appeared unfocused and sounded off-key. In June 2000, three weeks after his son was born, Blair was on the receiving end of a 'handbagging' by a rowdy bunch of hecklers at a Women's Institute rally in London who accused him of making an overtly political speech; the sure-footedness he usually possesses on such trying occasions was conspicuously missing. He was also noticeably lacklustre in his weekly Commons jousts with Tory leader William Hague, for all his faults a skilled parliamentary performer. And as anger among hauliers at rising fuel prices led to blockades of petrol refineries in early September, Blair appeared slow to react.

What was the cause of this sudden malaise? The answer, say insiders, is simply that the prime minister was 'completely knackered'. Blair's concerns that his domestic workload would be substantially increased by the arrival of a new baby had turned out to be well founded. Cherie, who was heavily involved with her fledgling chambers, had made it plain to her husband that she expected him to take his turn on the night shift when Leo woke up crying. This the baby did with unending regularity, according to friends of the couple. Consequently Blair, who frequently held meeting with members of his private office until after midnight, often spent half the night trying to get his new son to settle when it was his stint in the nursery. He would then often be back at work at six the following morning. Shortly after Leo's birth Blair had said, 'The thing is, you forget how tiny they are – and also changing nappies in the middle of the night.' 'He was utterly exhausted and it showed,' says a Number Ten source. 'He was demanding too much of himself and it affected his performance. It was a serious problem for a time.'

Alerted by his boss's obvious exhaustion, Alastair Campbell was open in his incredulity at the situation. Another who was vocal in her opposition to Blair's increased domestic duties was Anji Hunter. Although generally oblivious to the brickbats being aimed at her by her husband's private office, Cherie did feel that Anji had been unsupportive over the baby.

But wasn't this political correctness gone mad? In any normal marriage they would have been applauded for sharing child-rearing duties, but the circumstances were surely exceptional. Blair was a 'new man' before the term was invented, but there was, after all, a country to be run. One who voiced concerns at the time remembers, 'The whole thing was a farce. He was the leader of the country, for crying out loud. The last time I looked there was only one prime minister; there are lots of QCs. Cherie seemed to have got it into her head that she must practise what she had been preaching all her adult life. I truly think she had lost the plot if she believed they were like any other couple. She was certainly the instigator of it and Tony would not stand up to her.' Cherie provided an insight into her no-nonsense attitude to her husband's role in the family four years later during a speech in Iceland. After telling the audience how she had successfully cajoled her husband into taking paternity leave, she held up a cartoon by the *Daily Mail*'s Mac which showed her beating her reluctant husband with a vase to make him agree to take time off. It was, she said, an accurate portrayal of life in Downing Street. Then, in serious mode, she told the group of women lawyers in Reykjavik, 'We need to challenge the outdated practices regarding men and women in family life. Family responsibilities are not just women's responsibilities. I try to put that into practice in my own life.' This was all very well, of course, if she had not been married to a man who not only shouldered the burden of his own family, but that of his nation as well.

*

If being in power served to distance Blair from the electorate in the years to come, it was also responsible for Tony and Cherie losing touch with the friends who had been part of an important support system for them before the election. In their place came the political appointees, staff and gurus who formed a proprietorial circle around the couple. Their old friends felt increasingly forced out. Get-togethers have to be planned weeks in advance and cleared by Blair's Special Branch team. Although close to her mother Gale, Cherie's relationship with her sister Lyndsey is not warm.

Tony too found that friends from his pre-Number Ten days gradually stopped calling. Today, say Downing Street insiders, he has no real friends outside politics whom he can turn to for a chat or go for a drink with. Time constraints mean he sees his father only occasionally. Neither does he see much of his elder brother Bill and his wife Katie. Tony's sister Sarah also rarely visits. His children and his love of football, particularly his beloved Newcastle United, are his only real release from the all-consuming nature of the job. His staff describe the prime minister stopping suddenly in mid-sentence to wander into the Number Eleven garden to pick up Leo for a cuddle or share a few words with his daughter Kathryn as she bounces on the trampoline once much used by all his children.

As real friends from the past were allowed to slip away, the court turned in on itself. To those outside the circle it appeared increasingly that the control freakery and suspicion that had come to characterize New Labour was in danger of allowing those at its heart to lose touch.

6

2001: SPECIAL RELATIONSHIP

The awe that Tony Blair felt for Bill Clinton was matched only by the unswerving admiration Cherie had for Hillary. After their first meeting in 1997 Cherie had, using the language of New Age psychobabble that had increasingly become a mainstay of her vocabulary, told friends how she had witnessed the 'energy channelling' through Mrs Clinton. She was instantly smitten. The two women, so alike in many ways, were different in one respect at least. Cherie saw in Hillary the politician she had aspired to be. There was no doubting from their first encounter that the wife of the president was never going to be satisfied with being seen as purely an appendage of her husband. Privately, too, Hillary made no bones about her desire to pursue public office once her husband had left the Oval Office.

Not only did Hillary share Cherie's sharp intellect and her brand of conviction politics – characteristics not in evidence in either of their husband's approaches – she was also not afraid to be forthright about articulating her strongly held opinions. In addition, both women knew what it was like to be ugly ducklings, obliged because of media taunts to throw off a bluestocking image for a manufactured and airbrushed glamour that, to begin with at least, they had felt was at odds with their serious credentials. They had also both allowed themselves to be silenced, to a greater or lesser degree, in order to lend authority to their husbands. And, it should be said, neither was likely to win any popularity contests any time soon. But where Hillary also differed from her British counterpart was in the natural charisma she shared with her husband and an innate understanding of how to communicate her political vision. Cherie, profoundly skilled as she was in dry policy formulation, was transfixed by Hillary's ability to relay her passionately held beliefs in a way she never could. During the height of the scandal over Clinton's affair with Monica Lewinsky, Cherie had sat rapt as Hillary gave a speech about tug-of-love children. 'Cherie was mesmerized by her,' says a source. 'Hillary was so clear, so forceful in her message. In the background all this stuff about her husband and their marriage was being played out in the media, yet Hillary was unruffled and completely serene.' Cherie, who had idolized strong Labour women like Barbara Castle and Shirley Williams – before Williams incurred her derision by joining the SDP – had found a new role model.

Cherie felt thrilled that the formidable Hillary was so warm and treated her as an equal. In her company Cherie was for once able to break cover and ditch the charade she was forced to play out with others that she was not a vital political force within her husband's administration. Hillary, who occupied a similarly pivotal role in the White House, was an instant soul sister. By way of illustrating their meeting of minds, Hillary flew to the UK alone in the autumn of 1997 to attend a 'third way' conference at Chequers which had been the brainchild of the two first ladies. Mrs Clinton, who arrived early, sat up long into the night in front of a fireplace in the great hall discussing foreign policy and welfare reform with her new best friend. Cherie, says a Blair court source, was 'absolutely buzzing' after the exchange and thrilled that she was now an important part of the fabled special relationship between Britain and the US. Unfortunately, this was not to last. In late February 2001 the Blairs flew to Camp David to meet the new incumbent of the White House, the Republican George W. Bush, who had controversially been declared president-elect two months earlier after a protracted legal battle over vote counts in the election. On the Blairs' first day in the US capital, by way of contrast with the Clinton era, Cherie was left twiddling her thumbs as her husband and the new president held lengthy talks. That afternoon Bush's wife Laura excitedly told Mrs Blair that she had chosen the no-brainer Ben Stiller comedy *Meet the Parents* for the two couples to watch together that night. Times had indeed changed.

Cherie's distress over the election of Bush was palpable, not simply because she was by instinct and political ideology horrified by the thought of a right-wing hardliner running the world's only superpower. Her upset was personal too. She had relished the overt role she was allowed to play within the Clinton–Blair quartet, and she had hoped to continue playing her part if Democratic presidential candidate Al Gore and his wife Tipper, whom she regarded as being *simpatico*, got into the White House. Laura Bush, the homely former librarian, was as far removed from the ambitious, fiercely political Hillary as it was possible to be. Mrs Blair, who had privately branded Bush's narrow election victory 'theft', made little attempt to hide her dismay and outrage at the result. Tony, the political pragmatist, had already decided to take the outgoing Bill Clinton's advice, 'Get as close to him as you did to me.' But he was aware that the attitude of his wife to the new administration might prove a cause for concern if the Bush camp was to become aware of her increasingly vocal criticism of the new president.

As it became clear that Bush was about to win the disputed battle for the Oval Office, the British ambassador in Washington Christopher Meyer counselled members of Blair's staff and Cherie to moderate their tone. Meyer was seen by some in Number Ten and, more importantly by Cherie, as having become too cosy with the Republicans during the previous months. On the plane to Washington she had been vocal in her distaste for Bush and his band of neo-conservatives, saying at one point, 'Why do we have to be nice to these people?' It has been said that the Blairs also rejected a bust of Churchill they were due to give Bush as a present because they thought it wasn't of sufficient quality for the Oval Office. Not so. By way of letting her feelings be known about what she considered Meyer's impertinence, Cherie vetoed the gift, which had been chosen by the British embassy, on the grounds that they had not given anything so impressive to their friends the Clintons.

Once in Camp David Cherie was gracious and friendly, but she remained privately critical of Bush. Her antipathy came to the surface however in two subsequent encounters. When Bush stayed with the Blairs at Chequers in July 2001 Cherie could not hold her tongue any longer. In a diplomatic blunder that left her husband squirming with embarrassment, she tackled the president during a hitherto convivial dinner over the death penalty, of which she is a fierce opponent. She also pressed him on his record of signing more than 150 death warrants while he was governor of Texas. To his credit, her genial guest took this diplomatic faux pas in his stride. But the nadir for Cherie came when the Blairs were later invited to stay at the Bush ranch in Crawford, Texas. Cherie, who has an aversion to fresh air and the countryside, was disappointed to find that the president's home was in the middle of acres of barren scrubland while the house itself was a contemporary, arty building with masses of cold bare polished concrete and a minimalist lack of home comforts. Home on the range it most certainly was not. If the surroundings did not meet with Mrs Blair's approval, the company did nothing to lift her mood; Leo and his nanny were off in the original ranch house, some distance from the guest house they were staying in adjacent to the main building. Bush, Cherie complained to friends on her return, was uneasy with women and had studiously avoided getting into conversation with her.

Cherie was also infuriated by what she considered the appalling manners of the president when dealing with those who worked for him. She had watched open-mouthed as he summoned his domestic staff by alternatively whistling or clicking his fingers. Not only that, she was deeply offended by the chauvinism he displayed in his dealings with his wife. Bush, she told friends later, was in the habit of humming pointedly when he felt the first lady, who has an unfortunate tendency to witter, was talking too much. He would even butt in mid-sentence and tell his wife, 'That's enough of that now,' at which an embarrassed Mrs Bush would fall immediately silent. The contrast with the late nights spent discussing policies and their shared vision with the Clintons could not have been more marked. At 9.30 the Bushes went to bed, leaving the Blairs to retire to their guest house. There, they sat alone flicking through cable TV channels. To make matters worse, the Bush residence is dry; the president, a former heavy drinker turned teetotaller, has no alcohol in the house. Tony, who likes a glass of wine and the occasional whisky to wind down, was forced to make do with coffee. 'It was wretched,' says a Blair insider. 'Tony did his usual job of being charming and attentive, but Cherie was bored senseless and depressed and it showed. Not only did she have absolutely nothing in common with these people, she was having to hide a good deal of animosity to almost everything that Bush stands for.' The one area of shared interest was, however, Christianity, although even here Bush's Old Testament morality did not chime with either of the Blairs' more modern approach to God.

First ladies, of course, do have uses other than passing on their favourite cookie recipes or tips for the perfect eggnog. In November 2001 Laura Bush broke with American precedent by taking over from her husband his weekly radio address to the nation. As the US went to war on the Taliban in the wake of 11 September, Mrs Bush spoke of the brutal Afghan regime and counselled Americans to 'commit themselves to securing dignity and opportunity for the women and children of Afghanistan'. 'Only the terrorists and the Taliban,' she pointed out, 'threaten to pull out women's fingernails for wearing nail polish.' In a nation whose nail-bar industry is as large as the economy of a small industrialized nation, her words sent a chill down the spine of American womanhood. That was plainly the plan. Since Bush needed a public mandate to go to war, the hawks in his administration knew that they must garner the support of women, who are historically substantially less gung-ho than their male counterparts.

In Britain, Tony Blair too was preparing to break with tradition. In the week Mrs Bush canvassed support for her husband's war, Cherie Blair was about to do the same. On 19 November, six weeks after British and US troops invaded Afghanistan, she hosted a conference in Downing Street which was designed to 'lift the veil and show what has been happening to women in Afghanistan under the Taliban'. Like Mrs Bush, Cherie was seen as adding a female perspective on the issue but would it be too cynical to suggest that this was an overtly political act? If Blair wanted to appeal for the support of British women, there were several female ministers who could have done the job well enough. And while Mrs Bush's first lady title carried with it a limited constitutional role, no such position exists for the spouse of a British prime minister. That was the reason, we were told, Cherie refused to be questioned about her political beliefs and influence; she was not a member of the government, but a lawyer who just happened to be the wife of the leader and mother of his children. Mrs Blair, it seemed, was happy to play this highly political role, advocating British troops prosecute a war on foreign soil with the death and carnage that would undoubtedly follow, but not prepared to allow herself to be challenged as a politician who advocated such action would be. Again, it appeared that she wanted it both ways: making the most of the power she clearly exerted without those annoying incidentals like having to stand in elections, explain your actions in Parliament or face the questions of the media.

There is a widespread view that the Blairs are divided over the war against terror, particularly the invasion of Iraq by allied forces. This is significantly wide of the mark; in fact it is barely possible to pass a cigarette paper between the couple on this issue. Why if, as widely reported, Cherie is privately opposed to the war against Saddam, did she seek to convince the wavering international development minister Clare Short of the legality of the invasion, as Ms Short has claimed? As is evidenced by the plethora of memos which Downing Street sources insist Cherie has written to her husband on the matter, she actually added her significant legal weight to the case for war. Cherie was fully onside from the outset, not because of a strong political affinity with the US and even less the Bush administration, but for the very personal reason that she was profoundly moved by what she saw in New York in the days after the attack on the Twin Towers on 11 September 2001. She, like her husband, was also convinced of the need for action on the issue of Iraq.

*

For all the hundreds of people milling around in the huge and hastily erected tent on Manhattan's west side, there was an unnatural quietness about the place. Cherie Blair moved among the crowd, seeing every hollow face, every tortured expression. The makeshift building close to the river had become a shrine to those lost and missing in the days that followed the attacks on the World Trade Center. Each nation, including the UK, had a desk where those trying to trace a relative or friend could go for information. People walked in clutching hairbrushes, combs, pieces of dental floss to be processed by a special DNA team tasked with identifying those killed when two hijacked passenger planes slammed into the towers. Queues formed next to a children's centre responsible for trying to establish how many youngsters and babies had been in the building that fateful morning. Nearby, child psychologists crouched on tiny chairs counselling those whose parents had not come home.

Circling the building was an alleyway. Plastered to every inch of its walls were the thousands of photographs of those who were missing. As Cherie, lost in thought, shuffled slowly through the crowds taking in the faces of the victims, she was stopped by someone who recognized her. Would she, the person asked, stand next to a picture of their loved one and allow herself to be photographed? The picture might, she was told, appear on the TV networks or in the newspapers and someone might recognize the missing person. Cherie silently did what she was asked. She also laid some flowers next to the pictures of some missing Britons, but it was that moment being photographed next to a shimmering Kodacolor memorial that lived longest in the memory and when the conviction that the 'free world' must act against terrorism crystallized in her mind. If British forces must invade foreign lands, she decided, then so be it. The world owed it to those smiling faces pinned to the wall and to the people queuing inside clutching those pathetic mementos, the last physical evidence of lost life.

Tony Blair was in the Fitzherbert Suite of the Grand Hotel in Brighton preparing for his speech that afternoon to the TUC conference when the first plane crashed into the North Tower. His speech was scrapped and instead he gave a short address to his audience telling them, 'There have been the most terrible, shocking events in the United States of America in the last hours. I am afraid we can only imagine the terror and carnage there and the many, many innocent people who have lost their lives. This mass terrorism is the new evil in our world today.' By the time his train from Brighton arrived back in London, nobody was sure whether Britain might also be attacked by the terrorists. Blair had seemed not unduly concerned that he was in personal danger until it was pointed out to him that Downing Street, not just the centre of his government but the home of his wife and family, would be high on the list of potential targets.

In the ten days between the attacks on New York and the Pentagon and Blair arriving in the US he embarked on a round of diplomacy to shore up international support for dealing with the terrorist threat that culminated in whistle-stop trips to

Berlin and Paris. Now, three months after winning a second term with a massive majority of more than 160 seats, it would be the foreign stage that would dominate his thoughts and occupy his time. In New York Cherie accompanied Bill Clinton and Catherine Meyer, wife of the ex-British ambassador to the US, to a fire station where firefighters had lost ten of their colleagues. She was moved to tears by their stories and hugged every one of the men and their relatives. It was a new public side to Cherie, who had earlier in the month succeeded Princess Diana as the first non-royal president of the children's charity Barnardo's in fifty years.

Despite the traumatic scenes she witnessed, she remained strong, say those close to her. 'She was firmly of the opinion that she owed it to the people who had lost their lives that she should go to see what was happening there,' says a Downing Street source.

She was incredibly moved by what she saw and the people she spoke to. Like everyone else, she was in real shock. New York was eerily quiet despite everything that was going on and it affected everyone. But Cherie was very natural with the people she met who were grieving. It seemed to open her up. I don't think anyone relished the idea of having to go to New York so soon after the attacks, but Cherie was adamant that we must show our respect. The only time she broke down was in the fire station talking to those people. Somebody had brought a wreath in the shape of a helmet and Cherie met the wives of the men who had died. It was very hard. But seeing all those people really strengthened her resolve about Britain acting and supporting the US. That is why she was so supportive of what Tony was trying to do. There was never any disagreement between them about military action. She was as committed as him.

*

If Cherie's new charity role and the very real compassion she showed in New York were drawing comparisons with the late Diana, so too was her increasing interest in the spiritual and New Age beliefs, which the Princess had flirted with before her death four years earlier. A month after the World Trade Center attacks Cherie was photographed with an acupuncture needle in her ear. The needle, one third of a millimetre thick and with magnets at both ends, was pushed through her ear at the top in an area called the shenmen point which, in the language of Chinese medicine, translates as 'the gate to godliness'. In acupuncture a needle in this part of the ear is supposed to 'harness mental activity' and give confidence to the wearer. Diana had been seen wearing a needle in her shenmen point a year before her death. Cherie, says friends, was persuaded that the device would help her stay calm and relieve stress. She had also been having £120 'harmonising facials' with Bharti Vyas, which involved reflexology on the feet as a treatment for the complexion.

Picture the scene. The wife of our esteemed prime minister is lying motionless on her back on a thin mattress. She is wearing a large pair of goggles and a set of oversized headphones. Inside the goggles are red flashing lights which provide a series of kaleidoscopic images that appear before Mrs Blair's eyes. From the headphones comes a succession of strange, rhythmic noises. The bed on which she is lying is no ordinary one either; inside its mattress is a network of magnetic coils which will, she believes, help 'rebalance the magnetic field' in her body, while the 'alpha waves' from the goggles, she has been told, will tell her brain to relax.

Even in the unscientific world of New Age healing this £35-a-session process, called Magnetic Resonance Therapy, is considered controversial. Behind this unconventional procedure is Bharti Vyas, self-styled 'world renowned holistic therapist'. Vyas claims the treatment is 'highly effective in optimising the energy level of every cell, making them resonate faster, strengthening the body's functions, leading to growth in physical and mental wellbeing'. However Professors John Garrow and Vincent Marks were quoted in the *Mail on Sunday* pointing out that alpha waves are found in the brain; how they can be inserted into a pair of goggles leaves even the most eminent medical minds stumped. Second, there is absolutely no evidence that magnetic fields affect the body at the levels used in Mrs Vyas's treatment. The name for the cure itself seems to be a misuse, they say, of the term 'magnetic resonance imaging', a completely different technique which is used in hospitals to see inside the body.

But then a strict adherence to medical convention has never been part of Mrs Vyas's modus operandi. For starters she has no formal medical qualifications. Born in Nairobi, she wanted to train as a doctor but instead came to London after her marriage at the age of twenty and ran a delicatessen in Highgate. At thirty-five she trained as a beauty therapist, before setting up as a holistic guru to a growing band of ladies who lunch, who enjoyed Bharti's pampering treatments, such as her Flowtron leggings. Bharti described their remarkable properties: 'One might feel like Neil Armstrong stepping into the famous Flowtron boots, but there is no need to feel tentative because even if the person is not taking on the moon, post treatment they will feel ready to take on the world. With regular treatment once-a-month, for 90 minutes, the entire family can be kept relaxed and stress free.' Mrs Vyas rapidly built up a clientele of minor celebrities, such as television presenter Floella Benjamin and PR woman Lynne Franks, but Mrs Blair was her star convert. Their ten-year relationship, however, was about to hit the rocks. In early November 2001 Cherie officiated at the opening of the Bharti Vyas Holistic Therapy Training Centre in London's Marylebone. She was joined by Britt Ekland and Lady Helen Taylor, also clients of Mrs Vyas. Cherie cut the red ribbon and gave a brief speech. Her brevity was due to the fact that not all of the 200 people who turned up to celebrate the launch of the new centre were converts like herself. Bharti had omitted to tell Mrs Blair that she would be joined by a large contingent of Fleet Street's finest, all eager to find out the views of Mrs Vyas's most famous client on her unorthodox remedies.

Cherie was furious. The following day she fired off a letter to her publicity-conscious friend. She was uneasy at being used to promote her business. She had, she wrote, been expecting a quiet family affair and went on to call the event disorganized and shambolic. She threatened to boycott Bharti's salon for a few weeks as punishment for the abuse of her good name, but Cherie's immediate instinct to cut the indiscreet Mrs Vyas completely adrift was tempered by the realization that, if she had been a source of embarrassment so far, just imagine the havoc she could wreak if she was, to borrow a New Labour idiom, to go 'off message'. In politics, something on which Mrs Blair is well versed, the maxim goes that it is important to keep your friends close and your enemies closer. Mrs Vyas could in no way be seen as Cherie's enemy, but like those others to whose New Age dictums she had submitted herself, the colourful Bharti represented the possibility of considerable humiliation if she was to divulge the secrets of their relationship.

It is her questionable judgement about the people she puts her faith in that most frustrates even Mrs Blair's most ardent supporters. 'She seems to have no radar whatsoever for the sheer crackpotism some of them spout,' says one barrister friend. 'She has a fine analytical brain which is able to cut through complex arguments in court, yet she completely buys into this mumbo-jumbo. It is a complete conundrum.' Because Mrs Blair is not only a successful lawyer but also a part-time judge who has made no secret of her ambition to be appointed to the High Court her questionable judgement in her private affairs has unsurprisingly led to questions about whether she is fit to sit in judgement on others. Can somebody, it is argued, who has a tendency, at the very least, towards the gullible, really be the right person to sit in one of the highest courts in the land?

Where, too, do these false gods stand with Cherie's well-documented Catholicism? It surely cannot be appropriate in the eyes of the Church for a woman once called the highest-profile Catholic in the land to be seen to be dabbling in practices some of which can only properly be described as witchcraft. Did the subject of her routine of casting a circle in the manner of a white witch come up during her 2003 private audience with the Pope? One doubts it. Moreover, how does her behaviour sit with her husband's devout Christianity and quasi-Catholicism? The answer, according to friends, is that Blair has become used to his wife's foibles and tolerates them simply because he loves her. He has not, according to some, been immune to becoming involved in some of her more eccentric whims himself. It is said that during a 2001 summer holiday near Cancun in Mexico the couple took part in a rebirthing ritual in a Mayan steam bath, or *temazcal*, at the Maroma Hotel. It is alleged that the pair, wearing only swimming costumes, were guided through a ceremony that involved entering a brick-built tent-like structure and included bowing to the four winds as Mayan prayers were read out. They were supposedly invited to imagine animals in the steam of the bath, and to smear each other's bodies with watermelon, papaya and mud. They were then asked to make a wish – Blair's was, apparently, for world peace – and instructed to scream out loud to signify the pain of rebirth.

The Times journalist and friend of Mrs Blair, Mary Ann Sieghart, has frequently defended her against claims of crankishness. At the height of the Cheriegate scandal in 2002 Sieghart mounted a spirited case for the defence by claiming there is little difference between Mrs Blair's taste for New Age treatments and her Catholicism. 'The state of holiness that Catholicism inspires has parallels in the state of wholeness that holistic therapies promise,' she wrote. 'Both require water and incense to induce a sense of mysticism. Jesus washed his disciples' feet. Carole Caplin scrubbed the toxins from Cherie's body.' If her comparison of Christ and an ex-softporn glamour girl was not enough, Ms Sieghart then went on to claim that her friend's obsession with 'healing' was the result of sexual hang-ups that could be blamed on 'years of guilt-laden Catholicism'. 'Cleansing and purification are important features of both,' wrote Ms Sieghart, 'and are particularly powerful symbols to people who have been brought up to believe they must be purged of guilt.' Given the unstinting support of Ms Sieghart down the years, it is perhaps unsurprising that *The Times* is now the only paper Mrs Blair will read.

*

As we have seen, the education of their children has long been a touchy subject with the Blairs, who have understandably been concerned to preserve their privacy, but there comes a point when how a prime minister, particularly a Labour one, chooses to educate his offspring becomes a matter of legitimate public interest. Tony and Cherie Blair, like all parents, want what is best for their kids, and certainly their children have achieved well. Euan, the eldest, won a place at the prestigious Bristol University while Nicky has followed his father to Oxford, but the prime minister and his wife have found themselves the subject of fierce criticism over the advantages their children were given in getting there. In 2001 there were red faces at Number Ten when it was revealed that when Euan asked Cherie for help on a homework exercise that involved preparing for a debate on nuclear arms policy, his mother told a Downing Street official to track down the relevant information. By the time the aide reported back, Mrs Blair's request had led to an operation involving civil servants from two departments, and resulted in a fat briefing dossier which included two chapters from the *Strategic Defence Review* being delivered to the teenage Euan. When word of the exercise got out, Number Ten had to mount a hasty rearguard action to limit the embarrassment. The official Mrs Blair had asked was 'a bit too enthusiastic in contacting the MOD', said a press officer. But the question remained as to what Cherie was doing handing her son's homework enquiries over to Downing Street officials in the first place.

Far more potentially damaging for the prime minister however was the discovery that he and his wife had been using the services of private tutors to help their sons with their A-level and GCSE work. Moreover, these hired tutors were, by day, teachers at the £17,000-a-year Westminster School, arguably the leading private school in the country. The Blairs had already invited the condemnation of the left with their choice of the highly rated London Oratory for both elder boys, but while the Oratory was most definitely a cause for discontent among those in the Labour Party, Alastair Campbell included, who stuck determinedly to the comprehensive ideal, it could still at least be described as state sector. Westminster School, on the other hand, was a shining beacon of privilege and elitism, a monument to the tradition of the rich buying their children the kind of education that could only be dreamt of by their working-class counterparts.

It is no surprise that Blair, the product of a top public-school education who has seen at first hand the advantages it offers, has no inbuilt prejudice towards the private system. But what of Cherie, who never tires of pointing to the state education that offered her a way out of the relative poverty of her early life in Liverpool? Wasn't this a massive kick in the teeth for those like her who had been brought up to believe that all kids should be given the same chances as the children of rich professionals in London SW1? This was, was it not, the most shameful hypocrisy, worthy of the Tories Cherie so despised? Blair's cry of 'Education, education, education' came with an unspoken caveat: that those state schools and teachers so central to his government's policy might be good enough for the kids of those who elected him, but the prime minister wanted an insurance policy for his own children just in case. So, through the back door of Number Ten came the best teachers money could buy.

It was also further evidence of the myth that Cherie Blair was considerably to the left of her husband, a falsehood eagerly grasped by both sides of the political divide. For those on the right it was a useful scare tactic. Blair, they claimed, for all his moderate language, secretly had his strings pulled behind the scenes by his left-wing wife. The left, who have always remained suspicious of him, have willingly submitted to the self-delusion that for all Blair's Tory-boy credentials, Cherie will forever remain his Old Labour conscience. However, it is doubtful there was ever a case to argue that Cherie is any more radically minded than her husband. If it was ever true, then the pampered, moneyed world to which she so readily became accustomed has, without doubt, been responsible for her going native.

It was not just with regard to the schooling of their children that the Blairs laid themselves open to claims of double standards. As they sent out Christmas cards in late 2001 featuring a photograph of them with their children, a row broke out over demands for the prime minister to say if his son Leo had been given the controversial MMR vaccine. Not only would the fallout from the debate cause lasting damage to the government, it would lead to a previously unreported falling-out of Cherie with her sister Lyndsey. In 1988 the three-in-one MMR vaccination for measles, mumps and rubella had replaced the three single vaccines, but disputed research linked the injection with bowel disease and autism. Since its introduction there had been a flurry of claims from parents that their children had suffered harmful side effects and 2,000 British families were planning to sue the manufacturers. The claims, though far from being proved, led many thousands of parents to ignore the government's advice that the MMR jab was safe. The big question was whether the prime minister was sufficiently convinced of the safeness of the vaccine to allow eighteen-month-old Leo to have the injection. In the weeks that followed the Blairs faced a clamour for them to confirm that their son had indeed been inoculated. The issue was to become a bête noire for the prime minister, whose continued refusal to answer the calls led to the widespread assumption that Leo had not been given the injection.

The speculation was fuelled by suspicion that Mrs Blair's conversion to alternative therapies meant she would be predisposed to be wary of the vaccine. Indeed, it transpired that the gurus so influential in her life were all vehemently opposed to its use. Jack Temple, whose advice she often sought, had wholly unorthodox views about all aspects of immunization and argued that the MMR injection was not needed if a mother breastfed her baby from the moment of birth, thereby giving it natural immunity, he claimed, to all diseases. He offered a homeopathic alternative to the jab, and said, 'If women follow my advice their children will not need the MMR, end of story. I tell all my patients who are pregnant that when the baby is born they must put it on the breast until there is no longer any pulse in the umbilical cord. It usually takes about thirty minutes. By doing this they transfer the mother's immune system to the baby, who will have a fully functioning immune system and will not need vaccines.'

Others fiercely opposed to the vaccine were Carole Caplin and her mother Sylvia. For her part, Sylvia was adamant that it should not be given. 'I'm against it,' she said. 'I'm appalled at so much being given to little children. The thing about these drugs is the toxic substances they put the vaccines in. For a tiny child the MMR is a ridiculous thing to do. It has definitely caused autism. All the denials that come from the old school of medicine are open to question because logic and common sense must tell you that there's some toxic substances in it.' She advised parents that if they were determined to immunize their children, it should be done as three well-spread injections and at a quarter of the strength provided by doctors.

Meanwhile, under a barrage of criticism from the Tories, Mr Blair continued to refuse to be drawn on the issue. He described as 'horrible' the campaign being waged against him and in a statement said,

> The advice to parents to have the MMR jab is one of scores of pieces of advice the government supports, in matters ranging from underage sex to alcohol abuse or smoking, to different types of advice for the very young on a huge range of activities from breastfeeding to safe play. The reason we have refused to say whether Leo has had the MMR jab is because we have never commented on the medical health or treatment of our children. Once we comment on one, it is hard to see how we can justify not commenting on all of them. The suggestion that the Government is advising parents to have the MMR jab whilst we are deliberately refraining from giving our child the treatment because we know it is dangerous is offensive beyond belief.

He was not helped by the fact that a sizeable number of his own MPs, when asked, seemed happy to confirm that their own children had been given the inoculation. Moreover, the Queen had set aside her own privacy concerns about her children when in 1957 she had confirmed that Prince Charles and Princess Anne, then aged eight and six, had been given the polio vaccine, which had been dogged by claims it had been responsible for the death of children in the US. The Tories were quick to pick up on the Queen's lead on the issue of public health. Conservative MP Julie Kirkbride said, 'The precedent set by the Queen is highly significant and if Tony and Cherie really want to boost confidence in the Government's policy on the MMR vaccine, then they should say whether Leo has had it.'

Blair's stubbornness was by now a major political issue harming his government. Why, if Leo had been given the jab, did he not just admit it like the Queen had done forty years before? It was not, surely, going to open the floodgates as far as intrusion into the health of his children was concerned. But Blair was not driving the issue; his wife was. Cherie had taken, once again, a hard-line stance that their children must be allowed their privacy. But her attitude was not only miring her husband in charges of hypocrisy; more seriously it was encouraging parents already worried about the scare stories surrounding MMR to forgo the vital immunization for their children.

Mrs Blair's sister Lyndsey, a lawyer turned homeopath who has set up an alternative-health business with their mutual friend Carole Caplin, was also vehemently opposed to the MMR vaccine. The sisters fell out over the MMR issue when Lyndsey accused Downing Street of leaking private information about her family to justify the Blairs' position. The fall-out culminated in a bitter and high-volume row between the two women. The incident was the start of bad blood between the sisters which has seen them have little contact in recent years. Cherie attempted to mend fences by inviting her sister to a celebration of her twenty-fifth wedding anniversary with Tony. The small private party at Chequers was exclusive to those who had been guests at their 1980 wedding. Lyndsey, who had been one of those present to see the couple marry, refused her sister's olive branch and snubbed the occasion.

Blair's silence over the issue was in stark contrast to that of his chancellor and rival for the Labour leadership, Gordon Brown. When Brown's wife Sarah gave birth to their daughter Jennifer prematurely on 28 December 2001 the couple were refreshingly candid about their experiences. Brown's obvious and natural joy at the birth of his first child was far removed from Blair's taciturn display in front of the waiting media as Cherie went into labour with Leo eighteen months earlier. There would be no vans with blankets at the window for Brown, no sneaking out of the back entrance of the hospital. The Blairs had been at pains to ensure that the first happy image of the doting parents and newborn was released only once they had all been coiffed, made-up and subjected to the sympathetic light and airbrushing of the celebrity photographer. The Browns' simple grace was a welcome contrast to those faux off-guard shots by Mary McCartney, with their scrubbed and sanitized 'naturalness'. Brown, playing against type, was for once stripped of his trademark brooding countenance. Emerging from the hospital in Kirkcaldy where Jennifer Jane had been born by Caesarean section weighing just two pounds four ounces, he unselfconsciously spoke to reporters of the myriad emotions that had characterized the previous long hours. 'It's a superb feeling,' he told the waiting newsmen. 'I know every father says his baby daughter is the most beautiful in the world, but she is and we are so delighted.' He also gave permission for the doctor who performed the operation to explain his reasons for delivering Jennifer seven weeks early because of difficulties the thirty-seven-year-old Sarah had experienced with the pregnancy.

The cynical might suggest that Brown's generosity in opening up his emotions to public curiosity were specifically aimed at causing the maximum discomfort for the prime minister, whose own demands for the privacy of his son's health issues had been so badly received. But the emotion and pride coursing through Brown was clearly no act. Here was a glimpse into the private man so removed from his formidable public exterior. The episode only served to set in sharp relief the fundamental psychological differences between the men. Brown, unlike his rival, shunned personal publicity, but his performance when placed in the spotlight was refreshingly free of the gloss and spin that had come to be associated with Blair. Brown's quiet dignity in the subsequent weeks would win him friends on both sides of the political divide. Ten days after her birth, Jennifer Jane died from a brain haemorrhage. She had appeared to be doing well and gaining weight, but her condition suddenly deteriorated. She was baptised in the special baby-care unit of an Edinburgh hospital by the vicar who had married the couple eighteen months earlier. At the baby's funeral in early January at the Fife church where Brown's father had been minister the chancellor's grief was palpable. Yet, when a request for privacy would have been greeted sympathetically, the family permitted the press to take pictures. It was an act of bravery which sent the message that the Browns would not hide their grief, but lay it open as a public tribute to their lost child.

Tony and Cherie were in the congregation to hear Brown's brother John speak poignantly of a daughter who had brought her parents 'a joy so deep, a love so immediate and intense, that the anxiety, the loss that followed, are almost unbearable'. Looking at the photograph of the sleeping one-hour-old Jennifer on the cover of the order of service, the Blairs were deeply moved. The tragedy had rekindled memories of the real friendship the men had before their shared ambition opened up the gulf between them. The warm words they spoke in private were heartfelt and sincere. But both knew they were but a temporary armistice.

7

2002: THE QUEEN OF DOWNING STREET

Huddled together in the freezing cold, Tony and Cherie Blair held hands and swapped worried glances. Several thousand feet up over Afghanistan in the bare metal confines of an RAF Hercules transporter, the prime minister and his wife were experiencing an uncomfortable flight in rudimentary net seats strung around the inside of the fuselage. It was an experience they wouldn't forget in a hurry. Nerves among the Blair party were already jangling when they were given their pre-flight instructions three hours earlier as they departed India for what remained a war zone. The couple and their entourage were told the plane would not be heated inside because of the risk from heat-seeking missiles. They were also warned they must remain completely silent for the duration of the flight. If enemy listening equipment on the ground picked up human voices, they were told, chances were they would be blown out of the sky. These were hardly the sort of safety announcements likely to make for a pleasant flight. In early January 2002, just eight weeks after the fall of the Afghan capital Kabul, the Blairs flew into the country for a whistle-stop meeting with the new Afghan leader and to visit British troops.

It was not a trip to relish; there were still pockets of resistance within the country and those opposed to the US-led coalition were armed with sophisticated anti-aircraft missiles. Troop-carrying planes are not known for their levels of comfort either. Inside, the drone from the engines was ear-splitting and they were constantly buffeted by air turbulence as they passed over the Hindu Kush mountain range separating the country from its neighbour Pakistan. As their aircraft approached the Bagram airbase north of Kabul shortly before 11 p.m., the ground below was pitch black. The threat to their plane was so great, judged army security experts, even being illuminated by the runway lights would put it at extra risk. So, eerily, the pilot made a bumpy landing in the dark accompanied by the first audible sign of the stress they had silently endured during the previous hours – a spontaneous sigh of relief from the entire contingent. Once on the ground, the party was told to walk in single file off the tarmac without deviating from a narrow path which had been cleared of mines. If they had been in any doubt before, they were now only too aware of just how dangerous a place they were coming to. One of Blair's staff says,

> It was a terrifying experience. There was no question that it was a risk flying in there, but I don't think anyone thought just how frightening it would be. It took some guts for them both, but particularly Cherie. Naturally, all the security measures were in place, but I don't think anyone was really prepared for that flight into Afghanistan. It was very eerie sitting in silence in the freezing cold. It is expected that prime ministers have to make these trips sometimes, but Mrs Blair could have backed out and, to her credit, she saw it through. There was a real sense of dread as we took off and I'd be surprised if they hadn't thought of their children back home and what would happen if something had gone wrong. Everyone was incredibly relieved when we got out of there.

Blair became the first Western leader to visit the country, so recently a pariah of the world, since 1979. So dangerous was his visit that no advance notice of the trip was given and the prime minister's party was on the ground barely three hours before they were back in the air and heading away to safety. Their journey had required no little bravery but for Blair it was a moment of personal satisfaction. In the wake of

9/11 he had undertaken eight weeks of gruelling diplomacy to gather support for the attack on the Taliban, who were known to harbour Al-Qaeda, the perpertrators of the attack. During that time he had held 54 meetings with foreign leaders, been on 31 flights and covered more than 40,000 miles. He had stood shoulder to shoulder with Bush in his determination to deal with Afghanistan's appalling record of sponsoring international terrorism and the systematic abuse of the human rights of its own citizens. In the process Blair had faced a barrage of criticism that the conflict would prove a military disaster, unwinnable in the long term, and accusations that domestic issues were being sidelined in favour of his activities as an international statesman.

There was also another effect of the gruelling last few months: Blair was physically and mentally exhausted. Those close to him say he went without sleep for up to forty-eight hours at a time as he sought to secure support. There was virtually no time for rest. Jetting into and out of the world's capital cities, sometimes in the space of only a few hours, there was little time for sleep on the plane; instead he would be faced with another folder of briefing documents to study before his next meeting. By the time his mission reached Afghanistan he was pale and drawn, despite a short and desperately needed post-Christmas holiday in Egypt.

The prime minister, according to sources inside Downing Street, has an enormous capacity for work and an average day will stretch sixteen hours with few breaks. He almost never gives in to tiredness even if he is patently exhausted. Instead, Cherie tells his staff when he is tired and needs to go to bed and regularly unceremoniously throws his courtiers out of the Number Eleven flat late at night. A Downing Street source says, 'Cherie will often just march into Tony's study in the middle of a meeting and say, "Right, everyone out. Leave him alone. He's tired and he's going to bed." Nobody argues when she is in that sort of mood and certainly not Tony. Cherie is absolutely right, of course. She can tell when he needs to call it a day. Tony would never tell his team that he needed a break. Cherie performs the Rottweiler role, but it is in his best interests.'

During the short stay on the ground at the airbase the prime minister met the interim leader of Afghanistan Hamid Karzai, as well as British soldiers who formed part of an international peacekeeping mission. With him throughout was Cherie. Her appearance at his side was not only a statement of personal support for her husband, but also unqualified endorsement of his action in backing so wholeheartedly the American military response post-9/11. But if US action against Afghanistan had been driven by fundamental self-interest, Mrs Blair's visit had a distinctly moral dimension. As a human rights lawyer she was appalled by the abuses of freedom under the Taliban and was particularly motivated by her desire to improve the lot of Afghan women, who had endured years of suppression. Under the Taliban women had been banned from studying at school and university, forbidden from working as doctors, nurses and lawyers and even stopped from wearing brightly coloured clothes. Her husband's role in their tentative first steps to freedom was a cause of enormous pride for Cherie.

By way of illustrating her very real solidarity with oppressed women in the region Mrs Blair had joined the prime minister on his tour of Asia that concluded in Afghanistan but had also taken in Bangladesh, India and Pakistan. Their trip came at a time of increased tension between India and Pakistan, and another task for Blair was to act as mediator. However, as if to highlight the potential dangers of their visit, five soldiers, a policeman and nine Islamic militants had been killed in skirmishes between the neighbouring countries during the days before the Blairs flew in. Despite the risks, Mrs Blair had made a point during the trip of drawing attention to the plight of women disfigured by acid attacks. The practice was responsible for horrific injuries to women who were considered to have shamed their families by being unfaithful or simply refusing to wear a veil. Cherie made a personal visit to the Acid Survivors Foundation in Bangladesh to meet its leaders and some of the victims of this barbaric custom.

What she encountered was deeply shocking. Many of the women had been left blinded or had their faces melted away, but for Cherie it was a cause she was determined to highlight. 'Nobody would relish going to a place like that,' says a friend. 'But she was brave and she did it and what's more she hugged every one of those women. But did we read about it in the papers back home? Of course not; the whole thing was ignored. It is not a side of Cherie the press is interested in writing about.' Indeed, the trip to Asia did not pass without criticism. Blair faced demonstrations in the Bangladeshi capital Dhaka from protesters who accused him of being the 'mastermind of killing Muslims across the world'. Mrs Blair, too, was not immune from brickbats. She was accused by the Indian press of being 'stand-offish' after reporters were denied access when she visited a school, law centre and temple in Bangalore. It led the *Times of India* to complain, 'The visitors seemed slightly hostile and the venues she visited were a "no tresspasser" zone for Indians. It did leave a touch of the old colonial trace. She refused to even wave out to the people waiting when she visited a school for poor children.' Downing Street was quick to point out that she was visiting strictly in her role as the wife of Mr Blair, but this only served to illustrate what a cleft stick Mrs Blair found herself in. On the one hand she was genuinely concerned with raising awareness of causes clearly dear to her heart, but her continued silence in front of the media meant that not only did she appear aloof and cold, she was unable to exploit publicity for the issues she cared about. For the Blairs there was also a juxtaposition that no Western tourist fails to register: after their visits to the poor and the brutalized they would return to the grandeur of their luxury hotel suite. In Bangalore they stayed in the £750-a-night presidential suite of the Windsor Manor hotel, with its own butler, chef and multigym. And for her meetings with, among others, the acid survivors, Mrs Blair had packed a £20,000 wardrobe of hand-made ethnic outfits by leading London designer Babs Mahil. Travelling as well in her entourage was her ubiquitous hair-dresser André Suard.

*

Cherie returned to London frustrated by the limitations of her public role and walked straight into another skirmish in her ongoing war with the media. The previous month the Blairs had complained again to the PCC, this time about coverage of Euan's application for a place at Oxford University. The couple reported the *Daily Telegraph* over a piece in its diary column, Peterborough, which said their eldest child wanted to study at the university's Trinity College, whose president was Cherie's old friend and colleague Michael Beloff QC. The Blairs claimed the article, which had been followed up by the *Daily Mail*, 'unnecessarily intruded' on seventeen-year-old Euan's time at school. Once again the PCC found for the prime minister and his wife, but this time there was a difference. In a coded but strong warning to the Blairs, the commission stressed the diffi-culty of protecting children who 'compromise' their privacy by making public appearances and acquiring a public profile in their own right. The PCC was referring to an episode which clearly showed the ambiguity of the Blairs' approach to the privacy of their children. As the members of the commission were deliberating on the complaint, Cherie had taken Euan and his girlfriend to the gala premiere of the film *Iris* at the Curzon cinema in Mayfair. In front of the banks of photographers and TV news crews, Mrs Blair, her son and his friend marched up the red carpet where they were greeted by the star of the film herself, Kate Winslet.

It was a classic illustration of the trade-off made by the Blairs over the privacy of their children. Mrs Blair was apparently happy for her son to be photographed by the world's press at a glamorous show-business event because it gave him the chance to hobnob with international movie stars and, no doubt, impress his new girlfriend no end in the process. But by allowing his picture to be splashed all over the tabloids, she could hardly be described as protecting his privacy. The PCC appeared to agree, stating in its judgement, 'Privacy is best maintained when not compromised in any way.' The row was exacerbated by comments made by William Hague's successor as Tory leader, Iain Duncan Smith, in an interview with his local newspaper. Mr Duncan Smith claimed the prime minister 'uses his children ruthlessly' and added, 'Once you open the doors to your children it gives the press an excuse for intrusion. I don't want my children to grow up like that and I guard my family because I know what will happen if I don't.' The Conservative leader and his wife Betsy consistently refused to allow their children Edward, then fourteen, Alice, twelve, Harry, aged eleven, and eight-year-old Rosanna to be photographed. Downing Street, on the defensive, was forced to hit back: 'As the media well know, the Prime Minister jealousy guards the privacy of his family and does all he can to keep them out of the public eye where possible.'

In the future Mrs Blair would demand privacy rights that would have put her children on the same footing as the Princes William and Harry, but in the meantime she was increasingly accused of displaying signs of a faux regality that sat comfortably with a predisposition towards the imperious. Indeed, on a visit to a hospital a nurse presented to the prime minister's wife dutifully performed a neat curtsey. But to a large extent Cherie was also the victim in a farce that had her cast in the role of the Queen of Downing Street. In so many ways her part did mirror that of the monarch. Like Her Majesty, Mrs Blair was subject to a prohibition – self-imposed up to a point – on voicing her opinion in public, especially on anything political. Then she was given duties most frequently associated with members of the royal family: opening hospitals and schools, even launching a ship in Hull. Few people had ever heard her speak. Rather like the Queen Mother, who in the absence of any firm evidence to the contrary, was given a broad northern accent on *Spitting Image*, Cherie's puppet on the satirical ITV show was furnished with the Scouse enunciation of a Toxteth barmaid. In fact, in the years since she left Liverpool as a nineteen-year-old, she had worked assiduously on eradicating all oral traces of her Merseyside roots.

Those who sympathize with Cherie's position say she is damned if she does and damned if she doesn't. It is impossible, they point out, for her to be judged fairly when it has been deemed necessary for the public to be kept in the dark about the person she really is. One friend says, 'It is a deal with the devil that Cherie and Tony made. They both worried that she would be crucified if she dared to talk openly about her convictions, so for years she did what was wanted of her and kept quiet. As a consequence she is accused of being regal and aloof. Frankly, she can't win.'

*

If the Blairs' detractors needed evidence of what they saw as the couple muscling in on royal territory, it came with the death of the Queen Mother in March 2002. In the days before her funeral Blair allowed himself to become immersed in an unseemly and at times farcical imbroglio that once again aired his tendency towards shallow personal aggrandisement and an obsession with public showboating. The unbecoming episode began on Sunday 31 March 2002, the day after the Queen Mother's death at the age of 101. The senior parliamentary official Black Rod, Sir Michael Willcocks, who was responsible for overseeing the funeral arrangements, was heading from his Oxfordshire home to a meeting he had called of Palace of Westminster staff when he was phoned by a Number Ten official. The member of the prime minister's staff wanted to know what role Mr Blair would play in the forthcoming ceremonies to mark the Queen Mother's death. The prime minister's people seemed to be angling for their boss to perform a major role in the proceedings and the official wondered aloud if Blair might greet the Queen at Westminster Hall, where her mother would lie in state, or even meet the coffin itself. Willcocks pointed out there was no scope for changing the long-established plans for the ceremony, and that the only role for a prime minister was to lead the tributes in the House of Commons and join other MPs for the arrival of the coffin. But Blair and his staff were in no mood to accept a brush-off. What is previously unknown is that Blair was under pressure of his own. Cherie, anxious he should reprise his successful centre-stage performance at Diana's funeral and in the process boost his approval rating in the country, was adamant he should have a higher profile. Blair, of course, is no shrinking violet, and with his wife egging him on Downing Street staff began a five-day bombardment of Sir Michael and his staff with calls repeating the PM's case for a central role in the national day of mourning. Even during the minutes before the casket arrived at Westminster, the manoeuvring continued. The prime minister proposed to walk from Downing Street to meet the coffin and only abandoned the plan after Sir Michael again advised against it.

Unsurprisingly, given the thriving Westminster rumour mill, word of this undignified episode was already beginning to circulate. Heading the queue to pour opprobrium over Blair were the *Telegraph* and the *Mail*, the two papers Cherie had so publicly tangled with. Downing Street, realizing the potential for more unflattering headlines, came out with all guns blazing in a bid to shoot down the story. Alastair Campbell went into overdrive, threatening editors and demanding a retraction of allegations he claimed were completely fictitious. Insiders insist that Campbell was also being pushed by Cherie to demand apologies from the papers involved, but Blair's tormentors stood firm. Then a fundamental and humiliating mistake was made: Campbell, unable to get the newspapers to back down, made a complaint to the PCC. Campbell subsequently drew considerable flak for this error, but his friends insist he was in fact dead against the idea of involving the commission, knowing as he did the true story of the behind-the-scenes posturing that had gone on. But despite counselling strongly against the move he was overruled, not by the prime minister himself, say sources, but by Mrs Blair, who was convinced by her previous successes that the PCC would rule in her husband's favour. Not for the first time, she made a serious error.

At his office in the Palace of Westminster Sir Michael Willcocks knew Blair was holding a smoking gun. He had watched in astonishment as Number Ten continued to deny that it had tried to exert any influence on him and in the end he could remain silent no longer. His sensational memo on the row blew Blair out of the water. Every embarrassing detail of his unsuitable manoeuvres and attempts to place himself centre stage was laid bare. Campbell was told by the PCC that the PM's case had been shot to pieces and, humiliated, Blair withdrew his complaint. Campbell, whose ignominy was lapped up by his many enemies in the media, was boiling at being pushed into making such a basic error. At Buckingham Palace the Queen viewed her prime minister's posturing with distaste. Five years earlier Her Majesty's personal detestation of Diana had so separated her from her people that it had allowed Blair to step in as her unlikely saviour; now she was only too aware of how formal grieving for one of the royal family's own should be conducted. This time Blair was surplus to requirements.

If the fallout damaged Blair's relationship with the monarchy and his standing in the eyes of the public, it also marked a turning point in his relationship with Alastair Campbell. Campbell was furious that he had been forced to deny accusations that were so patently accurate. While it should be

pointed out that only his most myopic friends would defend
this inveterate spinner against claims that he has on occasion
been economical with the truth, Campbell the pragmatist was
only too aware of the battles that were worth fighting and
those which required a hasty retreat. He felt he had been
skewered by his boss and, more particularly, Cherie, who
had been adamant in the face of all evidence to the contrary
that they must not back down. As the farce played itself out,
Campbell was left to carry the can.

The national press, which to a greater or lesser degree had
been largely supine in the face of the brutally efficient Blair PR
operation led by Campbell, hit back in a backlash that was all
the more vicious for the now tainted love that had once existed
between it and New Labour. By way of shifting attention from
the rising clamour about government's spin, Campbell, as the
embodiment of Labour's obsession with the black art, had
been forced to give up his role as the PM's official spokesman
in 2000 in favour of a post directing operations from behind
the scenes. But the move was little more than cosmetic and the
scepticism of the media had festered. With this new round of
hostilities, Mrs Blair's role was again placed under the microscope. Her chairing of the Millennium Summits was only now
seized upon and came in for a barrage of negative headlines;
as did another slip of the tongue in February 2002 when she
used 'we' when talking about the government at the end of
one of the Number Ten seminars she chaired. She was criticized
for everything – from wearing a low-cut top at the Queen
Mother's funeral to going hatless and yawning throughout the
service of thanksgiving at St Paul's for the Queen's golden
jubilee in June.

Nor, as had been noted, had the Blairs endeared themselves
to the Queen and Prince Philip when they broke with protocol
and conducted an impromptu walkabout in the garden of
Buckingham Palace at the party and rock concert to celebrate
the jubilee. An unlikely mediator in the *froideur* that followed

between the royals and the Blairs was none other than young Leo. While the Balmoral visits remained the cause of mutual dread on the part of both host and guests, Leo's birth brought a thaw to the proceedings. The Queen was instantly smitten with the little blond boy on their first meeting, so much so that she positively looks forward to seeing Blair junior during the summer holidays. Says a Blair courtier, 'She adores Leo and when he was a baby she was always holding him and cooing like a doting grandmother. He certainly helped relations between the Queen and Cherie, in particular, because he gives the two of them something to talk about.'

Even those who had been loyal disciples were now turning on the couple. At the *Daily Mirror* Piers Morgan had never forgiven Mrs Blair for robbing him of his exclusive over her pregnancy while Cherie's cack-handed attempts to get Morgan's boss to sack him brought the bad feeling into the open. Morgan responded by publishing a list of the 'most irritating people in Britain' (the prime minister's wife featured prominently). In the petty tit-for-tat dispute that endured until Morgan's eventual sacking in 2004 Cherie responded by switching a campaign for Barnardo's, of which she is patron, from the *Mirror* to the more on-message *News of the World*.

Even in the *Sun*, which for the most part remained pro-Blair, the right-wing Richard Littlejohn regularly used his page to vilify the PM and, more particularly, Mrs Blair, whom he christened the 'Wicked Witch'. His diatribes against her were invariably illustrated with grotesque cartoons of her in full Cruella De Vil mode. Consequently Littlejohn, who announced he was joining the *Daily Mail* in 2005, is such a figure of hate in the Blair household that Cherie will now not even brook his name being mentioned within her earshot. Downing Street staff soon learnt to dispose quickly of copies of the *Sun* left hanging around Number Ten when Cherie entered the room. Littlejohn, she once told a friend, her words dripping with contempt, 'is a man with a very small penis who hates and despises intelligent women because they make him feel inferior. How awful it must be for him that the editor of the *Sun* is a woman.'

It was into this febrile atmosphere that Cherie rushed headlong in June 2002 when she joined Queen Rania of Jordan at the launch of a £500,000 charity appeal in London for Medical Aid For Palestinians. A few hours earlier nineteen people had died when a Palestinian suicide bomber detonated a device on a bus in Jerusalem. Among the dead were several children. The two women were asked for their response to this act of wickedness and Queen Rania spoke in tactful diplomatic tones. Delaying the political peace process, she said, 'inevitably exposes more innocent civilians on both sides to grave danger'. Mrs Blair's response was anything but diplomatic. 'As long as young people feel they have got no hope but to blow themselves up, you are never going to make progress,' she blurted out. Her comments were all the more provocative because, unlike Queen Rania, she omitted to condemn the killing of innocent men, women and children. The opprobrium inspired by her remarks was swift; within hours Mrs Blair was forced to issue an apology and a statement making clear her condemnation of the bombing. But it was too late. Cherie was mauled by Jewish groups and the media. Her offence, it seemed, had been to open her mouth and say what she felt. Whatever the cause of her outburst, it was a monumental mistake at a time when her husband's government was pushing both sides of the conflict to find a peaceful resolution.

Mrs Blair was not, however, without her defenders. She could always rely on her friend and occasional mouthpiece Mary Ann Sieghart of *The Times* to strap on the Semtex and wander into enemy territory for the cause. It was, Sieghart conceded, a serious blunder, but the first Cherie had made in eight years as the wife of the Labour leader. Mrs Blair, she said was 'mortified, but ought to console herself with the knowledge that, under intense and continuous pressure, she has until now succeeded in behaving pretty impeccably'. But those who argued that she was not a politician had failed to grasp a crucial point: if Mrs Blair hosted policy seminars at Number Ten; if she made public pronouncements on behalf of the government over the war in Afghanistan and controversial statements about the Palestinian conflict, her role could only be seen as de facto political. The truth is, say insiders, that Cherie had become so stifled by the rule to keep quiet that she was beginning to rebel. Once it had been enough for her to know that her influence was felt behind the door of Number Ten; now she yearned for a more public role. But this desire put her at odds with those like Campbell who had believed from the outset that a more high-profile, more outspoken Cherie would be hugely risky for Blair. For her part, Mrs Blair increasingly eyed her husband's private office team with suspicion and feelings of resentment.

But while she hankered for a role that gave her the freedom to speak on the issues that moved her, Cherie was still equally determined that she should not become public property. In 2001 she had used her considerable influence in an attempt to scupper a Channel Four documentary about her life being made by Linda McDougall, the wife of Labour MP Austin Mitchell. Angered by what she claimed were investigations into the life of a 'private person', she set out to have the programme stopped. Channel Four's deputy chairman Barry Cox, an ex-neighbour of the Blairs, received a flurry of complaints from Cherie and he contacted the programme's commissioning editor to warn that no more of Mrs Blair's friends should be contacted without his permission. Cherie also issued strict instructions to friends not to give interviews on pain of being cut off. The programme went ahead, but not without public accusations by McDougall of control freakery inside Number Ten. Ironically, it was this dogged determination to preserve her privacy at all costs that was about to plunge Cherie Blair into a very public scandal – and provide her husband with the most serious crisis of his premiership so far.

8
THE GURU

It was not, by any means, an outfit lacking in that all-important wow factor. Carole Caplin's ensemble for a family dinner with her friends Tony and Cherie Blair in the south of France had been carefully chosen for the occasion. Underneath her skirt she was, as is her wont, devoid of underwear – her habit of going au naturel is well known among her acquaintances – but it was her blouse that drew the eye. Loosely patterned with a floral motif, it was to all intents and purposes completely sheer. Underneath this see-through top the lovely Carole wore only the golden tan she had spent the previous hot days topping up by the pool.

It was an overtly sexual display and one which Tony, the only man present at the dinner, could not have failed to notice. But at least one of those present was unhappy with Ms Caplin's choice of attire. As the group, which included the Blairs' children, sat down to eat, Cherie's mother Gale finally exploded. 'I don't think that outfit is appropriate dress at a family meal,' she told a startled Carole. Caplin replied that she could see nothing wrong with it, and was supported by her mother Sylvia, who was also a guest of the Blairs at the borrowed holiday villa near Le Vernet. Mrs Booth would later describe the holiday at the house loaned to the Blairs by their friend Sir David Keane as a 'nightmare' and 'the worst ever'. She had not only been upset by the incident at dinner, but was also displeased by the habit of Caplin and her sixty-seven-year-old mother of sunbathing by the pool wearing only tiny G-strings. So embarrassed was the Blairs' teenage son Nicky that when his parents were out sightseeing one day he complained to his grandmother that he and his friends, who had joined him on the holiday, were unable to use the pool because of the Caplins' displays.

Throughout the pre-dinner row Cherie was silent as her mother and friend argued, but Gale's intervention was to a large part motivated by a desire to look out for her daughter. She, like Carole, knew that less than a week earlier Cherie, at forty-seven, had lost what would have been her fifth child. She had suffered a miscarriage in August 2002 at the Number Eleven flat as she and Tony prepared to join the children, who had already left for the continent. She was rushed to the Chelsea and Westminster, where Leo had been born two years earlier, to undergo surgery under general anaesthetic. Now, just a few days later, she looked drawn and tired and was still coming to terms with the grief of losing her unborn child. Cherie had known for a few weeks that she was expecting but had been waiting to tell her husband. Ten days before miscarrying the baby she had cradled a newborn on a visit to a maternity unit in Durham with her husband. Tony joked that she should put the baby down: 'Oh dear, she will be getting broody again. I'm getting worried about this,' he told the baby's mother.

Cherie, who say friends has never felt comfortable with her body image, was at a low ebb, realizing that in all likelihood her age had been a critical factor in the loss of the baby. Carole's provocative display in front of her husband was at best tactless; at worst it bordered on the cruel. But what was Cherie's reaction to Carole's social faux pas? At that stage, say friends, Mrs Blair was seemingly so completely in the thrall of the mesmerizing Miss Caplin that she did not react to it. Gale Booth wore no such blinkers. She has always been deeply sceptical about Caplin and her mother. There is, say friends, little love lost between the three women. Gale was also privately suspicious of Caplin's manoeuvring to place herself as close to the prime minister as she had long been to his wife.

For Blair's part, he had initially been dismissive of Carole, and when her colourful past as a soft-porn model had been so publicly revealed at his first Labour conference as leader in 1994 he was annoyed that his wife's lifestyle adviser had been responsible for shifting the focus from his performance in front of the party faithful. In the following years he had studiously kept his distance from her. 'Frankly,' says an insider, 'Tony didn't like her very much and found her over-exuberance irritating. Cherie would try to persuade him to get Carole to give him massages to help him relax, but he never seemed keen.'

However, the prime minister's attitude to Caplin warmed considerably, sources say, after another Blackpool conference eight years later when Bill Clinton arrived to address the Labour Party. Blair had, insiders reveal, recently begun having stress-relieving massages from Carole at Downing Street and Chequers. She also devised an exercise regime for him and regularly put him through his paces in one-on-one sessions at Number Eleven. Blair was so impressed with her that on a visit by Clinton to Chequers in the summer of 2002, when the former US president complained of lower back pain, he recommended a massage from Carole. She was ecstatic at the prospect of working her magic on Clinton but when she arrived at the prime minister's country residence she raised eyebrows with her choice of attire. 'She was wearing a skintight black catsuit,' says a source. 'She looked like a cross between Emma Peel and an extra in some sort of under-the-counter video. There was a sharp intake of breath when she bowled up, not least from Clinton himself.' So enamoured was Clinton with her massage technique and the series of stretches she showed him that when he joined Blair at the Labour conference he told Tony, 'I wish I could have Carole again for that exercise.'

It was during that same conference in the autumn of 2002 that Carole's influence over Blair himself first became evident. Caplin, who had been choosing the prime minister's outfits and shopping for his clothes, picked a rather garish red and purple tie for him to wear for his speech. She laid it and the shirt she had chosen out for him on his bed and went to her own room. But when Blair's team of advisers, including Alastair Campbell, saw the tie they warned him not to wear it because it clashed with the red backdrop of the conference platform. On hearing this, Mrs Blair immediately rang her friend Carole, who in turn was on the line to Blair himself within seconds, instructing him to ignore the advice of his team and wear it. He did as he was told by the persuasive Miss Caplin, much to the chagrin of Campbell et al. Another example of Caplin's input had been on display earlier that year at the Commonwealth summit in March. Blair made headlines by wearing a risqué creation by the British designer Paul Smith: a shirt featuring an image of a naked lady on the inside of the cuff. Once again pulling the strings was the flamboyant Carole. Blair's attitude to his wife's friend was suddenly warm. 'He used to pretty much ignore Carole,' says an insider. 'Now whenever she rang up he would be all friendly, saying, "Hello, darling," and being chatty.'

Mrs Blair, according to friends, was sanguine about her husband's burgeoning closeness to Carole. Alastair Campbell and his partner Fiona Millar were not. They had come to loathe and despise Caplin. Employing the barrack-room banter he affected inside Number Ten, Campbell had been heard loudly to declare, 'I'd give her one, but she's a fucking liability.' Millar detested Caplin and complained that her own advice to Mrs Blair was constantly ignored as Cherie took counsel from Carole instead. She was also furious that both Carole and Sylvia blatantly ignored her instructions to contact the prime minister's wife through her. Fiona schemed with others within the Blair court about how to rid themselves of Carole's annoying presence, but was scuppered at every turn. Not only did both Blairs show no sign of distancing themselves from Caplin, they grew ever more reliant on her.

Caplin's advice not only extended to the exercise classes she separately oversaw for the Blairs and the buying of their clothes; her position at the heart of their court also inspired her to flex her political muscles. She would, say insiders, long before Jamie Oliver thought of it, spend long hours lecturing the PM on her theories about improving the diet and fitness of the nation's schoolchildren. She was also keen to push, as she had done with his wife, her views on holistic medicine and its incorporation into established medical practice. By the end of 2002 Caplin had made herself virtually indispensable to both Tony and Cherie. But how did she manage to establish herself so close to the centre of government? The answer, say those who watched her inexorable rise, is that her hold over the Blairs was achieved by a practised ability to put herself in a position of power over those she seeks to influence. The relationship is built on control. It is this control over Cherie, and later her husband, that remains the central factor in the tale of Caplin's rise.

*

Carole first met Cherie in 1989 when Blair was the shadow cabinet's employment spokesman. Carole and her mother Sylvia were running Holistix, the company they had set up to promote an alternative approach to diet and health issues. In the years before she met the future first lady of Downing Street, Caplin, the daughter of middle-class parents, had been a young woman with a clear mission: to find fame and money as quickly as possible. She and her sister had been brought up by their mother when their gambling and adulterous father Michael Caplin abandoned his family and fled to South Africa. Carole, the prettier of the sisters, was her mother's favourite. She left school with few qualifications but with a determination to succeed. Her methods would stretch conventional boundaries, but her training in the art of manipulating those around her would stand her in good stead for her future.

In the early 1980s she started work for a telemarketing company called Programmes Ltd, which acted as a front for

to the growing number of women open to these new approaches. But their big break came when Tony Blair was appointed Labour leader and Cherie, who knew Carole through her interest in alternative treatments, asked Caplin to help her lose weight and choose a wardrobe befitting her new role. Carole took on her new job with gusto. Those who know her say she was tireless in her efforts to make herself indispensable to her new employer. According to one acquaintance:

> Right from the beginning Carole approached it like a full-time job. She would go out seeing designers to choose outfits for Cherie; she found her a hairdresser and would even go to the supermarket to do the Blairs' food shopping. Not only that, she made a point early on of getting very close to Cherie. She would ring up eight or nine times a day, asking how she was, wanting to know what she could do for her. She was relentless and it was all part of getting herself as close to her as possible. The way she approached it was highly professional. Both Carole and her mother made their life's work Cherie Blair. It was amazing to behold. Cherie is a domestic disaster. Her household skills are next to nothing. She can't really manage very well. Her homes have always been a mess and she is always running late. Carole brought some order and got Cherie a lot more organized.

From the outset, Caplin badgered designers to give her client huge discounts for the publicity they would receive by having the wife of the Labour leader wearing their creations. Cherie, whose eye for a bargain is well known to her friends, was grateful for the help. Over the years the two women developed a modus operandi in London's premier stores. If Mrs Blair was shopping alone, she would go in and try on a number of outfits or pairs of shoes, but would not buy anything. Instead Carole would contact the shops after Cherie had left and attempt to negotiate large reductions on her client's

behalf. Her shopping for Mrs Blair was not restricted to
London, with Carole making regular trips to Paris to seek
out suitable clothes. But increasingly designers whispered that
Caplin's aggressive attempts to secure reductions were winning her few friends. Some refused to dress Mrs Blair as a
consequence and in 2004 designer Lindka Cierach, who had
regularly supplied the prime minister's wife, ended the relationship after she revealed that discounts of up to 50 per cent had
been sought and heavy-handed demands made for her to sign
a confidentiality agreement. One couturier who regularly sold
clothes to Mrs Blair, said,

> She and Carole had it down to a fine art. Carole would
> come in hugging and kissing everyone and then launch into
> a pretty nasty and crude little spiel about how good for our
> image it was to have Cherie wearing our clothes. Once you
> agreed a discount she would come back and try to push the
> figure lower. There is no doubt Cherie knew what she was
> doing, but it suited her to have Carole do the bartering.
> Nothing was ever good enough; they wanted more and
> more discounts until it just got silly. To be honest, it was
> all rather tacky and left a nasty taste in the mouth. I wish I
> hadn't got involved really because I don't think Cherie
> wearing our clothes helped us at all. And to be frank,
> despite the fact I played the game with Carole with all the
> hugs and fakeness, I really despise that woman. She's like a
> shark in a nasty Afghan coat.

*

Given the embarrassment caused to Blair when Carole's colourful past as a soft-porn model was revealed at his first
Labour conference as leader, how was Caplin allowed to get
so close to the couple? Surely even the briefest examination
of the evidence suggested that a girl with her dodgy past
had the potential to cause trouble as long as she remained
within the circle. Indeed, from the very outset many within

New Labour felt Carole was an accident waiting to happen. They recall being astonished that she had managed so successfully to inveigle her way in. One said, 'It seemed obvious to me from the first twenty seconds of our conversation that she was false. She seemed full of fake charm and was spouting this complete New Age gibberish. She seemed deeply paranoid too, banging on incessantly with these weird conspiracy theories about major conglomerates and food companies. I thought she was loopy, and that she had the steely-eyed look of someone who had seen a chance and was not going to let it slip.'

Others tell how her constant mantra is of her loyalty to the Blairs and the price she has paid as a consequence. An acquaintance relates a previously untold story about when she was introduced to Carole at a time when Caplin's involvement with the Blairs was first under the spotlight. Carole, by way of illustrating her dedication to her employers and the trauma she had already gone through for them, relayed to her a tale. It is, perhaps, one of the strangest stories surrounding Miss Caplin. With a suitably grave expression and in a hushed tone, Carole told how soon after Mr Blair became leader of the party she was woken in the middle of the night by men banging on the door of her flat in Swiss Cottage. While her mother slept on, Carole claims she was taken away under cover of darkness, still dressed in her nightie. She described her kidnappers as being from the 'intelligence services' and she went on to say she was held by them for three days and subjected to prolonged interrogation. Her mother, said Caplin, had no idea where she was and was beside herself with worry. After her three-day ordeal Carole was returned home unharmed. It is a story Carole and Sylvia have repeated to friends, one of whom said,

Carole was vague as to what she was questioned about, but said it was something to do with 'national security'.

It seems that they were supposedly trying to establish if she was some sort of risk. It was clear she was implying they were from Special Branch or MI5 or something. It was, quite frankly, the most bizarre thing you could ever wish to hear, but it is no joke. Carole and her mother told the story in all seriousness. It was meant to be believed despite the fact it sounded completely far-fetched. Why, for example, did Sylvia not call the police when her daughter went missing for days on end? I was very much of the opinion that she wanted to demonstrate how she had kept quiet about what she had put up with for the Blairs. It was as if she was hinting that she had some hold over them because of this incident, but I have to say I have never heard anything so weird in all my life.

Another question is why the ferociously intelligent Mrs Blair, a barrister and would-be High Court judge, was not moved to dump her guru before she could cause her and her husband more embarrassment? That she didn't says much about the character of the prime minister's wife. There were several reasons for her reluctance. One was her natural belligerence coupled with disdain for the press. When faced with what she sees as an ultimatum Cherie will invariably dig her heels in despite the potential consequences. She was determined she would not be forced into getting rid of a woman she considered a friend merely because of the derision and hilarity in the media over their association. It is no exaggeration to say that, despite the glad-handing and schmoozing of the media that all prime ministers and their partners must do, Cherie hates most journalists. Her dislike dates back to her childhood, when the relish with which her father's excesses were reported on an almost daily basis by the tabloids was the source of acute embarrassment for his daughter. Those who know her well attest that she loathes being told what to do by anyone, her husband included, so the thought of her bowing to pressure from the yellow press is complete anathema to her.

Another reason is that while the ever more bizarre therapies that Carole introduced Cherie to clearly laid her open to ridicule, Mrs Blair has no real idea of how these diets and New Age fads appear to the general public. She is untouched by the thought that her behaviour might seem to those most traditionally loyal to the Labour cause that of a self-obsessed woman with too much money and time on her hands. It is, says one who knows her well, her blind spot. Carole had also, to give her her due, performed wonders for Cherie's look. She had taken her out of the unflattering outfits she had been ridiculed for when left to her own devices and styled her in elegant creations by designers like Ronit Zilkha and Paddy Campbell. She chose ensembles that disguised Cherie's broad hips and sturdy legs, softened her features with subtle make-up and got her weight down with their gym sessions. But, more that that, Carole went out of her way to be a friend to Cherie.

It is a little-known fact that, despite her position or possibly because of it, Cherie Blair has few close friends. She has never been naturally gregarious; she has the capacity to appear cold and humourless to those who meet her for the first time and she retains a reticence occasionally disguised by over-the-top displays of affection that at best appear forced and are described by one source as 'occasionally downright embarrassing'. Suffice to say she does not make friends easily. In Carole it appeared she had found someone who, despite their seeming chalk and cheese personalities, had her best interests at heart. Says a friend,

> For all Cherie's perceived chippiness, she is essentially insecure, particularly in her relationships. A major factor of her friendship with Carole was to do with the feeling that she, Cherie, could have such a beautiful and assured friend and that Carole would be interested in her. It might sound strange given all Cherie's achievements, but it has always been a feature of their relationship and it was very

much the case at the beginning. Cherie has always been impressed by Carole's looks and self-confidence. There was something of the playground about their relationship: the dowdy, swot girl being taken under the wing of the prettiest girl in the class. Carole is, of course, as sharp as a tack and was completely aware of this.

One example of Cherie's schoolgirl-like infatuation with her mentor was on display with her visit to the Chelsea Flower Show in 2002. Rather unwisely and to the horror of fashionistas Cherie and Carole wore matching white pixie boots.

It should also be stated that there is another insecurity that those detractors of Carole Caplin within the Blairs' circle point to as a major reason for Cherie's loyalty. It says much, too, about the hold Caplin has exerted over her. By the time her husband became leader of the party Mrs Blair had subjected herself, at the hands of Carole, to a series of strange ceremonies and techniques striking in their similarities to those Carole was responsible for putting into practice when she was employed by Exegesis. Cherie, according to those close to her and surprisingly for one in her position, displays a basic lack of understanding of what the press might consider a story worth chasing; but even she was aware as she moved from party wife to public figure in her own right that what Carole could tell about their relationship would be tabloid dynamite. In short, as a Blair insider puts it, 'Carole knows where the bodies are buried.' This alone was reason enough for Cherie to want to remain on the right side of her new best friend.

*

A dark-haired woman reclines in a scented bath while another sponges her body with slow movements. The scene, described here for the first time, could be straight out of one of those epic productions of the life of Cleopatra. It is, in fact, real. The woman lying undressed in the water is the wife of the future prime minister. The other is her 'personal assistant' Carole Caplin. Despite the intimacy of the bathtime sessions, there is nothing sexual about them. The treatment is part of a 'pampering service' which Caplin started as a sideline while working for Programmes Ltd. The idea was to give massages to customers, but on occasion the pampering went beyond a back rub. One former employee of Programmes, Behar Kavamoor, reports how he joined an Exegesis course during which he was made to crawl on his hands and knees and bark like a dog. Later he began working as a salesman for the company but after two weeks he quit. What happened next was a novel twist on traditional industrial relations. Kavamoor claims that in a vain attempt to get him back into the fold, Programmes bosses sent him round to Carole's flat. There she scrubbed him in her bath and, wearing a silk dressing gown, lay down next to him on her bed while they talked about the company. 'She didn't touch me, but it was all very suggestive,' he recalls.

Those who know Cherie well say she allowed herself to be scrubbed in the bath by Carole on more than one occasion. 'At that time Cherie would do absolutely anything she was told by Carole,' says a friend. Caplin has also mentioned the baths to friends. So, too, has Sylvia Caplin, who, embarrassingly for the Blairs, described her own bathtime 'pamper sessions' with the prime minister's wife in a rare newspaper interview in 2003. The two-hour induction was meant, says Mrs Caplin, to teach the art of cleaning one's skin properly. It was the same principle used during a 'toxins shower' which was reported to have occurred at the north London gym where Cherie met Carole for workouts. Carole told Mrs Blair the purpose of the shower was to wipe 'impurities' from her body. Both women entered the shower while Carole scrubbed Cherie's body. The scene was witnessed by Sue Harris, a former business partner of Carole. She told the *News of the World* she also saw Carole sitting astride a topless Cherie while she gave her a massage.

One tactic used during Exegesis courses was persuading

recruits to reveal intimate details and secrets from their personal lives; this provided trainers with an effective means of control. It was a skill Caplin took with her when she eventually left the cult. Those who know the two women say that within weeks of their first meeting Caplin had persuaded Mrs Blair to divulge details of her sex life with Tony. She was cajoled into talking about how often they made love, in what positions, and how good it was. Not only that; Cherie was shown a series of sexual exercises she was to do with her husband that were supposed to release her 'energy channels', as well as intimate massage techniques aimed at improving their love life. It was at this time, claims Carole's ex-business partner, that she and Mrs Blair were taken by Carole to see another practitioner who told the women to visualize bats protecting them. Sylvia Caplin also conducted a questioning session with Mrs Blair that involved her quizzing Cherie about her sex life. Again, to the fury of Downing Street spin doctors, Mrs Caplin outlined in the *Daily Telegraph* the questioning to which Mrs Blair had submitted, and which Caplin senior described as 'everything from bowels to bereavement'.

But how could someone like Mrs Blair, who undoubtedly possesses a sharp mind, put herself in such an invidious position? Once again, the root of Cherie's attraction to the world of alternative therapies can be traced back to her childhood. A friend says,

She still carries a hell of a lot of emotional baggage from her childhood. I believe that the most important and damaging event in her life was her father abandoning her. It screwed her up completely. I think from that moment on she has somehow considered herself to be lacking something. I truly believe there is part of her that thinks that she must not be a proper person if her father could just walk out on her. Ever since, she has been looking for something that would make her more whole. It is a major character flaw caused by her father and it has left her open to those who want to exploit it. She is just flailing round in the dark looking for something that will make it all right again.

It is this insecurity that those friends of Cherie who distrust Carole claim she has used to gain control over Mrs Blair, an insecurity illustrated by a previously untold story. A friend of Cherie reports that she was with the two women when Carole suddenly exploded with rage. 'You have got fat again,' she shouted at Mrs Blair. 'Look at your hips! You look a fucking mess. What's going on with your hair?' The tirade, says the friend, lasted close to a minute. She says today, 'Carole systematically tore Cherie to shreds. Every aspect of her physical appearance was destroyed. Carole was going absolutely ballistic. What was most shocking of all was that it came completely out of the blue. It was personal, brutal and painful.' Equally shocking was Cherie's reaction to this verbal assault. 'She just stood there meekly and took it,' says the friend. 'She was trying to placate Carole and saying she would try harder with her diet. It was quite a pitiful sight, I can tell you.'

Some members of the Blair court blame Caplin for the excessive dieting that resulted in Cherie looking overly thin in the twelve months after Tony became leader of the party. She was not, they insist, anorexic, but friends did worry whether her dieting was not in the best interests of her health. Caplin recently admitted she was seen as being tough, explaining that as a fitness trainer her clients want her to motivate them to eat and exercise correctly. One friend of Mrs Blair says, however, 'Cherie was simply trying to keep Carole happy. Carole was very strict with her.' Other members of the Blair circle recount similar verbal volleys from Carole directed at her boss over her appearance. One said, 'From day one it was Carole's tactic. She knocked Cherie down to build her up again, the sort of classic parade-ground stuff. Very quickly Cherie came to rely on Carole for everything. She didn't feel she could make any decision without Carole's say-so. Carole is not intellectually bright, but she is an expert in the laws of the jungle. She has developed a sort of hypnotic presence that she used to good effect on Cherie. Basically, I believe Cherie became so messed up by her that she spent the next several years trying to please her tormentor.' It was a strategy that would sow the wind and reap the whirlwind.

9

CHERIEGATE

The whirlwind came in the form of the Cheriegate scandal in the dying days of 2002. In its wake would be left questions that went not only to the heart of the Blairs' friendship with Caplin, but also their complicated relationship to the truth, the making of money and, crucially, their own marriage. They also laid themselves open to accusations that they had used civil servants to mislead the media on their behalf. Not only did they emerge from the wreckage with their credibility damaged irrevocably but, as we shall discover, with their relationship under more strain that any time before or since. The events of those days would play a part in Blair's planned decision to resign, and leave his wife so emotionally bruised that she fell victim to loneliness and a misery that would have lasting consequences.

*

In the autumn of 2002 Cherie decided that the family needed some financial security for the time when her husband was no longer prime minister. It was, as are many of Mrs Blair's financial schemes, rather muddled in its thinking. Tony Blair will, on his departure from Number Ten, be the beneficiary of a very healthy pension. Moreover, this will be dwarfed by the millions on offer from publishers desperate to win the rights to his memoirs. And, as ex-world leaders including John Major and Bill Clinton will attest, the capacity to cash in on the international speaking circuit is limitless. So there was little real financial imperative in Mrs Blair's decision to buy two flats in Bristol, one earmarked for their son Euan, who had recently started a degree course at Bristol University, the other as an investment.

But there was another reason for Mrs Blair's keenness to exploit the booming housing market. For at least the last eighteen months she had been complaining to friends that, in her own words, she and her husband were 'broke'. This was of course not strictly true. The Blairs did not have a mortgage, other than the small loan outstanding on their constituency house Myrobella in County Durham, nor did they owe money to anyone, but Cherie was increasingly frustrated by their lack of financial clout when compared to their new, and very rich, friends. The patronage of people like Cliff Richard had given the Blairs a taste for luxury hard to sustain even on their hardly insubstantial joint income. Coupled with this were the very large sums Cherie had taken to spending on her wardrobe, her domestic staff and her array of New Age therapists, not to mention her ever-present hairdresser, whom she decided must visit her not only in the morning but many evenings as well. Then there was Carole Caplin, who it was reported was earning up to £5,000 a month from the Blairs for her advice on health, fitness and diet, as well as her duties as Cherie's stylist. These outgoings meant there was little left over. Cherie became increasingly irritated by the brake that she inevitably had to apply to their spending, particularly as she was still exercised by the annoyance she felt over missing out by selling their Islington home before the property market took off.

It was against this background that Cherie Blair, wife of the prime minister, leading barrister and part-time judge, employed the services of a convicted fraudster and confidence trickster to help her purchase the flats she believed would offer a nice nest egg for their retirement and, in the meantime, provide a not insubstantial monthly rental income. Peter Foster was a crook of tabloid legend. The former boyfriend of 1980s topless model Samantha Fox, the Australian had been jailed in three continents for a series of get-rich-quick scams usually relating to fake diets. One such product was a herbal tea called Bai Lin, which Foster falsely claimed aided weight loss. Miss Fox, unaware of the falseness of his evidence for the efficacy of the tea, unwittingly helped Foster market it. When the fraud came to light in 1988 on the TV show *That's Life* Foster fled the country but was eventually jailed on his return to the UK in 1995 over another slimming con. He also served a prison sentence in the US for conspiracy to commit grand theft and was being pursued in the Australian Federal Court over a diet scheme said to have fleeced investors of £1.4 million. He was considered such an undesirable that when he returned to the UK from his home on the Australian Gold Coast via Malaga at the end of August 2002, he was refused entry and served with notification that he would be removed from the country. But lawyers for Foster in London obtained an injunction against the Immigration Service and lodged an application for a judicial review. In the meantime Foster was granted leave to remain in Britain. It was while he was awaiting his eventual deportation that Mrs Blair used Foster as middleman in the flats deal.

Foster's unlikely journey into the lives of the prime minister and his wife had begun eighteen months earlier on the tropical island of Fiji. Foster had moved to the South Pacific paradise from Australia to avoid a string of creditors. At the luxurious Sheraton Hotel the exiled con man met a glamorous economics professor from California State University called Leah Marcel who, in a delicious irony, was in Fiji to act as an election adviser to the island's New Labour Party. She became his girl-friend and Foster, with his trademark show of extravagance, donated £50,000 to the party's funds. But when his donation was revealed in the local press and Foster's background came to light, it scuppered the chances of its leader Dr Tupeni Baba gaining power. It was a story that would have uncanny parallels with his next attempt at making high-powered friends in politics. Foster's new girlfriend happened to drop into a conversation that she had a friend in Britain who was one of the oldest friends of Tony Blair's wife Cherie. Her name, Professor Marcel told him, was Carole Caplin. Foster logged the information and began formulating his next scam.

A year later, in the summer of 2002, Foster was in London and by July he had engineered a meeting with Miss Caplin in a cafe on Chelsea's King's Road. Foster, who was already planning another slimming venture in the UK with a product called Trimit, did not waste his chance. He began his charm offensive against the latest victim, visiting the upmarket stationery shop Smythson in Bond Street to buy a seventy-three pound notebook for her. 'Babes,' he told a business associate, 'love expensive gadgets.' If his plan to get the Blairs to help him promote his new business was to work he would have to move fast. Foster and Caplin quickly became lovers, with Foster moving into Carole's flat in Holloway. Opportunity knocked for him in the middle of October when Mrs Blair took her children to Bermuda on holiday. The trip was a classic Blair freebie. Cherie agreed to speak at a 'Women in Public Life' conference on the beautiful Atlantic island in return for the Bermudian government covering her air fare and putting her party up at the well-appointed Government House for a nominal fee of just fifty pounds.

It was while she was enjoying these genteel surroundings that Cherie's mind turned to her eldest son Euan, who had just begun university life in Bristol. Mrs Blair rang her friend Carole to ask her to view flats in a large prestigious new block in the city she was considering for her son. Foster jumped at the chance of escorting his new lover on the trip west and a week later his scheme to befriend the first couple was well in hand. He was already in email contact with Cherie. His opening gambit was calculated immediately to catch Mrs Blair's attention. He emailed her that he could save her a fortune if she let him carry out the negotiations for the purchase of the flat on her behalf. The offer was gratefully accepted. It would prove to be a costly mistake.

Foster, by way of impressing investors in his new company, had already traded on his connection with Mrs Blair, but some of those who had put up money became suspicious and demanded their cash back. One was the ex-Liverpool and England footballer Paul Walsh. When Foster demurred, Walsh took his story to tabloid fixer Max Clifford, who called in the *News of the World*. By the end of November both the *Daily Mail* and the *Mail on Sunday* had also become aware of Foster's involvement with Caplin and claims that he was acting as Mrs Blair's financial adviser. In Downing Street it was known that the link between Foster and the Blairs had been picked up by the press. In fact, Special Branch detectives had warned the prime minister and his wife that a newspaper, said to be the *News of the World*, was attempting to set a trap to photograph Foster with Mrs Blair. But what nobody on Blair's staff knew was how close Foster had been allowed to get to the first family. When detectives, who spoke to the Blairs separately, told them about his criminal convictions, Mrs Blair did not take the opportunity to tell her husband that Foster was involved in the purchase of the two flats. Blair himself told the police, 'I don't know this guy from Adam.' The prime minister only knew that his wife planned to buy a flat for their son from the trust fund they had set up with the proceeds of the sale of 1 Richmond Crescent; at this stage, Downing Street is quick to point out, he was unaware of how the negotiations had been handled.

Cherie's decision to keep quiet was about to blow up in her face. On 30 November a middle-ranking civil servant called Danny Pruce was on duty in the Downing Street press office when he received a series of faxed questions from the *Mail on Sunday*, which was planning to break the story about Foster's involvement with Mrs Blair. Alastair Campbell, who was ill at home with gastric flu, was contacted, and he called Blair, who was in Newcastle for a meeting of Labour's National Policy Forum. Campbell asked him if the allegations made against Mrs Blair were true. Blair spoke to his wife on the phone at Chequers and called Campbell back. Cherie, he told his adviser, had never used Foster for financial advice and he had not assisted in the purchase of the flats. Relieved, Campbell briefed Godric Smith, one of two official spokesmen for the prime minister, who had been taking his children to the Arsenal–Aston Villa football match. The story, said Campbell, was wrong and should be shot down by the Number Ten spin machine. But the *Mail on Sunday* was undeterred. The next day it reported that Foster had indeed negotiated the sale of two flats in a six-storey apartment building called The Panoramic in the upmarket Clifton area of Bristol. Foster, the paper reported, had saved the couple about £40,000 on the flats, which were valued at upwards of £250,000 each.

Despite the claims, Campbell, spurred on by Mrs Blair's original denial, was adamant the story should be stopped in its tracks before others repeated the allegations. Downing Street, he decreed, would employ its best efforts to undermine the piece and stifle any follow-ups. The story would be dead in the water. That Sunday Blair's press office repeated the line they had been given by Campbell and the strategy appeared to work. The following morning only the *Daily Mail* followed up the story and the BBC studiously kept it out of their bulletins. When the political lobby journalists gathered two days later to be briefed again, Tom Kelly, the second of the prime minister's official spokesmen, went further and insisted that any negotiations for the sale had been carried out by Mrs Blair and her lawyer only. Political journalists, privately briefed by Campbell and his team that the allegations were trumped-up charges by the *Mail* stable which was intent on discrediting the prime minister by attacking his wife, bought the official line and ignored the story. The *Guardian* loyally did Downing Street's bidding and told its readers the day after the story broke that it was 'just another smear on the Blairs'.

But on Thursday 5 December Mrs Blair's version of events was blown to smithereens when the *Daily Mail* published a series of emails between Foster and the prime minister's wife in which he laid out how he had managed to negotiate down the price of the flats from £297,000 each to £265,000. Mrs Blair was clearly thrilled with his efforts. She told him in one message, 'I cannot thank you enough Peter for taking over these negotiations for me.' In another email after he had sent her forms to fill in, she wrote, 'You are a star. I have sent them off.'

In Downing Street there was pandemonium. One insider describes the atmosphere that morning as being 'nothing short of out and out hysteria'. Alastair Campbell, who had been attempting in previous months to improve the tarnished image of the government's Information Service, was once again beside himself at being put in such an invidious position. After misleading news organizations and being so blatantly caught out he knew Downing Street would be savaged. 'They'll fuck us all now' was his only comment to one colleague as the story broke. The Blairs returned from a rare night out at a theatre in the West End just as the first editions of the *Mail* came off the presses. Tellingly, Mrs Blair's first call, made well after midnight, was to Caplin. She would, Mrs Blair assured her, remain her friend. Nothing had changed. Next on the phone to Carole was Blair himself, telling her that she and her mother would stay part of the inner circle. Within the next forty-eight hours, the prime minister would make the same call to Sylvia Caplin. She and Carole, he told her, had his 'total support'. The next morning Campbell stood over Mrs Blair as she logged on to her computer and showed him all her correspondence with Foster. But despite the looming scandal she was not contrite, say insiders. 'At this stage Cherie seemed quite unconcerned about it,' says one. 'She was very much of the opinion that it was a case of the press stirring things up. She didn't seem to think she had done anything wrong. I don't think she fully registered how serious things were.'

She was to have gravely miscalculated the mood in Westminster; the atmosphere in the press lobby was fevered. Those journalists who had swallowed the Downing Street denials of the story and failed to report it were now out for blood. In Whitehall, as they gathered in the Regency surroundings of what had once been William Gladstone's music room, Tom Kelly cut a lone figure in front of the hordes of political editors and reporters from television, radio and the press. He began by going on the attack and accusing the *Daily Mail* of conducting a personal vendetta against Mrs Blair. It was a valiant but ultimately doomed attempt at deflection. The statement he read out next confirmed Mrs Blair's involvement with Foster and thereby blasted a gaping hole not only in the credibility of the prime minister's wife but also the government's information machine. Whichever way it was looked at, the bottom line was that the media had been lied to. Adam Boulton, political editor of Sky News, waited for Kelly to finish and growled, 'If you people just come here and tell us lies the whole system has broken down.' In the rest of the media the howls were even louder. In the days that followed, Kelly, like Godric Smith a career civil servant, was said to have considered resigning. The position of the two men was perilously close to untenable. If they could be accused of feeding lies to the media they were supposed to serve, what was the point of them? The media was not alone in its anger. Both men were livid at the mess they found themselves in and the focus of their fury was Mrs Blair.

For her part, Cherie was still adamant that her involvement with Foster was a private matter. In the statement given to the media after the emergence of the emails in the *Daily Mail* she continued to insist that Foster was not her financial adviser and that she had met him only once by chance. She 'regretted any misunderstanding' caused by her previous statements, but said this had been due to her desire to keep a private matter out of the public domain. But her assertion that she had done nothing wrong was not helped by what appeared to be obvious discrepancies between her account of her dealings with Foster and the facts. She said she had only dealt with the con man for 'a couple of weeks' and that the price per flat had dropped from £295,000 to £269,000 during discussions before Foster became involved. Both statements were untrue. 'He was simply the boyfriend of a friend who was helping me out when I was busy,' she added. In reality there had been email traffic between the two of them for upwards of six weeks. Foster's financial advice had also stretched to him advising that they should not attempt to pay the lower rate of stamp duty applicable to property worth up to £250,000 because the Inland Revenue was monitoring sales. 'So to try and do something could be risky and unadvisable,' he said. However, he added, 'Either way you are a mile in front.' He ended one email by offering the services of his accountant Andrew Axelson, who was himself awaiting an Old Bailey trial on money-laundering charges of which he was eventually cleared, to arrange the mortgage. 'I am happy to take the burden off you and make this happen with the minimum of fuss,' Foster signed off. Mrs Blair's insistence that she had been unaware of Foster's criminal convictions also laid her open to claims of dissembling as Foster himself claimed that he had been open with her about his past. Carole Caplin had also discussed his record with Foster at their very first meeting.

As false rumours began to circulate in Westminster that Campbell had been behind the deception, he demanded a second statement from Mrs Blair later that day in which it would be made clear that 'She and she alone is responsible for any misunderstanding between the Number Ten press office and the media.' Campbell's fingerprints were however all over a series of briefings which appeared in the papers that weekend, quoting Downing Street sources as saying that Mrs Blair was guilty of ignoring the advice of both Campbell and Millar and of insisting that she had to get the sanction of Caplin before making any decisions. Campbell, the press reported, had counselled some months earlier that Caplin was trouble and her relationship with the Blairs should be ended. The atmosphere inside Number Ten was one of intrigue and suspicion. A raging Campbell was open in his derision of Caplin and determined that he would not take the flak for what he considered Mrs Blair's uneasy relationship with the truth. Some newspapers reported that, despite Cherie's denials, she had in fact known about Foster's past when she made use of his services as a negotiator.

The story was clearly not going away; nor were the allegations that the wife of the prime minister, and by implication Blair himself, had been mendacious. While these claims were of the utmost seriousness for a barrister and part-time judge – some legal colleagues went as far as to suggest Mrs Blair should have been subjected to a Bar Council investigation – they were infinitely more damaging to Blair's credibility. The 'no smoke without fire' argument was compelling. Was it believable, it was asked, that Blair, in spite of his other commitments, knew nothing of his wife's negotiations over purchases totalling half a million pounds? In fact, he really was unaware of how the flats had been bought and it says much about the little time available to him for personal matters that he did not involve himself in the details of such a major investment. It was only as the scandal broke that the prime minister became aware of the extent of Cherie's involvement with Peter Foster.

If the Blairs and their advisers were hoping Foster would resist wading into the storm, they were sadly mistaken. His original plan had been to persuade Mrs Blair to offer the services of her children in promoting his diet scheme in schools. The Children's Education Programme was supposed to involve a national tour of schools to make youngsters aware of the risks of obesity. In fact it was merely a ruse to promote Foster's company and his latest slimming products. Foster, it was reported, even got as far as arranging a meeting with Euan, but it was cancelled when the PM's son overslept. Foster was also aware that the Blairs' teenage daughter Kathryn was at the time a little overweight. He planned, it was said, to put her on his diet and exploit the subsequent publicity. But if Downing Street was mortified by revelations of the Blairs' links to him, Foster himself was sanguine about being thrust into the limelight again. As the scandal broke in Britain he was emailing an Australian newspaper columnist to boast of how he had broken into the circle of the first family. Initially he had kept quiet in public, but he was now preparing to come out in the open. The Blairs were also unaware of an added problem. Carole Caplin had also decided to make the most of the publicity coming her way by hiring a public relations man called Ian Monk. Monk, a former *Daily Mail* executive, had a murky past himself. After leaving the *Mail* he became deputy editor of the *Daily Express*, but left the paper under a cloud when his wife Anita was arrested with two pre-publication copies of a biography of the Duchess of York which Monk had acquired and which his wife was about to sell to the *Sun*. Through Caplin, Monk was also advising Foster. This triumvirate of crook, former glamour girl and ex-tabloid journalist presented a very nasty problem for the Blairs. As the scandal deepened, Monk would also be behind a series of leaks damaging to Mrs Blair.

The revelations about Foster's history did nothing to bring about the demise of his relationship with Miss Caplin. As has been noted, Carole knew all about his shady past from the beginning of their affair and, more importantly, she was pregnant with his child. Like her boyfriend Carole saw the chance to cash in. She had been keen to trade on her association with the prime minister's wife when promoting her new company

Lifesmart, which offered a range of alternative health, fitness and dietary advice to paying clients. Now, her role as the conduit between Foster and Mrs Blair had thrust her further into the spotlight. Her childhood dreams of wealth and fame were, she hoped, about to be realized. Bizarrely, throughout the episode Carole continued to be Cherie's only trusted adviser, extending her role to include giving Mrs Blair advice on how to handle the media. Cherie's decision to listen to Caplin ahead of Alastair Campbell and Fiona Millar brought her relationship with her former friends to a new low. Campbell's decision to allow the media to blame Cherie for the Foster debacle only intensified the hostility. For her part, Fiona was already thinking about quitting her job, unable as she was to control Cherie. She was only too aware that the battle she had been waging with Caplin, whom she loudly derided, for the heart and mind of Mrs Blair had been lost for some time.

When the initial revelations broke, Campbell and Millar had attempted to question the prime minister's wife but had been told in no uncertain terms that the issue was none of their business. Meanwhile, Carole, who had got her friend into the fix in the first place, retained Cherie's ear, but her parlous advice on handling the media only served to illustrate the perilous position Mrs Blair had got herself in by listening to her lifestyle coach instead of those charged with the task. A week after revealing the story of the flat deal the *Mail on Sunday* ran an interview with another of Caplin's former boyfriends, Israeli-born Doron Dalah, the brother of one of Cherie's favourite fashion designers Ronit Zilkha. Dalah described how easy it had been for him to become part of the Blairs' circle through his relationship with Miss Caplin. He told of being invited to Downing Street and Chequers for dinners with the Blairs, and of being given the free run of their Number Eleven flat. Cherie, he said, was so trusting of Carole that she would give her blank cheques to fill in. When the paper approached Caplin to ask her about her ex-boyfriend's comments, she made a series of serious allegations about him. Now, on top of the story that someone unknown to the Blairs could get close to them so easily, the paper could add Caplin's claims about his character. But despite Carole's blunder, her position as Mrs Blair's closest adviser appeared unchallenged.

A wise counsel would have advised the prime minister's wife to lay all the details of the affair out in the open, but instead Cherie became increasingly mired in scandal as more and more embarrassing details leaked out. On 9 December her assertion that she had known nothing of Foster's past was shot to pieces by Foster's own lawyer, who revealed he had spoken to Mrs Blair on 22 November in a conference call with Carole Caplin about the immigration proceedings against his client. The conversation took place while Foster was still negotiating the purchase of the flats. Mrs Blair, caught out once again, said she was merely seeking to reassure her friend Carole that the case was being handled properly by the solicitors. It later emerged, however, that Foster's lawyer had contacted Heather Rogers, a colleague of Mrs Blair at Matrix, to ask her to help. In the event she was too busy. Not only that; it was separately revealed that documents relating to the immigration case had been faxed to Downing Street by Foster's legal team, although Cherie maintained that Carole had requested the papers and she had refused to look at them.

Mrs Blair's initial misleading of the Downing Street press office was now compounded by accusations of obfuscation and blatant lying as the drip, drip of information began to submerge Number Ten. Instead of fizzling out, the story only gained momentum as more and more 'killer facts' emerged. Throughout the episode Blair's team of advisers had operated the strategy of keeping the prime minister out of the direct firing line; despite Foster's claims to the contrary in the days to come, Blair had never met the con man or indeed spoken to him. If Cherie had to take some flak, the prime minister's own reputation, though undoubtedly injured by association, would, they hoped, not be fatally damaged. So Mr Blair stayed resolutely quiet on the subject and it was several days before he mounted any sort of defence of his wife. His delay, though politically important if he was to distance himself from the row, did not go down well with Cherie.

Those close to her insist today that Mrs Blair was bullish when the allegations about Foster first materialized. Even in the face of the anger of her husband's own press officers, who believed their reputations had been thrown to the wolves by her decision to allow them to mislead the press, she was firmly of the opinion that the purchase of the flats was a private matter. To her cost she had held to the belief that the privacy of her son and where he was going to live while at college were the most important issues. Consequently, she was evasive and unhelpful even with those whose job it was to extricate her from the morass. Once again her natural stubbornness had kicked in. The result was that, far from being repentant, Mrs Blair gave the impression of being strangely unmoved by the drama she had unwittingly cast herself in.

A source says, 'To begin with Cherie was completely unapologetic. She said she was too busy to bother with the whole thing and that she had too much on her plate to let it affect her.' But as the days passed with ever more damning evidence that she had been, even if her actions are viewed generously, less than open about the affair, the mood of the prime minister's wife became darker. 'She visibly wilted,' says one insider. 'It happened so quickly. She had been ready to tough it out, but as you watched her you could see the realization in her that her reputation was being torn to shreds. When it finally dawned on her, she buckled. It hit her very hard indeed. She is a strong person, but whatever you think of the way she behaved, and she did make a bloody hash of it, it was hard to see someone who was so obviously devastated by what had happened.' Another friend of Mrs Blair says,

'She suddenly felt incredibly alone. She was the villain of the piece; she was being accused of openly lying and she felt nobody believed her.'

Undoubtedly the most devastating realization, court insiders say, was that those Cherie believed had lost faith in her included her husband. Those close to the Blairs believe that the affair was by far the lowest point in their marriage. One friend describes the episode as 'a dark moment between them' only compounded, say sources close to the couple, by the fact that Mrs Blair was already at a low ebb. She was, they say, still coming to terms with her miscarriage in the summer and had been down for some time. The fallout from Cheriegate only served to deepen the unhappiness she was suffering. At a time when those around them expected the couple to pull together to weather the storm, there developed a fissure in the relationship that became obvious to their friends. It has been one of the only times, before or since, that the pressures of their very unusual position have been on display.

Insiders believe that Blair, facing what was turning into the lowest point of his premiership so far, was privately incredulous at his wife's behaviour. Like others who know Cherie well, Blair was aware that his wife was prone to trust those she hardly knows, but he was nonetheless astonished by how naive she had been. Of equal concern to him, however, was her unwillingness to reveal the truth when pressed and her reluctance to take the advice of Campbell and Millar as the crisis escalated, preferring to stick with the counsel of her friend Carole. Blair's silence in public on the issue was motivated by political expediency. In private, his lack of support left her feeling isolated. A friend adds,

Cherie is a tough cookie. She is not easily beaten, but there was a negativity in her home. She doesn't have many friends, but she felt particularly alone then. Tony was angry and he was not helping her. His staff turned on her as well and she could feel the animosity. She really felt she could not trust those around her because there were leaks coming from the inside that were aimed to discredit her. It sounds dramatic, but I really think she felt her home had become her prison. In the end she didn't have the strength to fight because she was already feeling down. When push came to shove I think Tony let her down.

A previously unreported incident serves to illustrate just how strained relations between the Blairs became. As the episode rumbled on Blair feared a continuing seepage of damaging revelations about his wife's wheeler-dealing. Against Cherie's will he sanctioned senior Downing Street aide Hilary Coffman to conduct a lengthy questioning of his wife behind the closed door of Number Ten. Cherie, who felt humiliated by the process, was asked about every aspect of her life, her private finances and particularly her relationship with Carole and Sylvia Caplin. At the centre of the questioning was the vexed issue of the deals done by Carole on Mrs Blair's behalf with a long list of designers and fashion houses. Cherie was forced to detail at length the freebies she had received and the huge savings made. Coffman was also instructed to question Carole Caplin. In a sign of the mistrust that existed between the two camps – Cherie's on the one side and Blair's private office on the other – Carole told Coffman that she would not submit herself to questioning without her solicitor being present. As if all this were not enough, insiders reveal that Cherie has had to submit to having her personal email monitored by Downing Street to this day. She must also carry with her a small electronic box and wire which she has to connect to her computer before being allowed to send emails. This is all, according to one source, to 'protect her'.

The experience of being forced to face embarrassing questions from a member of her husband's staff was deeply wounding to Mrs Blair, particularly as she no longer felt his staff had her best interests at heart. To add to her misery she was also feeling guilty because, as the scandal hit the headlines, Carole lost the baby she was expecting. Cherie, say insiders, blamed herself because she believed the brouhaha over her involvement in the affair had contributed to her friend's miscarriage.

A further insight into the tension not only inside Number Ten, but also in the Blairs' Number Eleven flat, was provided by Cherie's friend and protector Mary Ann Sieghart in *The Times*. As the crisis headed into its third week even Sieghart was moved to ask whether the prime minister's wife had been 'legalistic' in her response to her husband's staff when she was asked whether there was any more to come out. 'Nobody,' she wrote, 'even those close to her, can explain why Cherie did not own up to the conference call she held with Carole Caplin and Peter Foster's solicitors.' Mrs Blair's friends – probably even her husband – were baffled by the omission, she said, adding, 'Blair has, for the first time, lost his normal cool and is raging privately, in a way his staff have never seen . . . She, meanwhile, is crumbling under the pressure and the guilt. Downing Street is in turmoil.' While Ms Sieghart loyally laid the reason for Blair's anger at the door of the press, in particular the *Daily Mail*, she also laid bare the chasm that had developed between Cherie, Campbell and Millar. They had fallen out over Caplin and her mother, said Sieghart, and now Cherie was loath to take their advice.

Another thing Mrs Blair appeared loath to do was pass up the opportunity of a freebie. Ms Sieghart said the issue touched on a 'raw nerve' – Mrs Blair's attitude to money stretching back to her impoverished childhood. This was undoubtedly the case, but wasn't there another possible explanation for the unseemly affair? Foster's emails made it plain that he had used the Blairs' name as a lever with the property company to force down the price of the flats. Could it be that Cherie Blair had become so used to such deals, so adept at asking for and receiving favours as a quid pro quo for the sale of her celebrity, that she no longer considered this barrow-boy way of operating as anything other than completely normal?

*

As the setting for the entrance of Tony Blair's éminence grise into this unlikely drama, it could not have been more fitting. Shuffling through the late-afternoon gloom of Christmastide, two men edged off the pavement and slipped discreetly into the portals of 70 Whitehall. One of the figures was Lord Falconer, friend of the Blairs and then Home Office minister. The other was Peter Mandelson. Neither man wanted to be seen answering the call for help from Number Ten, so they entered through the door of the Cabinet Office and navigated their way through a series of doors into Number Ten. Despite being forced to resign from the government, Mandelson was and is a trusted ally. As Blair sought to extricate his wife, and in the process himself, from the Cheriegate debacle, Mandelson's skills in the black arts of spin and media manipulation would be desperately needed. He would also, naturally, empathize with Mrs Blair's position. After all, he had been forced to quit two ministerial posts because he hadn't told the full truth.

Once inside the building, they moved through the door into Number Eleven and on to Number Twelve, situated at the end of Downing Street. Seated in an untidy office dominated by a hatstand with a claret-and-blue football shirt hanging limply from it was communications director and Burnley fan Alastair Campbell. The personal statement Cherie would give in a little over four hours would be composed in these cluttered confines by the three men, with Campbell, reprising his role as tabloid journalist, tapping away at the keyboard of his computer. Next door, in the stateroom of Number Eleven, Mrs Blair was attending a children's Christmas party hosted by the chancellor Gordon Brown. Watching the genial former ITN political editor John Sargeant acting the role of Santa Claus, she could be forgiven for being in a less than festive mood. As Downing

Street sought to draw a line under the events of the previous days, Cherie had been railroaded into agreeing to make a public appearance that night to explain herself. When the idea was first mooted Campbell and Millar had considered going to a friendly paper, but when Blair called in Mandelson he argued that the prime minister's wife should speak over the heads of the newspapers directly to the public. A televised statement, he argued, would give her the opportunity to demonstrate to the public her remorse and allow her to plead with them for understanding. Now with the lawyer Falconer helping to formulate the wording of the sections about Foster, the three men put the finishing touches to this mea culpa with Fiona Millar adding the most memorable line: 'I am not superwoman.'

Less than an hour before she was due at a charity event for the education and childcare charity Partners in Excellence Mrs Blair left the Christmas party to be given the draft of her speech. The event at Westminster restaurant the Atrium on nearby Millbank was to be the platform she would use to make her public apology. She was expected to make her entrance at 6.30 but as the clock ticked down Cherie was having second thoughts. Not only did she feel she had been backed into a corner by her husband and his advisers, she was still desperate not to give her detractors in the press the satisfaction of seeing her ignominy played out on millions of TV screens. She was also terrified by the prospect of facing the cameras and the court of public opinion. As the time drew closer for her to set off by car for the Atrium, Mrs Blair told Millar she wasn't going to go through with it. There followed a tense twenty minutes as her aide and former friend tried to talk her round. As Millar's frantic attempts continued, Sky News went live at 6.30 p.m. in preparation for what they thought was the imminent arrival of the PM's wife. Finally, accompanied by Millar, a drawn and tense Mrs Blair arrived forty minutes late. The fight gone out of her; she faced the cameras and, like an actor, dutifully delivered someone else's words of remorse.

It was a mesmerizing performance. In scarlet blouse and black jacket, Mrs Blair's nine-minute soliloquy was a master-class in the persuasive art of the barrister. This time, however, she mounted the case for the defence with herself as counsel, defendant and self-styled victim. Shot through with emotion, it was all there: the regret, the defiance, even the tears. Mrs Blair aimed her arrows at the heart of other busy working mums. They, like her, knew what it was like to 'juggle a lot of balls in the air'. They too understood that occasionally balls got dropped.

What, on colder assessment, her performance lacked was fact. Few of the questions that remained about her dealings with Foster were answered, except for one new admission: that she had looked at court lists to find out which judge would be hearing his case. This was Cherie's Princess Diana moment, full of wide-eyed pleading but short on detail. A survey carried out by London radio station Capital FM after her speech showed that most had been impressed by her performance but few thought she was telling the truth. 'Sometimes I feel I would like to crawl away and hide. But I will not,' Mrs Blair told her audience. It was the first time many people had heard her voice. Her delivery was precise, her tone deeper than expected and betraying only a hint of her Liverpool heritage. She was keen, too, to reiterate her continued links with 'my friend Carole'. Her only input into the speech had been to write in no fewer than seven references to Caplin.

The strategy was simple. While the prime minister's wife must distance herself from Foster, she must keep Carole onside. Already there were rumours that Carole's adviser was in negotiation with newspapers to sell her story. The last thing the Blairs needed now was Carole dropping them further in it. 'I choose my friends carefully,' said Mrs Blair. 'And Carole Caplin has been a trusted friend and support to me as I have tried to adapt to the pressures of my public role and to do Tony and the country proud. When she told me she had a new boyfriend and seemed happy with him and later was expecting his baby, it really didn't cross my mind that he was going to land me in the mess I am now, and anyway I don't think it's my business to chose my friends' friends. In any case, what Carole told me was that he'd been in trouble in the past but was a reformed character. Maybe I should have asked her more questions but I didn't.'

Cherie said that Carole had told her Foster had been in trouble over trading standards offences, but added, 'I had no idea that he had been in jail in more than one country, including this country.' She also continued to deny that Foster had ever been her financial adviser. However, she went on, 'I should not have allowed a situation to develop where Tony's spokesman said he [Foster] played no part in the negotiations and I take full responsibility for that. Obviously if I had known the full details of Mr Foster's past I would not have allowed myself to get into this situation.' She admitted to two mistakes. One was to allow someone she barely knew to become involved in her family's affairs. Of the other, she said, 'My immediate instinct when faced with questions from the *Mail on Sunday* ten days ago was to protect my family's privacy and particularly my son in his first term at university living away from home. This instinct, which I think any mother would have, and my desire not to open myself up to any and every question the press should choose to ask me, led to this misunderstanding in the press office and I think they know I did not in any way set out to mislead them.' It was this first mention of her son that brought the catch in her voice as she clearly held back the tears that had been so close to the surface during her entire speech.

Few could have failed to be moved by the spectacle, but when the raw feeling and the mawkish prose of her puppet-masters Campbell and Mandelson was stripped away what were we really left with? With the benefit of cool reflection, hadn't this public purging been yet another display of those much-maligned New Labour staples, smoke and mirrors? Beyond the sentiment were more half-truths and prevarications. And just how real was the role she had cast herself in, the hard-pressed mother crumpling under the burden of bringing up a family and just trying to offer a little financial security for their future? At a time when the government was making known its openness to university top-up fees, how many mums seated in the audience or struggling to make ends meet at home could have imagined spending upwards of a reported £50,000 a year on a lifestyle guru, or wouldn't leave the house without having their hair done by their personal stylist? And who would buy two flats worth half a million pounds without even going to the trouble of viewing them or discussing the purchase with their husband?

And how real was the emotion? Did arch-manipulators Campbell and Mandelson direct and choreograph her like a Hollywood starlet? Did the speech include brackets between which was inserted the instructions: 'Weep now'? Those close to Cherie insist her emotions were all her own. But were those tears she fought back when she mentioned her son for him or for herself? She certainly could not be blamed for shedding a self-pitying tear, but those who know her well point to another emotion – raw anger as she parroted Campbell's and Mandelson's lines. She was angry that, as she saw it, her detractors had been allowed their pound of flesh. Her ego had also been severely bruised.

Arriving back home she was downcast. Blair was returning to Downing Street by car as she gave her performance and watched Sky's reruns on the TV in Campbell's office. Both men believed her statement would be enough to calm the storm. But, as she trudged up the stairs to the flat, Cherie was preoccupied by another thought. For as long as her husband had been in office she had made no secret of her fervent wish to become a High Court judge. She was also known to be keen on the job of lord chancellor in a future Labour government.

Earlier in 2002 she had even half-joked that she could be the first woman to be appointed the nation's most senior law officer. Now those hopes lay in ruins. There were even murmurings from some within the judiciary than she should resign her place on the bench as a recorder.

*

Two days later Campbell was attending a Christmas party thrown by News International. On the way out he was handed a first edition of the *Sun*. The paper, one of the few still sympathetic to the Blairs, was running the transcripts of a series of phone calls between Foster and his mother Louise Pelloti, who lives in Ireland. Foster, who had previously strenuously denied that he would cash in on the scandal, was negotiating to sell his story for £100,000 to the press. The discrediting of Foster was a welcome development to those inside Number Ten, but in his phone calls to his mother and in his subsequent televised statement Foster continued to cast doubt on Mrs Blair's version of events. Not only did he insist that he had met her three times – a claim she denied – he also contradicted her assertion that she had not read the papers concering his deportation faxed to her office by his lawyers. He went further, alleging that she had not only studied the file, but had given him her legal opinion on the case. Here, if it were needed, was conclusive evidence of her fall from grace: a little over two weeks earlier there would have been no contest over who to believe. It would have been the word of the prime minister's wife, a respected QC, barrister and part-time judge over an inveterate liar and con man with a record of fraud on three continents. Now, it was too close to call.

10

2003: FALLOUT

In the half-light of a January afternoon a car stops briefly at the electronic gates of an imposing manor house, then as they open sweeps through up a long drive. As the vehicle draws to a halt a bodyguard steps out and opens the door for the prime minister's wife to emerge and dart into the building. It is an operation planned with secrecy and almost military precision. Today, like every Friday afternoon for the past several months, Cherie Blair has been driven by a police minder from Downing Street down the A24 into the Surrey countryside. Her clandestine appointment is with Sylvia Caplin in her apartment in Burford Lodge, a Grade II-listed eighteenth-century mansion on the outskirts of Dorking. In the weeks since she became enmeshed in the Cheriegate scandal Mrs Blair has come to rely heavily on these hour-long visits. Once inside Mrs Caplin's neat home, she is ushered to a chair in the centre of the living room where large stones are placed at the feet of the prime minister's wife. Then, while she watches silently, Mrs Caplin goes into a trance and summons up voices from the spirit world to offer their advice. It is this beyond-the-grave guidance that in these recent bleak times Cherie has latched on to. In her miserable state she hopes these ghostly exchanges will offer her succour and salvation.

*

As the fallout over her relationship with Peter Foster finally began to dissipate, Cherie's spirits remained low. For the first three months of 2003 she was utterly despondent. Those who saw her regularly during this period were genuinely concerned about her health. So racked with guilt was she over dragging her husband into the messy affair and so mortified at seeing her own reputation slain by her own hand, she struggled to cope. She appeared to those inside Downing Street to be in an almost constant state of distress, bursting into tears at all times of the day and leaving for court or her chambers in the morning with her face still red and blotchy from crying.

Her husband's mood remained black too. With Britain gearing up for war in Iraq, Tony Blair resented the distraction of the Foster imbroglio. And while he was worried about Cherie's continued anguish, he had, say Downing Street sources, temporarily lost patience with his wife and the advisers and gurus who increasingly populated her court. With the focus of his attention on shoring up United Nations support for an attack on Saddam Hussein, Blair had little time to devote to his troubled wife. Into the void came Sylvia Caplin.

By way of expanding her repertoire of alternative therapies, Mrs Caplin had added two years earlier a new string to her bow, that of 'channelling', a technique which had become popular among New Age devotees. The channeller claims to be able to go into a trance and become the medium for spirits, taking on the voice of a dead person. Many channellers say they remember nothing of the conversations they have while speaking for the dead. Mrs Caplin describes her psychic sessions, for which she charges £100 an hour plus expenses, as 'spiritual release' and claims to be able to communicate with the afterlife. Her disciples report that she makes continual reference to 'the light up there' while she is conjuring up these spirits.

One visitor to Sylvia's flat next door to Surrey beauty spot Box Hill describes a typical channelling session with Mrs Caplin. 'It is all very impressive when you arrive,' she says.

Once inside, Sylvia shows you into a very normal-looking room and you sit down. There are photos of her daughter

Carole all over the place, but there is nothing weird or out of the ordinary, except that on the floor are what looks like a pile of rocks. She calls them crystals and they are something to do with channelling energy. I remember Sylvia as being very skinny and equally bossy. She begins to meditate and invites you to do the same, then she begins to summon up spirits, dead people from your past. She keeps talking about 'the light up there' and kept telling me to feel it going through my body and to imagine its roots going down to the middle of the earth. She told me to draw eight circles around my head in my mind and that they would protect me. Once she told me she had made contact with a very close friend of mine who had died some years ago. It was pretty upsetting. She didn't start speaking as the person or anything, she just said she was making contact with her. I was recommended to see Sylvia by a friend and I did it out of curiosity. I have a pretty open mind about these things, but I have to say that for me the whole experience was less than fulfilling. I didn't feel our sessions achieved very much. A lot of the time I really didn't know what she was talking about. When she wasn't channelling she talked about sex the whole time, saying that it was a very important part of one's well-being and competence in life. She said it is essential in making sure your mentality is well balanced.

Friends of Mrs Caplin tell how Cherie regularly faxed up to eight pages of questions at a time for her to channel. One of Sylvia's claims is that she has taught herself to 'heal' patients by proxy, purely by thinking about them. Ironically, and sadly for Mrs Caplin however, her powers have not, it seems, stretched to improving her own health. She has been plagued by illness and has had half her bladder, her womb and part of a lung removed. She has been struck down by a rare form of cancer, a lung infection that came close to killing her as well as an incurable colon disease. Visitors to her home report that she uses oxygen to treat her shortness of breath.

Surprisingly perhaps the influence exerted by the Caplins over Mrs Blair showed no sign of diminishing despite the events of the previous weeks. Cherie's loyalty was all the more extraordinary when viewed alongside the further embarrassment caused to both the Blairs by a fly-on-the-wall TV documentary Carole agreed to take part in as the story of Foster's involvement with Cherie broke. The BBC1 programme, *The Conman, His Lover and the Prime Minister's Wife*, was aired in mid-February 2003 just as the Cheriegate scandal had appeared to be running out of steam. But the prospect of milking the episode was apparently too tempting for Caplin. As her friend Cherie's reputation was submerged by the crisis, Carole allowed documentary maker Lynn Alleway to follow her own every move with a camera. The eagerly awaited programme was to place the Blairs firmly back under the spotlight. Filming during the height of the affair between 12 and 22 December, Alleway was invited to stay with Caplin and Foster at Carole's flat to record the events from the couple's perspective. What emerged was, for the Blairs, an all-too-public insight into the farce in which they had cast themselves as leading players, with Foster and Caplin taking on the roles of charmless and occasionally witless accomplices. Most revealing were the late-night calls made by the prime minister to Miss Caplin. In one call, made the day after he had told the media, 'I'm not really getting involved in this anymore,' Blair is heard ringing at midnight and leaving a message which begins, 'Hi, it's Tony calling.' Foster tells the filmmaker,

Tony rings most nights – if not every night then every second or third night. They talk three or four times a week so I think he is trying to mend some bridges. Carole's secrets could sink them for ever and they're worried that she will sell her story one day and that's why I think they want to embrace her. I think they like her, but the machinery is saying you must embrace this woman. My

understanding is that there is a six-month plan: get rid of
me, then in six months' time they will ease Carole out.

For her part, Caplin, whose home was seen to be festooned
with dozens of photographs of the Blair family, made no sectet
of the animosity that existed between her and the most senior
members of the court. Of Alastair Campbell, she told Alleway,
'Amazing. Poor man. I actually feel sorry for him because right
now I think he really has always had a real bee in his bonnet
about me and I don't say that with any sense of pride. I just
say what an incredulous [sic] waste of time.' She also admitted
being unsure about whether to trust her new lover or not. At
one point in the film she calls her PR to tell him to warn Foster
to stop talking to reporters. She confides to the camera, 'A lot
of people are absolutely terrified about what he is going to
come out with.' Those fears did not take long to be realized.
Asked whether Mrs Blair had lied about her version of events,
Foster replied, 'Yeah. Yeah, she has.'

The programme was to be the source of renewed embarrassment for the already embattled Blairs. As it was about to
air, Caplin announced she had fallen out with Alleway, who
had formerly been a friend, and that she and Foster were
considering legal action to have the film pulled. After seeing
a preview she said, 'My understanding of it was that it was
going to be called *My Friend Carole in the Eye of the Storm*.
I was appalled when I heard they'd renamed it *The Conman,
His Lover and the Prime Minister's Wife*. I feel completely
betrayed. They have tried to bring out the worst part of Peter
by carefully editing sixty-nine hours of film to put him in a
negative light. I have been friends with Lynn for twelve years,
but I cannot see how I can be friends with her after this.'

Insiders, however, reveal that there was more drama to
come. On the evening the documentary was broadcast, Carole
Caplin arrived at Downing Street in a highly emotional state.
'She was openly sobbing and saying she wished she hadn't got

involved in the programme,' says a source. Her tears, however, went largely ignored by Mrs Blair, who could barely contain her anger over the new humiliation she was about to endure. Cherie was also facing a more immediate dilemma – how she was actually going to watch the programme without incurring the wrath of her increasingly exasperated husband. Insiders say that Blair, in an untypical display of marital assertiveness, had forbidden his wife and family from watching. In the two-room farce that followed, Carole fled the building in tears while Mrs Blair spent the evening sneaking into her bedroom when her husband's back was turned to catch snatches of the BBC1 documentary. 'By that point Tony had completely lost patience with the whole situation,' says a courtier. 'He was livid that a story that was all but running out of steam had been given new life by this TV show. He issued strict instructions to Cherie and the kids that they were expressly banned from watching it.'

Carole Caplin's cooperation with Alleway, however, was not the cue for the Blairs to dispense with their increasingly troublesome friend. Far from it. Caplin and her mother remained at the heart of the Blairs' circle. They had both received unusually generous presents from the couple for Christmas, and mother and daughter were also guests at a dinner party thrown in the New Year at Number Eleven in their honour. Carole, never one to pass up an opportunity, was well aware that the public disgrace of Mrs Blair might have an upside. With her profile raised by the episode, and with Ian Monk feverishly working on her behalf, she was invited to be a columnist for the *Mail on Sunday*'s *Night and Day* magazine. Some would have demurred at an offer from the newspaper that had been the nemesis of their friend; Cherie had, after all, been engaged in a running battle with the paper, which had broken the Foster story. But Carole, ever the pragmatist, is not the type to look a gift horse nor a six-figure salary in the mouth. She took the job but made no mention of her new position to Mrs Blair. Aware that her career move might not go down well with Number Ten, Caplin made use of her first appearance in the magazine to mount a self-serving defence of her actions. With his application to stay in the UK rejected, Foster had headed for Ireland at the end of January, but was arrested on arrival, spent a night in Dublin's Mountjoy prison and was deported to Australia. In her *Night and Day* debut Miss Caplin, falling easily back into her role of loose cannon, further embarrassed the Blairs with her claims that 'powers that be' had been responsible for having her boyfriend kicked out of Britain. These 'mysterious people', she said, 'were acting to protect whatever they thought they needed to protect, but they've gone way over the top'. Foster, she added, had been 'treated like a hardened criminal on the run, or a terrorist. He's not raped anyone, he's not murdered anyone, it's nothing to do with drugs or children. He's just been a stupid git.'

Foster might have been halfway across the world, but if the Blairs thought his deportation would draw a veil over the unhappy episode they were to be mistaken. He took less than forty-five minutes to fire off the first salvo to the pack of Aussie hacks waiting for him on his arrival back home. Foster made a series of fanciful claims including that he had been introduced to the prime minister, an allegation which has always been denied. But worse was to come. Over the next few months, as his relationship with Caplin petered out, Foster continued his barrage of ever more colourful and lurid accusations. It should be repeated that Foster is an unreconstructed liar and villain who was in the process of trying to sell his autobiography to publishers, but that did little to mitigate the embarrassment he was so intent on causing the Blairs. In one calculated outburst he accused his ex-girlfriend of being in love with the prime minister and claimed that Caplin and Blair had regular long late-night phone conversations. Carole, he said, even chose the PM's underpants. 'The British people would be flabbergasted if they knew the extent to which Mr

Blair is reliant on Carole,' Foster told a Sydney newspaper. He went on, 'I was amazed and annoyed by the intensity of their relationship. They went for long walks in the woods around Chequers and they phoned each other at night, having long conversations. People think that Cherie is the ugly duckling who Carole advised with clothes and make-up and styling. The truth is that Tony relied on Carole too. Carole coached him on how to handle people, how to handle situations and how to present himself.' A year after his split from Caplin, Foster's claims were to become even more bizarre with his assertion, reported in the Australian press and repeated in the UK, that he was suspicious the baby his former girlfriend had been carrying before her miscarriage was not his but the prime minister's. His ludicrous comments were denounced as 'fantasy' by Carole.

*

As she struggled to come to terms with the catastrophic errors of judgement she had made, Cherie Blair fell back on the one true constant in her life – her religious faith. Desperate to find a resolution to her travails, she became convinced that what she needed to purge herself of the torment she continued to feel was papal absolution. She threw herself into trying to engineer a private audience with the Pope through her many senior contacts in the British Catholic Church and within weeks heard that John Paul II had granted her an audience and a private Mass in Rome to take place at the end of February 2003. Those who witnessed her distress believe she saw her trip to meet the pontiff as an 'emotional lifeline' during those dark days.

Despite his unofficial conversion to Catholicism, her husband might have been forgiven for not relishing the visit to the Vatican as much as his wife. The Pope had been a vociferous critic of US and British plans to invade Iraq. While the Vatican was quick to point out that Blair had been invited not as a world statesman but out of respect for his Catholic wife, the prospect of a public rebuke from His Holiness was particularly unwelcome given the huge anti-war sentiment at home and even within his own party. Cherie, however, was thrilled not only by the prospect of meeting the Pope herself, but that her children and husband would also be granted the honour. A source says, 'It is hard to overestimate just how significant the Pope's invitation was at that time. Cherie had been left absolutely on the floor by what she had been through and there were times when she was in despair and saying she didn't want to have do this job anymore.'

The Blairs flew to Rome and were put up in the spartan environs of the Pontifical Irish College, a seminary open to visitors for a modest sum. Blair's suspicion that his meeting with John Paul would be more political than spiritual proved well founded. During their fifteen-minute private audience the Pope told a squirming prime minister that an attack on Iraq would not only be morally unjust but also a 'defeat for mankind'. The 'tragedy of war', said the pontiff, was still avoidable, and he reiterated his position that the United Nations must be allowed to attempt to solve the crisis.

But while the papal lecture was not exactly welcome, the trip and the time he was able to spend alone with his wife convinced Blair for the first time of the very real distress she had been suffering in recent months. As he struggled with decisions that would define his premiership, the ongoing focus on his wife in the media and her unhappiness had been distracting. But Blair felt he had not given Cherie the time she deserved. In Rome the prime minister became visibly more relaxed as he escaped the febrile Westminster atmosphere to spend some much-needed time with his family. For Cherie, her hopes that this spiritual odyssey would lift the veil of gloom that had hung over her were realized. She returned to London revitalized and reinvigorated. The impression of a woman cowed and defeated by the events that engulfed her was replaced with one armoured in a new steeliness and determination no longer to be browbeaten by her detractors in the media. Those who know her well point to this time as the moment Mrs Blair made the conscious decision to create for herself a harder shell against the attacks directed at her. She would, she resolved, never again allow herself to be dictated to by those she knew she would never win over no matter how hard she tried. With this rediscovered resolve came a new approach: in future, she decided, she might as well be hung for a sheep as a lamb.

It was also payback time. In March 2003, a month after returning from Rome, Cherie reignited the long-running battle with the media over her children. She summoned PCC Director Guy Black to Downing Street as she sought revenge on those who had, as she saw it, been responsible for a campaign of vilification against her. Not only do her actions at this time say much about her desire for retribution, they also provide an insight into the Blairs' attitude to the privileges they believed were their children's by right. Mrs Blair's belief that the PCC should offer her children more protection than that afforded to others had been aired in a previous letter to the commission's chairman Lord Wakeham in which she had demanded a new privacy law and an end to press self-regulation. She is said to have dismissed the view that her family should be offered the same rights under the PCC code as everyone else. The children of prime ministers and other important figures, she said, should get a greater degree of protection. Wakeham had turned her down, but Mrs Blair was bruising for a fight.

After her humiliation over Peter Foster, Cherie was adamant that the press must pay the price. It must, she believed, be cut down to size and she became convinced that legislation was needed to restrict the media from reporting on the private affairs of public figures. She began pressing her husband on the need for a change in the law. One Downing Street source describes her demands on the issue as 'increasingly strident and shrill. She talked about little else and was being very demanding about it.' But Blair was well aware that the issue was a minefield. Not only was there no public clamour for such a bill, he also knew he would face a barrage of criticism in the media and allegations that he was restricting freedom of speech. Moreover, he was aware of something that, in her fury and embarrassment, Cherie had missed: her behaviour over the Foster incident was precisely the sort of conduct the press would use to justify their contention that the private dealings of public figures can, on occasion, have relevance to their public role.

Still, though, she pressed her husband on the issue until he agreed that they should meet the PCC to demand increased protection for their children. Guy Black was duly called to the Blairs' Downing Street flat. He later told authors Francis Beckett and David Hencke that when he arrived he had to manoeuvre himself across a floor covered with children's toys, as well as past the young Leo, who was playing with Carole Caplin. In the Blairs' sitting room were Tony, Cherie and Fiona Millar. From the outset he was aware that the meeting was unlikely to be convivial. Cherie, he reported, looked like a 'volcano that was about to erupt', but initially she left the talking to her husband. Blair explained to Black that he was very concerned about the pressure being put on his children and wanted his opinion on the best way to handle the situation. He explained that he wanted a complete ban on all publicity to do with them. What the prime minister was proposing was an agreement essentially the same as the one Prince Charles had reached with the media over Princes William and Harry. His suggestion was not that there should be an extension of the existing guidelines relating to children in general, but an alteration to give only his own children the status of the royal boys.

Black turned down the proposal, telling the prime minister that his children were not public figures in their own right and not heirs to the throne. While the PCC would willingly take up any complaint over breaches of his children's privacy, the prime minister, said Black, was not able to demand privileges exclusively for his own family. Throughout Black's response Cherie, he said, looked furious. At that point Blair was called away to take a call from the Russian leader Vladimir Putin, and as he left the room Cherie could hold her temper no longer and 'exploded'. She proceeded to launch into a long rant about the *Daily Mail*, which she described as a 'disgraceful' paper. Tellingly, her complaint was not about its reporting of her children but its treatment of Cherie herself. Mrs Blair told Black the paper said she had bought Tony a cheap bottle of wine for his birthday when in fact, she claimed, it was a 'very expensive bottle'. What, she demanded, was he going to do about it? Black, now bemused that he had been apparently summoned to Downing Street, in part at least, to discuss a complaint about the cost of a birthday gift, told Mrs Blair she should take her case up with the editor of the *Mail*, and if she was unhappy with his response she could make a formal complaint to the commission.

Cherie's mood when Black left was described by Downing Street sources as virtually 'apoplectic'. Privately, some within the Blair court felt that her fixation on taking on the press over the issue of their children had long verged on the obsessional. There was also a strongly held belief among many that Mr Blair had not been forceful enough with his wife in demanding they choose only the battles with the press that were worth fighting. One said,

It seemed like simple bad politics to pick fights with the press over trifling issues. Nobody would have denied Cherie her right to do everything in her power to protect her kids and we all supported that, but running off to the PCC at every turn over the most innocuous stuff was only ever bound to stir up trouble we didn't need. Tony should have been more assertive with her and warned her of the damage it was doing to him personally to continue constantly inciting the newspapers.

Certainly, Mrs Blair's recent painful brush with the media had not made her any less inclined to risk its wrath with continued displays of acquisitiveness and attempts to trade on her name. During a shopping trip in London she was reported to have tried on no fewer than six pairs of Manolo Blahnik shoes worth £1,800 before leaving the shop empty-handed. Carole Caplin, in their well-rehearsed ploy, later contacted the store to ask for a discount. On this occasion her attempts to negotiate a deal for Mrs Blair were rebuffed. Then in April Mrs Blair found herself at the centre of a row over her love of freebies when she was invited to Australia to speak at a legal convention in return for having her expenses covered. It was while in Melbourne that she received an invitation, along with her three youngest children, to visit the showroom of Globe International, a designer clothing company. As the family toured the premises, Mrs Blair was invited to pick out a 'few items' as gifts to remember their Australian visit. She didn't need to be asked twice. By the time Mrs Blair and her brood's orgy of freeloading was over, she had helped herself to no less than sixty-eight items worth more than £2,000. So huge was their supermarket sweep that staff had to carry the haul, which included polo shirts, jeans, T-shirts, pyjamas, pillowcases, a beach set and, bizarrely, an alarm clock, in five boxes. Aptly perhaps, a pair of pyjamas thought to have been chosen by Mrs Blair for the prime minister featured a character called Julius who is known to Antipodeans as the 'cheeky monkey'. Other shoppers reported hearing the teenage Nicky and Kathryn calling, 'We want that one, Mummy,' as they ran round gathering up their complimentary goods.

Given the furore she had caused by using Foster to get her discounts on the Bristol flats, Mrs Blair's excess down under just four months later was at best ill-advised, particularly as not only was she obliged to declare the gifts to customs officers on her return to the UK, but keeping them would have put her in breach of rules forbidding government members and their families from accepting presents worth more than £140. Within days of the news of the spree leaking out, Downing Street was forced to issue a statement saying Mrs Blair would be paying for the items from her own pocket, but despite the embarrassment she had again caused her husband, Cherie was unapologetic. Quite the contrary in fact. Ceaseless bad publicity had prompted her to come to the conclusion that whatever she said or did, no matter how blameless her behaviour, she would remain a target for certain sections of the media. Deeply irritated by what she considered to be the family's limited finances, she determined that she would make use of every opportunity to reverse this state of affairs. She had, she believed, seen her advancement in the law thwarted by negative publicity over her dealings with Foster, so now was the time to cash in and those who criticized her moneymaking endeavours could go hang. 'She was being offered very lucrative deals to speak at charity and business events around the world,' says a Downing Street source. 'She decided that she would start accepting some of the offers. She felt that she needed to provide a nest egg for the family for when Tony was no longer in office. She was aware it would attract criticism, but she figured she would get that anyway. I think the whole Cheriegate thing hardened her to the flak she gets.'

Cherie remained, however, no less crucial to her husband's administration. As Blair sought to prevent a devastating Commons revolt by his own backbenchers over the proposed war on Iraq that would surely have signalled the end of his premiership, his wife edged quietly from the shadows to step into the fray. In mid-March 2003 Mrs Blair watched her husband's opening speech in the crucial debate and, while the prime minister desperately glad-handed wavering Labour members in the Commons Tea Room, began a round of canvassing amongst the party's women MPs to shore up support. The tactic was simple and ultimately effective. Mrs Blair was a human rights lawyer thought, even among Blair's own backbenchers, to be to the left of her husband. Her conviction that going to war over Iraq's failure to comply with a series of UN resolutions demanding its disarmament was not only legal but morally justified was a powerful tool in talking round those suffering a crisis of conscience over the government's decision to side with the US and turn its back on the United Nations.

*

It had been a long and exhausting flight. Arriving home late at night after a twenty-four-hour journey from Australia Cherie Blair was tired and ready to fall into bed, but as she trudged upstairs to the first-floor living quarters of the Number Eleven flat she was greeted not only by her husband but also by an unexpected guest. Standing next to Tony was an elegantly attired Carole Caplin ready to welcome her home. It was not an altogether pleasant surprise. In fact, such was her astonishment at finding her beautiful friend and husband together Mrs Blair could only blurt out, 'What are you doing here?' After an embarrassed silence, the prime minister explained that Carole and her mother Sylvia had joined him for dinner. Friends of the PM's wife say that Mrs Blair appeared 'shocked' by the presence of the pair so late at her home, but Cherie had become more and more used in recent months to Miss Caplin spending time alone with her husband. By the middle of 2003 Carole Caplin had come to play an increasingly important part in the life of the prime minister. Not only was she regularly called on to give massages to Mr Blair, including at Chequers every Sunday as he struggled to deal with the political fallout caused by his decision to back the US in the war on Iraq – which began in earnest at the end of March – she had recently taken on a new role. For several months Blair had been receiving daily morning visits at Downing Street from a male fitness coach, a New

Zealander who worked with Carole at Holmes Place in Regent's Park, but Downing Street sources say that during the spring Miss Caplin had deftly engineered his departure and taken over the role of overseeing the prime minister's workouts herself. Alone upstairs with Carole at Number Ten, Mr Blair would go through a series of exercises using weights to tone up his physique.

The improvement in his body shape was evident later in the year when the Blairs went on holiday to Barbados, and Carole, employing a mischievous and deliberate double entendre, was happily boasting to friends, 'Tony's body is fantastic and it's all down to me.' Indeed, Miss Caplin, who had taken to calling the prime minister and first lord of the Treasury by the affectionate nickname 'Toblerone', was well used to adopting an overtly flirtatious tone when addressing Mr Blair. According to Peter Foster, he was once in the bath when he overheard Miss Caplin talking to the PM on the phone. Carole, he claims, told Mr Blair, 'I want your body.' Then, Foster says, she added, 'I mean when you get back to London you have got to get that weight off. I want your body in the gym.' More bizarrely, Foster alleged that his ex-lover had claimed to him that she had slept in the Blairs' bed at Chequers. Because Foster is undoubtedly a most unreliable witness, his allegations went largely ignored and have been written off as the wilder fantasies of the rogue he most certainly is. For once however he was, in part at least, correct. Number Ten sources confirm that Carole Caplin was regularly to be found asleep in the couple's bed in Downing Street. It was certainly not unusual for staff, called to the Blair's bedroom, to find Carole asleep under the couple's duvet. It should be pointed out that what Miss Caplin described as her 'power naps' never took place while Mr Blair was in the room; nor did she undress before sliding under the prime ministerial covers. What, though, was Mrs Blair's attitude to another woman slipping between her and her husband's sheets? According to insiders, Mrs Blair was seemingly unfazed by her friend's unscheduled siestas in the £3,500 Norwegian

king-size divan that Miss Caplin had herself picked out for
them when they moved into Number Ten. A Downing Street
source says,

> It became quite a regular occurrence. Of course everyone
> talked about it and Carole loved that. She would bang on
> about how short naps of fifteen minutes during the day
> were very healthy, but how many people would just get
> into a friend's bed and go to sleep? Sometimes Cherie
> was in the room, sometimes not. Carole would suddenly
> announce that she was tired and wanted a nap, then get
> into bed. Cherie didn't seemed to be bothered in the
> slightest that she was getting into the bed she and Tony
> sleep in. Frankly, I'm sure a shrink would have a field day
> with the whole set-up because a couple's bed is so private
> and intimate. It smells of them for God's sake. But I'm sure
> Carole did it purely to display how close she was to the
> Blairs and how intertwined she was in their lives.

Caplin was also quick to drop into conversations at the first
opportunity that she was so vital to the prime minister that she
did, indeed, even shop for his underpants. Not only that, but
while Mrs Blair was out of the country on one occasion Downing Street staff report that Carole arrived alone to spend the
evening at the flat sorting through Mr Blair's wardrobe. She
was also keen to point out to her friends that her influence with
the PM went beyond her role as fitness trainer and clothes
stylist. 'He relies on me because I am the only one he can talk
to,' she declared without prompting to one bemused acquaintance. What is undeniable is that as Caplin continued to cement
her position at the very heart of the court, she was allowed a
degree of autonomy not granted to others. Keen to make the
most of her heightened public profile, Carole added to her
Night and Day column a £75,000 appearance in *Hello!* magazine in which she talked breathlessly and in minute detail about
her role for Mrs Blair. Caplin, pictured in a £5,000 diamond

ring which was part of a set of jewellery worth £20,000 she had originally borrowed from Japanese store Mikimoto on Mrs Blair's behalf, told how she arranged Cherie's clothes and appearance six months in advance, even extending the detail to planning how Cherie would look getting in and out of cars and whether her clothes would crease or not.

Cherie had become particularly demanding about how she looked and had developed something of a prima donna attitude to protecting her stylish image. She was not immune to the occasional strop more suited to a musical diva than a political wife. Mrs Blair was, however, furious about Carole's appearance in *Hello!* and her habit of failing to seek her boss's approval before accepting offers from the media. Part of Cherie's annoyance was, say insiders, due to concern that Caplin was using their relationship as a means of promoting herself, but there was a baser human emotion operating too. Sources say Mrs Blair was riled that Carole was making large amounts of money from their connection, while Cherie, because of her position, made nothing. Her displeasure was evident, they say, when Mrs Blair saw the several pages of pictures featuring Carole in the edition of *Hello!* Caplin, Cherie pronounced, looked like Posh Spice. It was not meant as a compliment. But the prime minister's wife had long since given up trying to control the strong-willed Carole. For her part Caplin was convinced, say her friends, that she was indispensable to the Blairs, not least because of the money she saved Mrs Blair in furnishing her ever-expanding wardrobe. It was a service that both the prime minister's wife and Caplin were happy to extend to the wives of visiting world leaders. One such beneficiary of Carole's market-trader brand of haggling was Lyudmila Putin, wife of the Russian president. In the space of an hour and a half in the London showroom of Burberry, Carole, who accompanied the leaders' wives on the trip, negotiated a huge discount on more than £1,000-worth of designer clothes for the fashion-conscious Russian.

Mrs Blair also continued to rely on Miss Caplin to seek out ever more radical New Age therapies. One such treatment, for the perennial issue of her weight, took place in a private room at the salon of top London hairstylist Daniel Galvin. During the process, known as RejuvaSlim, Mrs Blair lay on a table while a Polaroid-style camera photographed her stomach. A thermal image-type picture was taken which supposedly allowed a therapist to examine Mrs Blair's digestive processes. Then thirty-two electrodes were attached to her body to remove, it is claimed, 'toxic waste'. Those marketing the treatment say the method reverses years of 'digestive abuse' to leave a 'svelte, youthful' figure without the need for exercise or a calorie-controlled diet.

Caplin, moreover, continued to have a hand in creating a trail of bad publicity for the prime minister's wife that owed much to the farcical. One such incident was so spectacularly misjudged and amateurishly handled that it was christened 'Lippygate'. Mrs Blair contrived to allow herself to be photographed by a women's magazine in the role of supine baby sister on the edge of her bed while Carole Caplin, assuming the part of glamorous older sibling, applied lipstick to her. The accompanying pictures of the chaotic Number Eleven flat also revealed Mrs Blair to be immune from the distractions of housework. The comic episode was conceived as an attempt to improve Mrs Blair's image in the wake of Cheriegate, but ended up raising more questions than it answered, not only about her judgement but also her behaviour. Cherie found herself back in the spotlight and once again the subject of negative comment.

The incident began innocently enough with a plan by Number Ten to begin ridding Cherie of the dreadful public persona she had acquired for herself. The plan was to use a friendly publication to focus on the charity work done by the PM's wife and portray a more caring, accessible Mrs Blair. A writer from women's magazine *Marie Claire* was duly invited to spend a day with Cherie and write a piece for its September edition. But there was a major flaw in the strategy: for nearly ten years New Labour had operated a journalistic no-fly zone around Mrs Blair. The result was that when she finally came face to face with this hitherto alien species she displayed a complete naivety about how they should be handled. Barbara Ellen, the journalist chosen by the magazine for the assignment, later wrote a fascinating account of the meeting in the *Observer*. Her version of events did not make comfortable reading for Cherie. She emerged as a highly strung personality – uncomfortable, awkward and still deeply in the thrall of Caplin.

According to Ellen, the prime minister's wife had, on their introduction at her legal chambers, at first seemed ill at ease. 'She came across as shrill and tense. A charm-free zone,' said the writer. Then, in the people carrier on the way back to Downing Street, a clearly overwrought Mrs Blair took it upon herself to try to lift the mood. She began serenading the bemused journalist and her photographer with her favourite show tunes. This, say Blair court insiders, is not at all unusual. Cherie will, they attest, break into song at the drop of a hat and often at the most unlikely moments. She also possesses an almost photographic memory for the lyrics of the most forgettable and disposable of pop tunes. On this occasion the experience was not altogether pleasant. 'At the time I was just relieved that Cherie had relaxed,' Ellen wrote. 'But even then there was a quite inappropriate mood of hysteria – Cherie singing away, rocking to and fro, clutching my arm, and laughing raucously straight into my face.' On their arrival at Number Ten the journalist and photographer were dismissed by an imperious Fiona Millar and told to come back after lunch. When they did, Millar was nowhere to be seen and a security guard showed them straight into the Blairs' flat. The place was a tip with children's toys scattered around the floor and boxes of papers shoved up against a radiator. Cherie appeared and after a moment's hesitation, and without clearing it with Millar, invited them in. What they found there was journalistic nirvana. In Millar's absence, Cherie introduced the women to Carole Caplin, who they were surprised to find in Mrs Blair's messy dressing room surrounded by Cherie's clothes and an array of what Ellen described as 'kinky-looking' ankle boots belonging to the PM's wife. At first Cherie sat down at a dressing table overflowing with tights, knickers and make-up, then ushered the journalists into her bedroom, where that most famous image of the prime minister's wife and Caplin was caught as they perched on the edge of the bed like two giggling schoolgirls. Here was Cherie Booth, human rights barrister and formidable mind, regressing to her teens as friendless bluestocking at last getting to hang out with the prom queen.

In PR terms the exercise could barely have been more damaging with its renewed evidence of Mrs Blair's reliance on Miss Caplin, of her tendency to behaviour that bordered on the slightly loopy and, tut-tut, her slattern's approach to the housework to boot. To make matters worse, Mrs Blair tried and failed to have her quotes changed after seeing an early draft of the article. Yet, astonishingly, on the advice of Caplin she passed up the opportunity given her by the magazine to leave out the offending lipstick moment. Once again the hand of the disaster-prone Carole was firmly on the tiller as Cherie made fullsteam for the iceberg.

Where was Fiona Millar during this whole fiasco? The truth is that Millar, like Alastair Campbell, had already conceeded victory to Caplin. She and her partner had simultaneously announced that they planned to leave their Number Ten jobs in the autumn. Cherie's treatment of Millar had hastened the departure of Campbell, who had previously threatened to quit over the way Mrs Blair had frozen Fiona out. Now, with Blair about to face some of the darkest days of his premiership over the Iraq war and the continuing fallout over the suicide of weapons inspector Dr David Kelly, he would have to do so without the man who had been his most trusted lieutenant. A year later, when Blair looked over the precipice and came within a whisker of quitting, it would be Campbell's absence that he would feel most acutely. The Lippygate affair served to bring into sharp relief the parlous state of relations between Mrs Blair and her former friend Fiona. Either Millar was happy to let her boss dig her own grave or she herself was proving a one-trick pony when it came to handling Cherie – capable of maintaining a jackbooted closed-door policy but unable to handle the finer details of a successful PR strategy.

Just when Mrs Blair needed an intelligent approach Millar was found wanting. Her years of sneering at journalists, and her taciturn manner meant there were few takers when she was given the task of making new friends for Mrs Blair in the media. Millar's approach had only raised hackles and alienated many from her boss, whose own natural charmlessness was in need of a positive gloss. Cherie had lost faith in Fiona anyway and it was little wonder that the ingénue Mrs Blair turned to Caplin for guidance. Cherie, say observers, was and remains incapable of accepting advice from anyone whom she does not consider a friend. It is an attitude that has led to her putting her faith in those she likes rather than those whose advice she would do better to listen to. That said, just how well-advised was this latest attempt to submit the prime minister's wife to the close inspection of the media? Not only was she plainly unsuited to such a exercise, her attempt to sell a new image of herself by opening her home and family to inspection drove a coach and horses through her argument that she should be allowed privacy because she was not a public figure.

11

2003: FALL GUYS

Such are the spoils of war. As the setting for an evangelical Blair masterclass, the amphitheatrical splendour of the US Congress could scarcely have been more fitting. Surrounded by his newest and most adoring disciples, the prime minister gave a performance brimming with quasi-religious fervour, chockfull of proselytizing zeal about the struggle between the forces of good and evil. Four months after standing shoulder to shoulder with George Bush and sending his troops to join the invasion of Iraq, Tony Blair came to Washington a conquering hero. Only the fourth British prime minister to be invited to address a joint session of Congress, Mr Blair's speech was interrupted by applause no fewer than thirty-five times and resulted in seventeen standing ovations. For today at least, he was the king of Capitol Hill.

Harrowdown Hill is a long way from Washington DC. Set amid rolling Oxfordshire countryside near the village of Longworth, it has at its top a dense copse of oak and ash. It is the place where Dr David Kelly chose to die. Outed by Mr Blair's government as the source of the now infamous BBC report alleging that the government had 'sexed up' its dossier on Iraq's weapons capabilities in order to strengthen the case for war, the weapons inspector had, over the previous days, seen his reputation and career shredded as he became the public fall guy in the battle between the corporation and New Labour. On a wet summer afternoon in July 2003 the government scientist walked for an hour from his home to the beauty spot he knew well. There he swallowed some co-proxamol painkillers, then cut his left wrist and waited. As Blair gave that momentous address, David Kelly was already dead. His body would lie undiscovered until the following morning.

In the first-class cabin of a chartered British Airways Boeing 777 en route from Washington to Tokyo the Blairs were in jubilant mood and still taking in the historic events of their brief hours in the US capital. Mr Blair had planned to get some much-needed sleep on the fourteen-hour flight to Japan, which would host the next leg of his round-the-world diplomatic mission. As always, however, he would not be out of contact with the world below. Attached to one of the porthole windows of the jetliner by means of suckers was a satellite pod from which an untidy series of wires led across the aisle to a telephone handset. This secure line is the prime minister's constant link to his Downing Street office while in the air. The call with the news of Kelly's disappearance came through as his jet was crossing the Bering Strait. Blair was told that the wife of the weapons inspector had called police when he did not return from a walk. The mood change could not have been more marked. Mr Blair 'visibly wilted'. The euphoria was gone instantly, replaced only with feelings of isolation and vulnerability.

His state of mind was not lifted by the fact that not only was he carrying a contingent of the British media with him on his plane, he was travelling without his most senior aides. Alastair Campbell, Chief of Staff Jonathan Powell and Director of Government Relations Sally Morgan had all boarded a flight for London from Washington. Shocked though he undoubtedly was by the news he had been given, Mr Blair was also angry at the predicament in which he found himself. The information reaching him from the duty staff at Downing Street was sketchy and he wanted to know what was happening. An irritated Blair demanded his people on the plane find out more. When one of his staff suggested that it would be difficult to establish the full details until London woke up, he exploded. 'I don't care. I'm awake. Wake them up,' he ordered.

Those who have worked for Mr Blair for many years report never seeing him so angry before or since. 'We were having great difficulty discovering what was going on back home because of the time difference and the fact that we were on the plane,' says a Downing Street source. 'Nobody seemed to know anything. The police were not being helpful and he reacted very badly to being left in the dark. He was under enormous stress and it showed.' Finally, in a series of desperate calls, the PM spoke to Defence Secretary Geoff Hoon in London, as well as Lord Falconer, his friend and the new constitutional affairs secretary, and Sir Kevin Tebbit, the permanent secretary at the Ministry of Defence. By the time an ashen-faced Mr Blair stepped onto the tarmac at Tokyo's Haneda airport he had been told that Dr Kelly's body had been found. Later, in the New Otani Hotel, he walked up to a Sky News cameraman and said he would give a short statement. Announcing an independent inquiry, he said, 'This is an absolutely terrible tragedy. I am profoundly saddened for David Kelly and his family. In the meantime, all of us, the politicians and the media alike, should show some respect and restraint.' It was to be a vain hope.

A few short hours earlier it had been the rapturous applause of his US hosts that had been ringing in his ears. Now out of a throng of journalists came the first of many difficult questions to come: 'Mr Blair, how does it feel to have blood on your hands?' His reception from Congress served merely to bring into sharp focus the contrast that already existed between Blair's standing in the US and British opinion. Dr Kelly's death and the subsequent Hutton Inquiry would become the focus of much discontent in Britain. The merits of the government's stated justification for sending troops into Iraq would have serious implications for Blair that stretched to the 2005 general election and beyond. His problems, however, were not restricted by any means to the political stage.

In September 2004, after rumours surfaced that Mr Blair

had come close to resigning in the wake of the death of Dr Kelly and the failure to find weapons of mass destruction in Iraq, Melvyn Bragg, broadcaster, New Labour peer and friend of the Blairs, gave an interview to the ITV News Channel in which he let slip that the PM's 'wobble' had been caused by 'personal and family' problems. For the prime minister and his wife, Lord Bragg's unwelcome disclosure threatened to expose a secret they have kept since Easter 2003 which involved a family crisis so upsetting it easily eclipsed any of the problems Mr Blair faced in the world of politics. It is a situation the couple have understandably gone to great lengths to conceal. Their actions in drawing a veil over the incident, however, go to the heart of their relationship with the media and the public's right, or otherwise, to know. Its significance cannot be overstated, yet despite details of the episode being more or less known by the media, it remains under wraps. Almost immediately, details were leaked to the press. For the Blairs, who naturally were seriously shaken by what had happened, there came the added distress of the prospect of details of their family business being divulged in the newspapers. Although Fleet Street editors came to an agreement with Downing Street that they would not publish details of the episode, for several days Number Ten was unsure whether one title might break ranks and run the story. 'All the stops had been pulled out to make sure the press stayed quiet,' says a Downing Street source. 'But to be perfectly frank, I don't think there was a real expectation that everything wouldn't become pretty much public knowledge quite quickly. The stress of it was awful for Tony and Cherie at time when they were already under enormous strain.' When the public voted in Blair's third election in May 2005, they remained in the dark about the episode. For the same reason that Fleet Street did not report the details of the crisis, they will not be discussed here.

*

In August 2003 the Blair family flew to Barbados for a summer holiday that, given the previous year, could not have come a moment too soon. After the strain placed on their relationship by the Foster affair the couple were grateful for the time they were able to spend together. At last they could talk about the most traumatic chapter of their marriage. When they returned home Mr Blair ordered that Carole Caplin be banned from visiting Downing Street. A member of the Downing Street staff was instructed to tell Miss Caplin her security swipe card, which she had used with impunity to let herself into the Blairs' home, was being confiscated. She was, she was told, no longer welcome in the seat of government. Mrs Blair would continue to meet Carole at the gym for their daily workouts, but Mr Blair was to stop immediately his own fitness sessions and massages with Miss Caplin, never to be resumed.

It was a sudden and unceremonious rejection for the previously ubiquitous Miss Caplin. Not only did it come as a huge surprise to Downing Street insiders but to Carole herself. Friends says she was 'utterly devastated' by her banishment. She was also furious and talked loudly to those close to her about how she had been 'used up and spat out' by the Number Ten machine. 'This is the reward I get for fifteen years loyalty,' she told one acquaintance. In public, however, she determined to put a brave face on her exile, insisting that her new high-profile media commitments meant she was simply too busy to be at the beck and call of the first couple. In fact, Carole was to be kept busy with Mrs Blair, seeing her nearly every day for their gym sessions at the Holmes Place club. She continued also to meet Cherie to tour the showrooms of designers like Burberry and Paddy Campbell in search of discounted clothes. Indeed, they developed a strategy to avoid being photographed together which involved them arriving and leaving minutes apart. They employed the ruse on a visit to the offices of Irish couturier Paul Costelloe a month after Carole was given her marching orders from Number Ten.

In truth, it suited neither woman to end the relationship. Carole was acutely aware that continued involvement with Mrs Blair was vital if she was to continue with her lucrative media work, including her magazine column. She was under no illusion that her musings on alternative health issues were only of any consequence as long as she was closely associated with her famous client. Likewise, attracting new clients was also dependent to a large degree on retaining her celebrity links. For Mrs Blair's part, she still relied heavily on Caplin's advice on clothes and certainly appreciated the large discounts her friend's upfront approach to shopping were able to deliver. It has been reported that Mrs Blair also approached confidentiality with renewed vigour, requiring designers to sign far-reaching agreements preventing them discussing the huge discounts she secured. She felt Carole's absence around Number Ten immediately, say sources. In the first days after Caplin's departure the notoriously disorganized Cherie was forced to enlist the help of the young Leo's nanny Jackie to choose and organize her outfits for her at Downing Street. It was not a success. But just as important, not only to Cherie but her husband as well, was ensuring that Carole remained loyal. Neither of the Blairs could risk her going public with the secrets she could undoubtedly tell.

Immediately, the Blairs sought to draw a veil over the casting out of Miss Caplin and that of her mother Sylvia. Court insiders report that in the months that followed Mr Blair never as much as uttered her name in Downing Street. Cherie, too, refuses to raise the subject of Carole's exit. A source says, 'It all happened so suddenly. Tony and Cherie came back from the Caribbean and out of the blue Carole was gone. It was very strange because Carole had become so important to Tony. She would buy his clothes, tell him what to wear and was always there to give him massages and his fitness sessions. He would talk to her on the phone a lot too. Then she was gone and he never talked about her again. It was as though she had never existed.' Caplin's banishment coincided with the prime minister appointing a replacement for Alastair Campbell. Sources confirm that Dave Hill, who took over Campbell's role of communications supremo, had identified Mrs Blair's guru as the cause of much of the derision aimed at the couple in recent months. Hill's partner, Downing Street staffer Hilary Coffman, was considered by Caplin one of her fiercest enemies within the Blair court.

Carole Caplin took the rejection badly. She let it be known that she now considered herself top of the list of Downing Street's 'undesirables'. 'Friends' who spoke to newspapers on her behalf, reported her as saying, 'How can I possibly continue to be the Blairs' lifestyle guru when I am no longer part of their lives? How can I style the prime minister's clothes when I am no longer allowed anywhere near him? And how can I realistically continue to work for people who allow their staff to brief journalists against me?' One source from her camp was also quoted as saying, 'It was because she was a friend to them as much as an employee that she is left with a profound sense of betrayal.' It was not, however, Carole's style to disappear quietly. She enlisted the help of Sue Corrigan, the journalist given the task of editing her column at *Night and Day* magazine, to pen a self-serving defence of her actions and an unalloyed attack on her detractors in the Blairs' inner circle. In it, Caplin tried to claim it had been her decision to stay away from Downing Street. Corrigan reported as well that Carole was in a state of 'near breakdown'. She had become the victim of a dirty tricks campaign, it was claimed, and attempts had been made by mysterious figures to access the details of her bank account. Corrigan compared Caplin's situation to that of the late Princess Diana and, even more strangely, implied that Carole might be bumped off. Elsewhere, Caplin was claiming that 'unwanted eyes and ears' were gathering information about her. 'I understand how that man Kelly felt. This is just scary. I'm terrified and I don't know why they're watching me like this,' she was quoted as saying.

Home Clear: Blair cruised to a 167 majority and a second term in June 2001, trouncing the Tories under William Hague. The Prime Minister holds baby son Leo as he, Cherie, Kathryn, Nicky and Euan (far right) stand on the steps of Number Ten.

(CHRIS ISON / PA / EMPICS)

French Leave:
Tony and Cherie take
a hand-in-hand stroll on
holiday in south-western
France in August 2001.
But wherever Blair goes
his office goes with him.
(REUTERS / CORBIS)

United in Grief: Cherie is comforted by former US President Bill Clinton
at a memorial for New York fire fighters killed in the September 11 attacks on
the World Trade Centre in 2001. (DYLAN MARTINEZ / REUTERS / CORBIS)

Goodwill Ambassador: Mrs Blair meets Bangladeshi villagers near Dhaka on a three-nation tour of Asia in January 2002. On the same trip she hugged the victims of acid attacks. But she remained frustrated by her role. (PA / EMPICS)

Queen of Downing Street: Mrs Blair welcomes Her Majesty to Number Ten for an official dinner to mark celebrations of her Golden Jubilee in April 2002. But behind the smiles there are tensions. (REUTERS / CORBIS)

Mea Culpa: An emotional Mrs Blair delivers her statement about the Cheriegate affair and her involvement with the fraudster Peter Foster at Millbank in London in December 2002. (REUTERS / CORBIS)

Rogue Trader: Peter Foster pleads his case in Australia, January 2003. He is said to have targeted the Prime Minister and his wife through his affair with Carole Caplin. (CAMERON LAIRD / REX FEATURES)

United Front: Blair stood shoulder to shoulder with George W. Bush in the war on terror, but Cherie was critical of the US President. The Prime Minister invited Bush and First Lady Laura to his County Durham constituency in November 2003.

(OWEN HUMPHREYS / PA / EMPICS)

Trusted Friend: Restaurateur Martha Greene became close to the Blairs, sending over regular food parcels to Downing Street. But her relationship with Cherie put her on a collision course with Carole Caplin.
(REX FEATURES)

Demonstration: In January 2005 Carole Caplin delivered a letter to 10 Downing Street protesting against the EU's plan to ban certain food supplements.
(PAUL GROVER / REX FEATURES)

Shellshocked: As the Sedgefield results are announced, Blair watches Independent candidate Reg Keys, the father of a Royal Military policeman killed in Iraq, make a condemnatory speech. The Iraq war had dominated the 2005 election campaign. (SCOTT HEPPELL / PA / EMPICS)

Media Circus: The world's press listens to Mr Blair speak outside Number Ten following Labour's historic election for a third term. Blair's majority, however, was slashed to 66 seats. (MATT DUNHAM / PA / EMPICS)

Third Time Lucky: Mr Blair holds four-year-old Leo as the couple and their children, Kathryn, Euan and Nicky (far left) celebrate Labour's election victory in May 2005.

Unsurprisingly, rumours that Caplin was considering writing a book about her relationship with the first couple began appearing in the press. As her PR man Ian Monk admitted she was considering offers a rattled Mrs Blair rang Carole to tell her she still considered them friends. The intervention of the prime minister's wife appeared to work. Within days Carole had parted company acrimoniously with the go-getting Monk. As she issued a statement through her lawyers that she had never had any intention of betraying the secrets of her friendship with the prime minister and his wife, Monk published a letter he had written to Caplin in which he accused her of using people other than him to brief newspapers and shot a gaping hole through her repeated argument that she had only employed his services to protect her from the media. 'I have enjoyed much of our working relationship,' wrote Monk, before adding in a transparent dig at his former client, 'in particular creating and exploiting the various media and commercial opportunities which you requested.'

The fear that Caplin might talk did nothing to improve the mood inside Number Ten and was responsible for Cherie slipping back into the unhappiness she had struggled with earlier in the year. Still tired and strained, she almost immediately headed off on holiday again. This time accompanied only by her daughter Kathryn, she flew to Italy for a hastily arranged stay at the home near Rome of Carla Powell, the wife of Lord Powell – once Lady Thatcher's most trusted adviser. She spent days playing tennis with her daughter and swimming in the pool at the lavish house in an attempt to lift her spirits, which friends described as 'very low'.

*

If Mrs Blair was feeling the strain then so too was her husband. As much as his wife he stood to be damaged by anything Carole Caplin might say should she break cover. He had also suffered a gruelling past year which, without doubt, had been the worst of his leadership. Not only had he made the decision to take his country to war against the will of the United Nations, he had also faced a backbench revolt by his own party and the resignation of two of his most senior ministers, Robin Cook and Clare Short. In the last month he had also had to endure giving evidence to the Hutton Inquiry into Dr Kelly's death, knowing that a damning verdict on the veracity of the government dossiers that had made the case for war would almost certainly lead to his departure from office. At the end of October Mr Blair attended an EU summit in Brussels. Heading back to Chequers on Friday afternoon, he was hoping for a short respite from his worries. He paid a visit to the gym over the weekend but at lunchtime on Sunday started to feel unwell. By the time he was rushed to the nearby Stoke Mandeville Hospital, he was doubled up. Although the Downing Street machine would attempt in the days that followed to play down the severity of the scare, those close to the prime minister say that Mrs Blair at least was convinced her husband was having a heart attack. 'It was panic stations at Chequers,' says a source. 'Cherie was very badly shaken by seeing him in that state. She really feared the worst. He did look absolutely terrible and it was really rather scary.' At the Buckinghamshire hospital he was told he would be transferred to a bigger heart unit at the Hammersmith Hospital. Mrs Blair insisted on going with him as doctors began almost five hours of tests to establish what was wrong with the fifty-year-old prime minister. Finally, they diagnosed atrial fibrillation, a condition in which the heart quivers instead of beating regularly. In serious cases the blood may clot and if the clot is then pumped out of the heart and into the brain, it can cause a stroke. For someone who, as a schoolboy of eleven, saw his forty-year-old father's life destroyed by a stroke, such a diagnosis was worrying in the extreme. To resolve the heart flutter Mr Blair was anaesthetized for twenty minutes while electric shocks were administered to his heart to get it to resume beating normally.

Downing Street, aware there was no hope of keeping such dynamite news secret, issued a statement about the heart scare but sought to downplay the events of the previous hours. The condition, they told the media, was 'relatively common'. Mr Blair returned home and was said to be 'laughing with his staff'. The condition should not, it was claimed, recur after his treatment. 'He suffered no damage and is fine,' said a spokesman. What he didn't say was that this was not the first time the condition of Mr Blair's heart had come into question. Insiders insist that a problem has been known about since he became PM. His friend Bill Clinton later let slip that Blair had confided to him as early as 1997 that he was suffering from a minor heart condition.

Seeing her husband taken ill and fearing that the next time could be far more serious, a worried Mrs Blair decided she must take action. She became convinced that the scare at Chequers had been caused by her husband's love of coffee. The Prime Minister had gone through cup after cup of the stuff over the previous few days at the EU conference, where he had taken part in a series of long meetings that often left little time for food. From now on, she decreed, Tony must no longer be allowed coffee. Not only that, in case he was tempted by the aroma of somebody else's espresso or latte, all members of the Downing Street staff would be banned from drinking coffee in front of him. His staff were also warned that they must refuse all prime ministerial appeals for the dangerous brew. Mrs Blair was supported in the ban by Carole Caplin, who rang her immediately after hearing the news to talk darkly about the dangers of caffeine. She was joined by an unlikely ally in the shape of Peter Mandelson, who also counselled against its evils. Within twenty-four hours of returning from hospital the order had gone out that in future the prime minister must only be served herbal tea. It is an edict that endures to this day, although one Downing Street insider let slip an admission that will land the prime minister in hot water over his choice of refreshments: 'I'm not one to tell tales out of school, but he has coffee in secret when Cherie is not around.'

Insiders report that in the run-up to the scare Mr Blair had been working, even by his own gruelling standards, increasingly long hours, existing on occasion on as little as four hours sleep a night. He was also still having his sleep interrupted by his youngest son, who would occasionally wake up during the night. Privately, the PM admitted he felt 'battered'. A month later he was ill again. After the Queen's Speech debate in the Commons two doctors were called to Westminster when Mr Blair complained of agonizing stomach pains, but a consultant surgeon who rushed to Downing Street on a motorbike diagnosed nothing more than a minor complaint.

*

The constant spate of bad news stories led Downing Street to become gripped by a state of near paranoia as evinced by an absurd act of heavy-handedness over a photograph of the young Leo that almost provoked an diplomatic incident. In an act of friendship Mr Blair had presented a photograph of his son to French President Jacques Chirac when they met for talks in Downing Street in November 2003. In fact Chirac and Leo had already become great friends, with the Blairs teaching their son to sing a Gallic version of 'Happy Birthday' for the French leader. But when a delighted Chirac showed off the picture, signed by the youngster himself, to the press, Number Ten demanded that newspapers not publish the photo, claiming that since Leo was no longer a baby, showing his face was a potential security risk. It was not, however, a consideration that would appear to have exercised the minds of too many inside Number Ten when Mr Blair held his four-year-old son aloft to the world's press as he celebrated winning a third successive term in May 2005.

Nor were the Blairs immune from allowing their other children to step into the limelight, provided of course that they got the chance to meet celebrities or members of the royal family. The same week Dave Hill wrote to editors about the picture of Leo, Euan Blair strode out in front of the cameras with his girlfriend Kate Sanders, daughter of a millionaire Somerset garden-centre owner, at the state opening of Parliament. And a month later the Blair children were at the centre of an embarrassing row involving the prime minister's wife and a Tory MP. The encounter took place at a reception for the world cup-winning English rugby team held in the rarefied atmosphere of the ornate Pillared Room overlooking Downing Street's gardens. Fellow guests at the party, including the England centre Will Greenwood, were said to have watched in 'shocked silence' as the prime minister's wife laid into Conservative culture, media and sports spokesman Julie Kirkbride. Ms Kirkbride, who had proved a thorn in the couple's side during the MMR row, had previously complained that members of her party had been left off the original guest list in favour of Labour ministers and MPs. Belatedly, she had been issued with an invitation, but it seemed Mrs Blair was not a welcoming hostess. According to Kirkbride, Cherie spotted her among the throng, marched over and shouted at her, 'If you wanted to come all you had to do was ask, you know. We haven't invited our children here tonight because we thought there would be complaints about it. So they haven't come now.' Kirkbride reported that she thanked Mrs Blair for inviting her, then walked away 'before she could carry on disgracing herself'.

If the season of goodwill did not extend to her political foes, Mrs Blair was in a generous mood when it came to her husband. She remained worried about him and told friends he looked 'gaunt and ill'. Cherie announced that the prime minister needed a holiday and cancelled a planned Boxing Day party at Chequers to fly him instead on a week's family holiday to the Egyptian Red Sea resort of Sharm el Sheik. She also invested nearly £3,000 on a Christmas present for Mr Blair. The prime minister was clearly missing the stress-relieving massages Carole Caplin had given him before her departure. His new cream leather Keyton Concept massage chair, presented to him by Cherie – which for once she had paid full price for – was her robotic replacement. It immediately took pride of place in his Downing Street bedroom, on hand for whenever he needed an automated back rub.

12

2004: MONEY MATTERS

Time had healed for the most part the fissure that for a brief moment had shaken the Blairs' marriage in the fraught and distressing days of the Cheriegate scandal; in the intervening months the prime minister and his wife had resolved successfully to put those painful events behind them. But the fault lines that exist even in this most solid of unions remained. By the summer of 2004 Tony Blair's premiership was shipping water so fast it seemed merely a matter of time before he was submerged by his many travails. Though cleared by the Hutton report, published in January, Blair remained under fire. There was widespread anger and claims of a whitewash as the BBC and its senior executives and governors took the fall over Dr Kelly's death. The corporation was heavily criticized by the judge for broadcasting a report on Radio 4 by its correspondent Andrew Gilligan in which the allegation about the 'sexing-up' of the dossier on Iraq was made. Blair's personal exoneration by Hutton should have left him strengthened, but instead he stumbled from one crisis to the next, never fully regaining his feet before being felled again.

At the end of January a rebellion by Labour backbenchers over government plans for university top-up fees saw the prime minister's 161-seat Commons majority slashed to just 5 when the measure was put to a vote. It was the biggest backbench revolt for fifty years and left his authority in tatters. In February Tory leader Michael Howard called on him to resign over the war. A second report into the Iraq conflict by Lord Butler, due in July, was being looked forward to with trepidation by Number Ten staffers, who believed Mr Blair would be heavily criticized over taking the country to war on the basis of flawed intelligence. With his personal approval rating at an all-time low and with the parliamentary party in mutinous mood, even Blair stalwarts began to believe he had become an electoral liability. There was widespread fear of humiliation in the forthcoming local and European elections, and Labour MPs began to worry for their seats at the next general election if their damaged leader remained. For Gordon Brown it seemed his time had finally arrived. Brown's closest aides cancelled holiday plans and rumours abounded that cabinet heavy-weights like John Prescott and Jack Straw had begun to cosy up to the chancellor in preparation for Mr Blair's imminent demise. At the end of May, with his own MPs speculating about how long he could go on, a YouGov poll suggested a majority of voters wanted the PM to stand down in favour of Mr Brown.

As his premiership took a standing count, the PM, in public at least, came out fighting. On 29 May, he gave an upbeat interview to the *Daily Mirror* in which he promised to soldier on despite his problems, but privately he was resigned to leaving Number Ten. Three days later, on 1 June, 2004, Tony Blair decided to quit as prime minister. His decision to walk away has been much denied since, not least by Mr Blair and more particularly his wife. That Blair, who was adamant that morning he intended to go, was talked out of his decision by his private office staff and by Cherie herself says much for the fragile and exhausted state in which he found himself. In the weeks that followed he would agonize over whether he had made the right decision in fighting on. The difference for Blair was that whereas in the past and in times to come his wife would have been the person he turned to as his true confidante and sounding board, now he felt unable to confide fully in her. At his lowest ebb, when he needed his wife's counsel most, Blair felt very alone. With few friends outside politics he could turn to, he sought guidance from those inside his court. Tellingly, however, and for the only time before or since, these conversations were hushed when there was a chance his wife might overhear. The Blairs flew to America on 8 June for a G8 summit in Georgia with the prime minister still desperately grappling with his decision. A source says, 'Before he left for the US he was as low as I have ever seen him. He was mentally and physically drained, completely wrung out and tired. It had gone on for months. I remember when he flew to Basra that January he looked really terrible – thin and ill. That summer he came very close to giving it up. Few people could take the pressure he was under. I think he felt pretty friendless and was particularly feeling Alastair's absence.'

For her part, the events surrounding her involvement with Peter Foster eighteen months earlier had brought about a change in Mrs Blair. When she had most needed her husband's support he had put his premiership first. At the same time she believed his staff, with Campbell as the orchestrator, had been allowed to throw her to the Fleet Street pack so as to draw them away from her husband. As a result Cherie had since then indulged in a series of feuds, not only with Campbell and Millar before their departure the previous autumn, but also with the press and the most significant foe of all, Gordon Brown. Indeed, some sources believe her fundamental loathing for Brown was a factor in Cherie lobbying her husband to battle on in the face of his many problems. Her determination that the chancellor must not get the upper hand was clear as Mr Brown readied himself to step into the PM's shoes and Mr Blair wavered. Cherie was said to have marched up to one of Brown's staunchest allies and, in a glaring eyeball-to-eyeball showdown with her finger jabbing into her opponent's chest, hissed, 'You have got to understand. We are going on and on and on.' Some within the court are convinced that Mrs Blair's insistence that her husband must carry on had as much to do with her own desire not to be beaten as what was in the best interests of the party or her husband. 'Cherie digs in and fights it out when she feels under attack,' says a Westminster source.

> She was determined that they should not give in to those people she hates. She has always seen herself and Tony as very much a team, and his failure would be her failure too. Tony has always been driven by the need to be loved by his party and the electorate. When he saw that love dying away it hit him incredibly hard and it made him want to get out. With Cherie it is about not letting anyone get one over on her. She is determined that when they leave Number Ten it will be on their terms and no one else's. For that reason alone I think she and Tony were on different wavelengths at the time. It's not that Cherie didn't want what was best for him, it's just that they were not on the same page for a while.

Privately, Mrs Blair was also highly critical of her husband's closest staff. Despite the souring of her relationship with Alastair Campbell, she has been at times a vehement critic of his replacement Dave Hill. There was little surprise then, when, after the 2005 election, rumours began circulating that Hill was to be sidelined. Likewise, Mrs Blair has been less than discreet about voicing her dislike of her husband's chancellor. One who met her for the first time was taken aback to hear Cherie describe Mr Brown as 'not our sort of person'. Her language to those she knows well has been, to put it mildly, considerably more choice. Brown's supporters, for their part, were under the impression that the chancellor had a deal to take over from Blair that summer, although this is strenuously denied by the Blair camp. But the UN vote in June which saw France, Germany and Russia put to one side their opposition to the war to support a British plan for restoring sovereignty to Iraq, buoyed the PM. A month later the Butler report, though highly critical of the government's use of intelligence, cleared Mr Blair of wilfully misleading the nation over weapons of mass destruction. Suddenly the talk inside Number Ten was of carrying on. Brown's camp believed, correctly, that a pivotal figure in persuading Mr Blair to stay on had been his wife. At the same time Mrs Blair herself went into print in the *Daily Telegraph* to put the chancellor in his place. 'We are not by any means at the end of the story,' she said. 'I don't think I'm hankering after a bungalow just yet.'

*

Lord Bragg's clumsy remarks in September served to illustrate just how fraught life at Number Ten had become in those dark days. Asked about suggestions that the prime minister had planned to stand down, the *South Bank Show* host spoke of the 'colossal strain' Mr Blair had been under. 'I think he was under tremendous stress,' Bragg said. 'He was being hammered in the press. Perhaps he had doubts about some policies, perhaps not. But in my view the real stress was personal and family, which matters most to him. And my guess is that the considerations of his family became very pressing and that made him think things over very carefully.' Bragg's comments shifted the focus back on to the Blairs' private life and it is not surprising that Mrs Blair reacted with fury when she heard of them. 'Melvyn's fucked us now,' Cherie exploded. 'She was apoplectic,' says a source. 'She was completely incredulous about what he had done and I think she really believed that it would mean all their secrets would be laid open for public consumption.' Within minutes a livid Mrs Blair was on the phone to Bragg to give him a dressing-down, described by one source as 'blood-curdling'. During the bawling out Cherie told the stammering and contrite Bragg, 'How dare you? You have no right to discuss my family's private life.'

The mortified peer, who during this verbal onslaught by all accounts was offered precious little opportunity by Mrs Blair to defend himself, decided to write a grovelling letter instead.

The missive, begging for forgiveness and promising no repeat of his indiscretions, was delivered to Number Ten the following day. But despite friends saying he was 'in despair', Cherie was in no mood to forgive and forget. Bragg, who had been rewarded with a peerage by Blair for his donations to the party, had hitherto been a firm favourite within the court. Now, Mrs Blair decreed, he could no longer be trusted. In private and to friends she went further, accusing him of being jealous of successful women, although it should be said there was to be an eventual rapprochement. Meanwhile, as false rumours began to circulate that the Blairs had sanctioned the leak to take pressure off the PM, a succession of cabinet ministers was wheeled out to pour scorn over the elaborately coiffed head of Baron Bragg of Wigton. One unnamed minister quoted in the press briefed simply, 'Bragg is an idiot.' The health secretary John Reid did however concede, 'Anyone involved in public life knows that there are all sorts of pressures, political, family. The prime minister is human like everyone else. He has ups and down periods, but that doesn't mean to say he goes round planning resignations.'

Cherie had added reason to be furious with his lordship. Two days after publication of his injudicious remarks, she was due to give her first ever live television interview – to plug her book *The Goldfish Bowl* about the spouses of prime ministers. Terrified about her long-planned appearance on Channel 4's *Richard and Judy Show*, she had been on a day-long media training course to learn how to handle appearing on TV. Bragg's blundering not only added to her sense of panic as the interview approached but also displayed the risks contained within her new policy of self-promotion. It would have been naive to imagine that, once comfortably ensconced on the sofa of the daytime TV show, she would not be questioned about the furore involving Bragg. It left Mrs Blair two options: either cancel her appearance and risk stoking up the story further (not to mention losing all that free publicity for her book – the

'Richard and Judy effect' had been responsible for a series of bestsellers) or appear as planned and hope for the best. Cherie decided to take the risk. It was hardly surprising, therefore, when co-host Richard Madeley got round to raising the subject of Bragg's comments. Mrs Blair's reply was as interesting as it was perhaps disingenuous. 'I don't know where Melvyn got it from, and to be honest I think he's mortified that he said it,' replied the prime minister's wife, before adding, 'We can't always explain what goes on in men's minds – I wish I could.'

Mrs Blair of course had a very good idea how Bragg had got to know about her family problems. Not only was he a trusted ally of nearly twenty years standing, he had been a guest at her fiftieth birthday celebrations at Chequers the previous week. He also happened to be married to Cate Haste, co-author of *The Goldfish Bowl*. Although both Blairs insist they never discussed their domestic problems with him directly, he was in a prime position to know what was going on in their household. And anyway the Blairs' family issue had been an open secret in the media world Bragg inhabits for more than a year. Technically speaking, Mrs Blair could argue that her response was not the blatant obfuscation it appeared to be. She could quite easily make a case, if accused of lying, that her answer had been to the question of how Bragg had found out about their problems, rather than the veracity of his comments. But her response to Madeley's question had been at best legalistic and calculated and at worst, mendacious. It should be pointed out that few could argue with her desire to do everything she could to protect the privacy of her family. Was she expected to sit in front of her TV interrogator and lay bare family secrets simply because she had been asked? Of course not. But once again Mrs Blair had put herself in the position of having to make public statements she knew bore little relation to the truth, this time in front of an audience of millions. On both occasions her pursuit of financial gain was at the root of the issue: previously with her use of Peter Foster

to secure discounts on the two flats in Bristol and on this
occasion with her desire and that of her publishers to use
television exposure to sell her book. Richard and Judy are no
doubt used to the litany of half-truths and cant served up to
them by the ragbag of celebrities, self-publicists and wannabes
who inhabit the world of daytime television; Cherie Blair,
however, remained a senior barrister and QC; she still had
hopes of one day being appointed to the bench of the highest
court in the land; she was the wife of the British prime minister.

As her husband fought for his reputation Mrs Blair once
again found herself the subject of jibes from her detractors
over her decision not to give any proceeds from the book to
charity. Cherie was unrepentant. She told friends, 'I worked
bloody hard on it and I deserve the money.' At the same time
she was again bemoaning what she perceived to be her lack of
funds. 'I'm absolutely sick of having no money,' she told one
friend. 'I've got a living to earn and a family to keep. You've
absolutely no idea how much it costs us to live.' Another
source close to her reveals, 'She very much sees herself as the
family breadwinner. She makes absolutely no apology for that
and good luck to her. But it is surprising how often when you
talk to Cherie the conversation turns to the subject of money.
Her friends just accept it about her. I don't know if I'd say she
is obsessed by money, but I would say she is very motivated by
it.' Her decision to add to the family finances through writing
meant selling and promoting herself, most notably through
the Richard and Judy appearance. The acutely self-conscious
Cherie had not relished the experience and her screen performance was polished if brittle. Three months after her husband
had been on the verge of resigning, Mrs Blair was asked about
the prime minister's future. Without missing a beat, she stated
there had been 'never a moment' when he had thought about
giving up his leadership. But for the 'private' Mrs Blair it was
another example of her putting her head above the parapet.

That she drew fire is hardly surprising, but that it came in the form of a thinly veiled attack on her personality and character from none other than the woman who had, until just a year earlier, been her gatekeeper and protector was particularly shocking to the PM's wife. Fiona Millar chose the pages of the *Guardian* to launch her broadside against her old boss. Restrained though her language was, it was nonetheless a scathing assessment of Cherie Blair by a woman who had formerly been one of her closest friends. Millar admitted she had left Downing Street after losing the battle for Mrs Blair's ear with Carole Caplin. Cherie's biggest mistakes, she said, were to have become involved with Peter Foster and to have stood by Carole 'after her full flakiness was revealed to the world on TV'. In a reference to Mrs Blair's book, Miss Millar went on,

> Even as a minnow in the goldfish bowl I found the require-
> ment to toe the line politically ultimately overbearing and
> suspect that the pressure to conform and perform in so
> many other ways took its toll on Cherie. Perhaps it contrib-
> uted to some of the ill-fated decisions as she struggled to
> assert her independence against the system which I repre-
> sented. My advice was increasingly ignored as I, a dour left-
> wing feminist, began to lose the battle for Cherie's heart
> and mind to the glossy sex-symbol Carole 'The Conqueror'
> Caplin and left Downing Street – a painful and much more
> complicated process than the tabloid soap opera it
> became . . . Most destructive of all, of course, was the mis-
> judgement of Peter Foster, the loyal but ultimately damag-
> ing decision to stick by Caplin . . . and to a lesser extent the
> [New Age] practitioners and the decisions about money.

Millar's comments also appeared to throw into question Mrs Blair's truthfulness in specifically denying to Richard Madeley that she had been subjected to pressure from inside Number Ten to dump Caplin. Her get-even assault on Mrs Blair was a rare betrayal for one who had been so close to the centre of the court. However, the timing of her volley was perhaps unsurprising. Both she and Campbell had been conspicuously missing from the guest list for Cherie's fiftieth birthday party celebrations at Chequers the previous week. The taciturn Millar could barely conceal her anger over the snub. 'I'm not going to the party because I haven't been invited,' she said. 'Alastair isn't going to the party because he hasn't been invited.' Two other names, however, were to feature on the list of invitations sent out in advance – those of Carole and Sylvia Caplin.

The extravagant birthday celebrations could have been better timed; Mrs Blair chose to hold her bash on the third anniversary of the 11 September attacks, despite it being two weeks before her actual birthday. In the event, Campbell and Millar might have thought themselves lucky not to be invited. On the evening of the party 150 pro-hunting demonstrators blocked the roads around Chequers and many of those invited had to spend much of the evening in the car park of the nearby Tesco superstore as the prime minister personally negotiated with the leaders of the protestors. Eventually, Mrs Blair declared that they must begin anyway, and their friends who had made it through were treated to a *This is Your Life* presentation on Cherie as well as a touching speech by Kathryn about her mother. Then, as partygoers helped themselves to an Indian buffet, Mr Blair, reprising his front-man role from his days with Ugly Rumours, joined the band to serenade his wife and guests with Elvis Presley numbers including his favourite, 'Blue Suede Shoes'. One guest revealed, 'I must say that when I saw Tony getting on stage with his guitar I really suspected we could be in for something excruciatingly embarrassing, but he was actually really good. He was patently loving every minute of it.'

*

Despite Mrs Blair's best efforts, her book, which gave virtually nothing away about her own life inside Number Ten, was not the success she had hoped. Substantially more lucrative have been the lectures she has since given around the world, but these have again left her open to accusations of profiteering and trading on her husband's name. It is noteworthy that while the feminist Cherie has always used her maiden name Booth for anything to do with her career, she has been apparently happy to capitalize on her husband's name to attract high-paying corporate guests to her lucrative speaking tours. As Mrs Blair began the drive to sell her book it was revealed that she had signed up with the New York-based Harry Walker Agency, which also represents Bill Clinton, Henry Kissinger and U2 singer Bono for speaking engagements. The most sought-after speakers with the agency like the former US president are reputed to earn up to £160,000 for a single appearance. Mrs Blair, it was said, would be likely to charge a not insubstantial £30,000 per speech. Her first three lectures after signing for the firm, which bills itself as 'America's Leading Exclusive Lecture Agency', were booked for October 2004. Her addition to the company's books was revealed in a leaked email sent to potential clients in the US. The round-robin message from the agency included a quote from the prime minister: 'She is an enormous source of strength and an extraordinary person in her own right.' Mrs Blair, the agency promised, would offer guaranteed 'value for money' and the email concluded, 'I know Cherie Blair would be a great success at your next event, so please contact me today for more information about her lecture topics and more scheduling opportunities.'

Lucrative though Mrs Blair's new venture clearly was, there were doubts about its wisdom. While former prime ministers Margaret Thatcher and John Major had both made consider-able amounts of money on the US lecture circuit, they waited until they had left office. Her new representatives billed her as 'noted British attorney and human-rights advocate', but it was the epithet 'and the wife of Prime Minister Tony Blair' that was meant to appeal to corporate America. Nobody believed that stateside captains of industry would be prepared to shell out £30,000 to hear the musings of a British lawyer if she didn't happen to be married to a man who, post-Iraq, had been christened by Americans 'the second most powerful man in the world'. Indeed, the convention of US insurance executives who hired Mrs Blair to speak to them made it plain that one of the primary reasons they had chosen her was so she could tell them all about life in Number Ten. While her husband remained in office, there was also the not insubstantial threat that her words could have embarrassing ramifications for his government.

Predictably, on touching down in the US to begin her tour, Cherie marched headlong and unblinking into a political minefield. In addition to her well-paid dates in Detroit, Mrs Blair also agreed to speak for free, and as Cherie Booth, to students at Harvard University. Just days before America went to the polls to vote on whether George Bush should be re-elected president, the wife of his closest ally stepped up to a speaking platform and attacked the legality of the administration's imprisonment of terror suspects at Guantanamo Bay. She also went on to criticize the arrest of a gay couple in Mr Bush's home state of Texas for defying a ban on sodomy, a law backed by Bush when he was governor, and called a US Supreme Court decision to overturn the ban 'a model for judicial reasoning'. Perfectly sound though her arguments were, spoken on foreign soil in the run-up to an election they were bound to spark controversy. Sensing this, perhaps, Mrs Blair had banned journalists from the speech and students had to show ID cards before being allowed in, but the attempt to keep secret her comments was in vain. Inevitably, details leaked out and once again Mr Blair found himself rueing his wife's blundering. While the speeches she made under her married name were scrupulously free of the controversial, for Mrs Blair to imagine that she could switch from lawyer to prime minister's wife at the drop of a hat was optimistic in the extreme.

But why, given in the not-too-distant future her husband would be free to make her the millions she craved by giving his own lectures once he had left office, has Cherie continued to put herself in the firing line with her schemes to make money? The answer is twofold, say observers. One has to do with Mrs Blair's natural vanity. Despite her early agreement to remain in the background, she remains driven by a desire to be seen as half of the prime ministership. 'She has never fully come to terms with having to remain in the background, taking none of the credit,' says a friend. 'Quite naturally, she has some-times felt the temptation to seek the recognition she feels she deserves for the influence she has not only on Tony, but on his government.' The other and more pressing reason for Cherie to risk more brickbats was the now urgent need to fill the Blair coffers thanks to their decision to spend £3.6 million on a house at 29 Connaught Square, close to Hyde Park. Once again, as with the infamous Bristol flats two year earlier, the driving force behind the purchase was Cherie. And once again she used a third party to handle the negotiations. Peter Foster had famously taken on the role in 2002; now Cherie turned to Martha Greene, the tough-talking New York-born owner of the Blairs' favourite restaurant Villandry. The two women had been introduced by Carole Caplin and used the same gym, but in the months since Caplin's banishment from Number Ten Greene had usurped her friend Carole as Mrs Blair's guru of choice. As Cherie sought to raise her profile in the US in preparation for her lecture tour, it was the brusque Miss Greene to whom she turned for guidance. It was also Martha who orchestrated a photo shoot with American style-bible *Harper's Bazaar* to coincide with Cherie's trip to the States.

Greene's reputation as a skilled and dogged networker had been steadily building since her arrival in Britain in 1981.

Starting as a secretary at advertising agency Saatchi and
Saatchi, she had risen through the ranks and gone into business
herself, launching her own film company before buying into
the ailing Villandry restaurant in London's West End in 1998
and turning it around. Her rise to the top had not been
achieved without making enemies. Her former business partner
Jeff Stark describes her thus: 'Martha is straight to the
point, no bullshit, and people either love her or hate her.'
Little wonder then that as Carole Caplin was increasingly
marginalized, it was the go-getting Martha who stepped into
her designer shoes. Inside Number Ten she became known
quickly and predictably as 'Carole Mark II'. Two years earlier
Miss Greene, a divorced mother of two, had been seated on
the prime minister's right when he celebrated his forty-ninth
birthday at Claridges in Mayfair; she had arranged the lunch
at the special 'chef's table' in the kitchen at Gordon Ramsay's
restaurant in the hotel. Cherie had celebrated her forty-eighth
birthday at Villandry and Greene had also done the catering
for the couple's twentieth wedding anniversary in 2000. Their
friendship was further strengthened when Mrs Blair assumed a
supportive role after Martha was diagnosed with breast cancer
in 2003 at the age of forty-six. Since then the Blairs had
become regular guests of Greene and her lover, travel executive
Ivan Ruggeri, at her town house a couple of streets away from
their former Islington home.

  Greene was responsible for resurrecting the *Harper's
Bazaar* shoot, which had been shelved in the wake of the
Lippygate fiasco. Where Carole had overseen a PR disaster
in the Blairs' untidy private quarters, Martha got Patrick
Demarchelier, the photographer most famously known as the
late Princess Diana's favourite, to photograph Mrs Blair in
a flattering Vivienne Westwood ball gown and Alexander
McQueen suit in the state rooms of Number Ten. But, like
Carole, Martha made few friends within the Blair court.
'Frankly,' says one, 'it was out of the frying pan into the fire.

Martha is possibly the most bossy person I have ever met. Cherie replaced one dominating character with another.' Greene's elevation did not, of course, go down well with the competitive Carole. Once the two women had been firm friends, with Caplin writing a rave review of Villandry in London's *Evening Standard*; now, the battle lines had been drawn. Caplin was furious to have her gym sessions with Mrs Blair cut to two a week. Where once it had been Carole Mrs Blair had spoken to up to a dozen times a day on the phone, now it was Martha. So secure in her new role as Mrs Blair's closest confidante was Greene, say insiders, that she began a campaign to push her old friend out completely. 'Martha started sticking the boot in Carole's choice of clothes, and began telling Cherie she should get a new style adviser,' says an insider. 'Carole heard about what Martha had been saying and went mad. There were several slanging matches between the two of them at the gym. It was all rather good entertainment and for a while Cherie seemed to quite enjoy them fighting over her. But in the end it was all becoming too silly and Cherie finally had to ban Martha from going to the gym anymore because she couldn't go there without her having another screaming row with Carole.'

Greene accepted the edict, secure in her new position. At Cherie's fiftieth birthday party it was Martha who sat next to the Blairs at their table. Carole, for once demurely dressed, was placed on the other side of the room with her mother and, according to one fellow guest, 'spent the evening looking miserable and shooting daggers at Martha'. It was also Martha who accompanied Cherie as her 'lady-in-waiting' on her lecture tour of the US. But most importantly Mrs Blair chose the American to negotiate the purchase of the house the Blairs bought to be their home when Tony leaves office. For Carole, who had formerly been involved in every major purchase by Mrs Blair – employing her not inconsiderable talent for nego-tiating reductions – it was a kick in the teeth. Worse still, her friend Cherie, on the advice of Martha, had purposely kept secret from her the fact she was buying a property. So hush-hush was the Blairs' involvement that phone lines into the house were listed in Greene's name. Caplin only discovered about the house when news of its purchase appeared in the newspapers. There followed, say insiders, a tearful confrontation with Cherie during which Carole complained, 'I have been your friend all these years and you couldn't trust me enough to tell me.'

Neither was moving to 'Millionaires' Row' a piece of information Labour spinners were particularly keen to share with the voters just months ahead of a general election. But when one newspaper got word of the Blairs' new des res it turned out to be, to borrow an infamous New Labour idiom, a good day to bury bad news. As it transpired, the details of the purchase of the Bayswater mansion trailed a distant second to another piece of news Number Ten image makers were keen to brush firmly under the carpet. For more than two months Mr Blair had been suffering a recurrence of the heart problems that had resulted in his collapse a year earlier. The prime minister had carried on working as usual, but his doctors told him in the early autumn that he would require further surgery to correct the 'short-circuiting' which affected his heart's rhythm and efficiency. Knowing there was no way they could keep the operation a secret, Downing Street decided to announce the planned surgery the day before the prime minister was to check into a London hospital. But both stories, they hoped, would be overshadowed by the headline news announced by the prime minister in a series of TV interviews that night. Blair, doing a tour of the major TV networks, revealed that he would fight only one more election before bowing out as leader. But he would, he insisted, serve a full third term if he won the forthcoming election. Mr Blair attempted to play down the operation, described as 'catheter ablation', which would be carried out to correct his atrial flutter. 'It's a routine procedure,' said the prime minister. 'It's not particularly alarming, but it's something that you should get fixed. I've had it for the last couple of months and it's not impeded me doing my work and feeling fine, but it is as well to get it done.' Of his decision to see out a third term, he said, 'The reason I want to stay is to see the job through. I do not want to serve a fourth term. I don't think the British people want a PM to go on that long. There have been stories that I will stand for election then stand down in a year or two. I'm clear that I'm not going to do that. I feel I've still got lots more to do and to give.' Gordon Brown, flying to Washington for a meeting of the International Monetary Fund, was not given advance warning of Mr Blair's announcement. He only discovered the news when he stepped off his plane in the US capital.

The diversionary tactic, working on the theory that the electorate is wont to be sceptical about voting for candidates who (a) have dodgy tickers and (b) lavish fortunes on themselves, was simple and effective. But the Blairs' problems over their new abode would not be restricted to the purely presentational. As soon as the deal was announced local estate agents declared that the couple had paid way over the odds. The five-bedroom house set on five floors and boasting a grand wooden staircase was, they said, worth no more than £3 million. Not only that; they had bought at the height of the market as prices were about to dip. Alarmingly for the Blairs, this assessment did indeed appear to be accurate. Four months after completing the sale, its value had slipped by £300,000. And if that was not enough, Connaught Square, it was revealed, went by the unwelcome nickname of 'downtown Kuwait City' because of its proximity to the Arab stronghold of the Edgware Road. The square, while boasting near-neighbours like Madonna, is also a notorious cut-through and bottleneck for traffic. Neither could the Georgian house, which directly fronts the pavement, be described even at a stretch as private. Meanwhile the couple, whose plan it was to rent out the property until Mr Blair left office, were not finding any takers for the £15,800 a month Foxtons letting agents were asking. Rival firms said the couple would be unlikely to find tenants willing to pay more than £8,000. All the while the prime minister and his wife were having to find the £13,500 monthly mortgage repayments on the house while it sat empty, not to mention the one-off £144,000 stamp duty. That, even on their substantial combined salaries, was a tall order. They had, according to reports, been granted the huge mortgage on the basis of Mr Blair's projected earnings once he left Downing Street, but for the time being it would be down to his wife to get out and earn enough money to meet their suddenly substantially increased monthly outgoings.

Given the pressure on their finances, it was perhaps unsurprising that Mrs Blair should continue to search out a bargain. Logging on to auction website eBay, she outbid five rivals to buy a pair of size six second-hand pink strappy sandals for £15, a 99p Winnie the Pooh alarm clock and two Disney videos at £1.99 each. And with £3,500 to spend on a car for Euan, Mrs Blair eschewed the newspaper ads and went instead directly to the UK headquarters of the car giant Ford. On this occasion any hopes of a discount were dashed when she was told the cheapest car the company made was more than twice the sum she was proposing. However, Cherie, despite the perennial embarrassment her quest for discounts has become to her husband, continued to hunt down a deal. While overseeing the refurbishment of the Connaught Square house in early 2005 she did, says insiders, a bit of business that owed much to Del Boy Trotter, arranging with the aptly named Baron Harris of Peckham to have her home carpeted throughout by his company, the discount chain Carpetright. Again Martha Greene acted as middleman. The fact that the multimillionaire Harris is a Tory peer, an ardent critic of the Blair government's policy over Europe and a campaigner against the EU constitution mattered not to Mrs Blair, it seemed, when there was a saving to be had.

The couple were also keen to pass on this spirit of enterprise to their children. Mrs Blair, particularly, has always been commendably insistent that her children should not be isolated from the real world because of their position. The two older boys have been encouraged to find work in the holidays when they are not studying and Euan was employed as a runner for a film company. In the summer of 2005 it was reported he would be working for three months as an unpaid intern in the Capitol Hill office of senior US Congressman David Dreier.

That is not to say the Blairs do not remain partial to introducing their children to the delights of the world's most exclusive holiday destinations, particularly of course if someone else is picking up the tab. During the 2004 summer break the Blairs undertook a marathon tour of the playgrounds of their wealthy and generous friends around the globe. Although once again they made charitable donations in lieu of the freebies offered by their well-healed benefactors, estimates put the notional cost of their month-long grand tour at well over £100,000. The holiday included an eighteen-day stay at Cliff Richard's six-bedroom mansion on the secluded Sugar Hill estate in Barbados. Travel experts said that if the prime minister had been paying to rent such luxury on the open market, the bill for their sojourn at Sir Cliff's place in the sun would have been a cool £45,000 alone. While on the Caribbean island the first family also had use of Heron Bay House, the holiday home of JCB multimillionaire and Tory backer Sir Anthony Bamford. Next was a brief stop in Greece for the opening ceremony of the Athens Olympics, and a stay on board the liner *Queen Mary 2* for which the Greek government picked up the bill; the Blairs were reportedly put up in a £2,000-a-night double-storey suite with butler service. But most lavish by far was their stay with Silvio Berlusconi, the Italian prime minister and billionaire. The couple managed a trip to his

twenty-seven-room palazzo on his private island off the coast
of Sardinia in the middle of their visit to the home of Prince
Girolamo Strozzi in Tuscany. So eagerly anticipated was the
Blairs' visit that Berlusconi sent his government's Gulfstream
jet to collect them and had one hundred Italian workmen
labouring right up to their arrival to ensure the villa he had
earmarked for the couple was up to scratch. That was only the
beginning of media tycoon Berlusconi's hospitality. He had
£30,000-worth of olive trees planted for their visit, laid on
helicopter and boat rides, gourmet meals and even a private
concert in their honour in a purpose-built amphitheatre on his
hundred-acre estate. Tony and Cherie could choose from five
swimming pools on Berlusconi's island, which even boasts its
own James Bond-style escape tunnel. The pièce de résistance,
however, was a £50,000 firework display in honour of his
guests which went on until 1 a.m. and featured red, white and
blue starbursts. It climaxed with the words 'Viva Tony' spelled
out in the heavens.

The Blairs were subjected to a barrage of criticism on their
return, accused of flagrant freeloading and derided for being
in the thrall of the rich and famous. Their arrival back also
coincided with a vitriolic attack on the prime minister by
former BBC Director General Greg Dyke, who had resigned in
the wake of the Hutton report. As well as accusing Mr Blair of
lying over Iraq, the one-time New Labour supporter and donor
accused Mrs Blair in his memoirs of ringing him when he was
a Manchester United director to get a cut-price team shirt for
her son. His friendship with the couple had broken down over
the war, he said, and when he had later met Cherie at Wimble-
don she 'looked through me as if I didn't exist'.

*

With the dust finally settling after the Foster scandal, Mrs Blair
now made another thinly veiled application for promotion
to High Court judge. During a speech in Iceland she told her

audience of women lawyers that only 6 per cent of judges in the British High Court were women. 'The fact that in my country almost all our senior judges are men is problematic not only for individual women who wish to advance to being judges, but it is also actually damaging for the notion of the rule of law itself,' she said. Given the trashing of her reputation, in the wake of the episode, her implied job request was, perhaps, a triumph of hope over reason and advancement in the law was something she, herself, would quite quickly go cold on in the coming months. After spending a lifetime dreaming of presiding in the nation's highest courts Mrs Blair has quietly, say friends, shelved her ambitions. The reason? 'She joined the international lecture circuit and realized the fortunes she could make for a few hours work,' says a source close to her. 'The plain fact is that being a judge simply wouldn't pay her enough.'

13

2005: THE SCOTTISH IMPATIENT

Arriving back in Downing Street from Manchester, the prime minister was tired and stressed. Marching into the Number Eleven flat in early February 2005, he sat in the living room that doubles as his office and decreed that before going home his most senior staff should be called in one by one. Chief of Staff Jonathan Powell, advisers Hilary Coffman and Sally Morgan, and Communications Director Dave Hill dutifully took their turns to troop in. And each time Blair launched into a tirade never before heard in his eight years tenure in the building. Such was his vehemence, as the prime minister laid into his team with unbridled ferocity, his voice reverberated around the building. For those around the prime minister it was a portent of the fraught and frazzled weeks to come. 'They were given the bollocking of a lifetime,' says a member of the Downing Street staff.

> To say he lost it would be a huge understatement. He wasn't so much angry as raging. He was annoyed about some minor glitch over the welfare reform package, but what came out was his anger over what he thought was a lack of focus three months before an election. Each one was called in and destroyed by the PM. They all came out looking completely pale. The whole thing was so completely out of character for Tony. He very, very rarely raises his voice, never mind a complete tantrum. Everyone was really shaken by it. He obviously needed to vent and it worked because he was calm and even quite relaxed afterwards, but it didn't last. He was as stressed as I've ever seen him during the campaign.

In the phoney war that preceded the formal announcement of the 2005 election the surefootedness that had characterized Blair's two previous campaigns was noticeably lacking. Blighted by the issue of trust over Iraq, beset by divisions in his own party over his leadership and afflicted by the physical and mental weariness from which few long-serving administrations are immune, Tony Blair's government needed desperately to reconnect with those who had put him into Number Ten. He needed the British people and his own party to fall in love with him again. The more arduous the task became, the more hopeless the goal, the deeper Blair slipped into the melancholy that was to come to characterize his mood over the coming weeks.

If Mr Blair, and just as significantly those running his party's campaign, was presented with an image problem in the run-up to 5 May, his wife was to find herself beset by a similar if not altogether unfamiliar difficulty. As New Labour strategists including Alastair Campbell, recalled to the ranks for the duration by his former boss, sought to put the brake on a personal-ratings slump that threatened to derail the prime minister's campaign, they had to decide what to do about the thorny issue of his first lady. As the lines were drawn up in the battle for Number Ten, Mrs Blair had confidently been predicting a high-profile role for herself. Her expectation of prominence was not merely wishful thinking on the part of the ambitious Cherie. The prime minister himself had given his wife assurances that she would be his 'secret weapon' in the campaign to win an unprecedented third term. Mrs Blair, who no longer found being pushed into the shadows by Labour image makers sat comfortably with her desire to be recognized for her huge impact on policy, was increasingly looking to a third term to step into the light. With her husband back in Downing Street but with his stated intention not to fight another election, she saw this as her final chance to get some of the public recognition she feels she deserves. This had been the tacit understanding between the couple since Mr Blair entered Number Ten for the first time. But Mrs Blair was quickly to find as the days drew closer to her husband launching the campaign proper that her role as leading lady had been relegated to that of little more than bit-part player. For this humiliation, an angry Cherie would hold responsible Campbell and Gordon Brown, who both, it cannot be denied, privately revelled in their revenge. In truth, however, Cherie had no one to blame but herself.

*

In February 2005 an overhaul of the Australian laws governing charity fund-raising was announced which became known in the local media as the 'Cherie effect'. It followed an episode so monumental in its bad taste, so unashamed in its moral ambiguity, that it will live long in the memory. In a compendium of PR blunders of the modern age there, at item one, page one, will be Cherie Blair's 'charity' lecture tour of Australia and New Zealand. She would return from her trip down under more than £100,000 better off, but in the process would take a chainsaw to what was left of her of her tattered reputation and eclipse the numerous occasions she has freely given her time to the many charities she supports.

The previous November, the Harry Walker Agency in New York had been contacted by a British-born, Australian-based businessman keen to book the prime minister's wife to appear in Australasia early the following year. On the surface at least, the offer made to Mrs Blair by Max Markson, a self-styled impresario whose business history can best be described as colourful, seemed tempting. She was offered a fee of £125,000, first-class return airfares, plus free accommodation and expenses in return for six speeches. In a letter to the agency Markson also offered the bait of extra cash. 'There may be the opportunity to arrange an additional number of small, say 30-person, round-table-style private meetings with high-wealth individuals which would generate additional income for Mrs Blair. If this would be an assistance to confirming the deal, I am happy to guarantee an additional amount of £20,000 for each of these functions,' he wrote. The event in New Zealand would be in the name of a children's charity called the Starship Foundation and the five events in Australia would raise funds for the Children's Cancer Institute of Australia. Mrs Blair would be the star attraction.

Markson's journey into Mrs Blair's orbit had been unconventional. He had started in business as a mobile disc jockey and pop promoter in Bournemouth before moving to Australia in the early 1980s, where two of his first moneymaking ventures were running a wet T-shirt competition and signing up the then fugitive great train robber Ronnie Biggs to appear in an advertisement for a product he claimed could cure baldness. An adept self-publicist, Markson had detailed other entrepreneurial exploits, including how he had toured dentists' surgeries to collect used fillings which he sold on to silversmiths, in his autobiography *Show Me the Money*. Since then he had become used to an enviable lifestyle in an exclusive district of Sydney thanks to his company Markson Sparks!, which had arranged speaking tours for Nelson Mandela, Bill Clinton and the former New York mayor Rudolph Giuliani in Australia. But in doing so Markson had raised some concerns in some of the charitable groups with whom he had become involved. One of these, the Queen Elizabeth Hospital Research Foundation, a pioneer of kidney transplants in Australia, had accused Markson of 'promising the world' when he arranged fund-raising events with Mr Giuliani as guest speaker. Although the foundation had, it claimed, been told it would receive substantial proceeds from the events, it had initially received less than £1,500. The foundation's chief executive Maurice Henderson accused Markson of promising more than £80,000 from the Giuliani tour. After protracted wrangling the charity was finally given £8,000, even though Mr Giuliani's fee was rumoured to be almost £125,000. Markson had also fallen out with the New South Wales Liberal Party over his cut of the proceeds from functions he staged to raise funds.

So it was that Mrs Blair flew into Auckland in February 2005 to begin her tour and stepped right into the middle of a row. It would go to the heart, not only of her cashing-in on her role as consort to the British prime minister, but also the argument about the ethics of celebrities profiting from charity events. There was also a separate issue, lost in the controversy over the payments, which raised further questions about her trip. Not only was Mrs Blair given police guards by the two nations she visited on the speaking tour, including close protection officers, Downing Street sources confirm that she also took Scotland Yard officers on the trip whose wages and expenses were covered by the British taxpayer. Two accompanied her in New Zealand with two going on ahead to Australia to assess any potential risk. By the time she finished her trip – in the Middle East state of Kuwait – she had no fewer than four armed protection personnel. Neither, sources reveal, is guarding Mrs Blair always the easiest of assignments. So absent-minded is she, say those close to her, that she invariably gives her bodyguards the slip. 'It happens most when she goes shopping,' says a source. 'She will wander around the store and her Special Branch officers will wait at the door. But she will forget about them and leave through another door. It happens all the time and drives them mad.'

Given her recent history, it was perhaps hardly surprising that Mrs Blair should begin her first speech with a gaffe. Speaking to 800 people who had paid between £90 and £380 to hear her speak for thirty minutes at a dinner at the Auckland Convention Centre, the prime minister's wife twice forgot where she was and confused her hosts with their arch-rivals in Australia. Once again British journalists were ejected from the hall before she began speaking, with Markson personally escorting them out. Those who stayed, however, were reportedly unimpressed. Mrs Blair, who had her picture taken with the local VIPs who had paid the highest prices to meet her, according to some guests used the speech as a blatant attempt to sell copies of *The Goldfish Bowl*. Others complained that her monologues were dull, with one protesting, 'If it had been a Broadway show she would have got the shepherd's crook after the first night. She read with the sing-song consistency of a kindergarten teacher.' But her faux pas in mistaking the nationality of her audience already appeared trifling when compared to newspaper claims on both sides of the world that Mrs Blair's fee was likely to be a third of the proceeds from the series of charity events. Moreover, these were not just any organizations but the charitable nuclear option – those for sick children. Nor did it appear that those arranging the tour were being completely transparent about who would be the biggest winner. The charity in New Zealand seemed confused as to whether Mrs Blair was actually charging a fee for her speech and a television interview with the NZ television channel Prime to promote the tour was also conducted on the strict understanding, said the show's anchorman, that the subject of her payment should not be raised.

Nor was she questioned about why she seemed so sanguine about trading on the Blair name when she had hitherto been so adamant that as a career woman she should be known by her maiden name. The inescapable impression that Mrs Blair's principles ran only as far as the bottom of her wallet was further underlined by the pictures of her children, including Leo playing in the garden at Downing Street, projected onto a screen behind the prime minister's wife as she talked about juggling her career with bringing up her family. Wasn't this a model of hypocrisy from the woman who had styled herself a 'tigress' to friends when describing her determination to protect her children's privacy? Had the Blairs not demanded that a photograph of Leo, given as a gift to the French president and happily displayed by him to the media, not be published because it could jeopardize her son's security? Most important of all, her decision to take part in the tour raised the issue of the principle of selling celebrity under the cloak of charity work.

Even for the staunchest defenders of the prime minister's wife, the financial facts of the episode did not make easy reading. It was reported as she finished her speaking engagements that the children's cancer charities named as the beneficiaries of the tour would not receive a penny of the ticket sales from the events. That sum, an estimated £200,000 would, it was claimed, be split between Mrs Blair, who would receive £100,000, with the organizer Max Markson taking the rest in profits and to cover expenses. The charities would receive about £100,000 from raffles, auctions and cash pledges made at the individual venues. Estimates had the cost of administration and wages at close to £160,000. Markson defended the trip and accused the press of stirring up the controversy. 'If Cherie Blair wasn't coming to Australia there wouldn't be that money raised for the children so it is sad, but that is the way of the world, that's the media,' he said. 'I have an impeccable reputation in this marketplace and the Fleet Street press have a go at me for political reasons – it's a way of dragging down Tony Blair by getting at me.'

As new and ever more grubby details emerged, Downing Street officials, in the absence of any other strategy that seemed to offer even the faintest glimmer of success, opted for a policy of silence. Mrs Blair, they said, was a private individual and not on government business. But nor were they in a position to refute any of the charges levelled against the prime minister's wife. The simple truth, insiders confirm, is that those responsible for protecting the image of the government and its leader had not been given advance warning by Mrs Blair of the financial details of the trip. They were as much in the dark as anyone else.

Her old enemy, Richard Littlejohn of the *Sun*, was in no

doubt who the winners and losers were in this complicated morality tale. His column featured a grotesque cartoon of the prime minister's wife with dollar signs for eyes clutching an overflowing trough of money on which was emblazoned 'Worldwide Wicked Witch Fund' under the headline TAKING CASH FROM KIDS WITH CANCER IS AS LOW AS IT GETS. The prime minister, he said, should be forced to explain to Parliament and the electorate 'why he thinks his bank balance should profit from a foreign children's cancer charity'.

It seems astonishing that Mrs Blair had not envisaged the storm her involvement would create, but as the story gained momentum on both sides of the world it dawned on her that she was appearing in yet another farce in which she was the author, director and star. She was, as is her wont, unwilling to take any responsibility for the mess in which she found herself. Instead she turned her fire on Martha Greene, who was about to find her new role of right-hand woman to the PM's wife already under threat. Cherie, say sources close to the American, laid the blame at Greene's door because it was to her that Cherie had delegated the job of organizing the trip in collaboration with Markson and the Harry Walker Agency. Martha, who had at the eleventh hour not travelled with Mrs Blair, spent hours on daily and increasingly tense calls to Cherie as she was forced to pass on the negative headlines the jaunt was making back home and belatedly attempted a fruitless damage-limitation exercise. 'Cherie was furious with Martha because the whole thing was a public-relations catastrophe,' said one source. 'Cherie had never met Markson and didn't know anything about his past, but she didn't like him from the start and Martha caught the flak for not checking things out properly. Martha was panicking and dreading ringing up Cherie to tell her the latest slagging she was taking in the media.'

It was not merely Cherie's detractors in the press who had pounced on her. She now became the focus of a political row, with the Conservatives wading in to attack what they described as her 'cash grabbing'. Sensing the opportunity to score some much-needed points against the prime minister only three months before the probable election date, Tory Chairman Liam Fox accused both the Blairs of 'feathering their own nests' while in Number Ten. And of Cherie he added, 'She is Cherie Booth in her professional life, but is Cherie Blair whenever there is cash to be made. The hallmark of the Blair years in Number Ten is one of vanity and conspicuous consumption. Their attraction to power, moneyed individuals and a wealthy lifestyle has put them out of touch with the people who put them in office. If Tony was ever brought down in a scandal it would be because of their love for the rich and famous.' The Tories entered the fray as an advert, sublime in its bad taste, began being shown on Australian television. Against the backdrop of a Union flag and to the theme of Handel's 'Arrival of the Queen of Sheba', it superimposed footage of Mrs Blair in stateswoman mode meeting the Australian prime minister John Howard and being driven around in a limousine. The regal theme owed much to a film of the Queen's state visit to Australia three years earlier. Over these images, a narrator announced, 'Cherie Blair, wife of the British prime minister Tony Blair, noted attorney, human rights advocate, Queen's Counsel and mother of four, will be in Sydney for one night only, February 12.' The advertisements, which appeared on the major Channel Nine station, advised viewers not to miss the 'once in a lifetime opportunity' of meeting Mrs Blair. Certainly, in both countries there appeared to be no shortage of people willing to part with their cash for the chance of being introduced to their VIP guest. In New Zealand its most wealthy citizens were, reveal those close to organizers of the trip, paying about £400 for the privilege of having their pictures taken with her.

To complete the farce and in an intervention dripping with irony the chorus of disapproval was joined by none other than that model of propriety Peter Foster. Revelling in his revenge and summoning up all the disapproval he could muster, he said of Mrs Blair,

> She's done it again, hasn't she? She's dropped herself right in it. I don't think she'll ever learn that there's no such thing as a free lunch. Sooner or later she'll have to pay in terms of bad publicity. She obviously still needs all the money she can get, but it's wrong to make it out of charity. I don't know who's advising her, but you have to wonder what on earth she is doing putting herself in the hands of Max Markson, who has already had questions asked about him in the parliament here. He's not the kind of person I'd like to be associated with.

Cherie, it appeared, had pulled off the seemingly impossible and allowed Peter Foster to set up camp on the moral high ground. Australian politicians also joined in the catcalls, with demands for greater transparency over charity fund-raising. South Australian MP Nick Xenophon called for promoters to be forced to detail exactly how the money they raise is spent. 'I think some people would be very annoyed if they knew how little actually goes to the charity involved with some of these events,' he said.

In the face of this barrage Cherie's innate defiance kicked in. Those close to her say she remained pathologically averse to accepting any responsibility for her mistake in taking on the tour. 'She did a pretty good job of shrugging off all the criticism she got over the trip,' says one who knows her. 'I don't think she expected to be given such a rough ride and I don't believe she thinks even now that she did anything wrong by doing the tour. She certainly expected to be criticized for making money out of who she is married to, but she figured that the benefits outweighed the pitfalls.'

Mrs Blair's new career as a globe-trotting public speaker was a welcome shot in the arm for the couple's depleted finances. In the course of the last two years Cherie had seen income from her work at the Bar dwindle. In 2000 her payments for legally aided work were a healthy £178,000, but by 2004 they had sunk to £26,500. The family's new Connaught Square home, which was supposed to earn them money before they finally moved in after leaving Downing Street, had instead been responsible for burning a huge hole in their finances. In an attempt to secure tenants the Blairs had spent close to £100,000 on renovations and decoration of the property. Even so, there were still no takers and they were forced to reduce the advertised rental price by almost £1,500 a week. Finally, at the end of March 2005, following six months of lying empty and after employing several agencies in attempts to rent the house, the New Labour-supporting film director Michael Caton-Jones took over the tenancy, paying a reported £2,000 a week .

Cherie returned to the UK from Australia undoubtedly richer, but the debacle was to provoke such strong emotions that aftershocks were felt by both the prime minister and his wife throughout the coming election campaign. Martha Greene, who, as far as Cherie was concerned, had to carry the can, could have been forgiven for not looking forward to her reunion with Mrs Blair, and the episode was to mark a cooling in the relationship between the two women. In future, Cherie announced to friends, she had decided to be more self-sufficient. She was already emboldened by increased confidence since Carole Caplin's departure and was choosing her own clothes and styling her own outfits. The wardrobe for her trip down under she had largely picked out herself and, while her ensembles could hardly be described as bargain basement, Cherie was proudly telling friends that doing her own shopping had actually saved her a fortune.

Increasingly, Caplin had been consigned to the fringes in the life of the prime minister's wife. By the time of the general election Carole had been sidelined to such an extent that she saw Mrs Blair no more than once or twice a week at the gym.

Even there, one of her colleagues would often oversee Cherie's workouts. For her part, Cherie confided in those close to her that she was prepared to give her former best friend 'bits and pieces to keep her out of trouble'. She was only too aware, say friends, that despite their increasingly distant relationship it was not in the best interests of either herself or the PM to sever ties with Caplin completely. The ongoing cooling of the friendship led predictably to renewed speculation that Carole might be tempted at last to cash in her secrets. Those close to her point to her hopes of launching a television career as the primary factor standing between her and the decision to tell all. In the summer of 2005 she was excitedly working on a pilot for a TV show called *Carole* for Channel 4 with the option of a series if the one-off proved successful. Her marginalized role did not, however, mean that the spotlight-loving Carole had gone quiet; indeed she retained the capacity to be a source of irritation and embarrassment to the prime minister long after she ceased to play a part in his personal life. In the autumn of 2004 she became an outspoken critic of controversial government proposals to licence a new breed of super casinos in the UK. She used her magazine column to lambaste Mr Blair over the scheme and spoke of her own father's gambling addiction and how it had wrecked her early home life.

At the beginning of 2005 Caplin embarrassed her old friends again by returning to Downing Street for the first time since her expulsion in a demonstration against the government's endorsement of an EU directive banning over-the-counter sales of vitamin and mineral supplements. Waving a petition emblazoned with the words BRITAIN WON'T SWALLOW THE BAN, she chose a décolleté top for her January visit to Number Ten with a Tory MP in tow. As photographers urged her to take her top off, Miss Caplin told reporters, 'It's nothing to do with who is in power. I would be here even if Mickey Mouse was in power.' Insiders reveal that Mrs Blair, who had been aware that her friend was planning to mount the protest, asked Caplin not to take part. 'Carole just completely ignored her and did it anyway,' says a source. 'It was very embarrassing for Cherie, but she has never been able to tell Carole what to do. Is anyone really seriously surprised that Carole Caplin behaves like a loose cannon? She loves to control people. Yes, she believes in this stuff about her herbal pills, but this was also an example of her warning them just how difficult she can be if they try to dump her out completely. She won't let herself be walked over by anyone.' The episode, however, only served to highlight the precarious state of the once-close friendship. Another source confirms, 'Bit by bit Carole was edged out. She stopped shopping for Cherie and they only saw each other when Cherie visited the gym and that was getting more and more rare because Cherie became so busy.'

*

Despite Tony Blair's political problems, as he formulated his strategy for the upcoming election he was buoyed by opinion polls which predicted he would still win a huge majority. In the months to come Blair would find himself increasingly rattled by Tory leader Michael Howard in a campaign that would mark a new low in the level of personal attacks aimed at a sitting prime minister. In the meantime, however, Mr Blair was preoccupied with a deadlier political enemy. In the wake of the U-turn over his plans to quit the previous summer, relations between the PM and his chancellor had reached their nadir. As Brown's camp briefed that Blair had not once but twice reneged on promises to step down before the end of a second term, the froideur that had long characterized their relationship increased. Downing Street sources reveal there came a point when the lines of communication between the two most senior men in government all but shut down. Blair, suddenly reinvigorated as he determined to fulfil his goal of being the only Labour PM to lead his party to a third successive term, moved to put Brown in his place. He was prepared finally to undergo a trial of strength with the chancellor. In his corner was Cherie, who like Blair had come to the conclusion that a public face-off would force Brown out of the shadows from where he and his supporters had been conducting a sniping campaign against the leader. Blair's team was sure that Brown would refrain from a straight challenge to the PM because his perceived disloyalty would damage his chances of winning support from the rank and file.

Blair's team set out to destabilize his opponent. There began a series of ploys aimed at undermining the chancellor. In February the prime minister's supporters leaked that Blair would reshuffle his pack after the election and relieve Brown of his power base at the Treasury, moving him instead to the Foreign Office. That would allow the prime minister to shift arch-Blairite Alan Milburn to the post of chancellor. A month earlier Blair had torpedoed a major and long-planned speech by Brown on world poverty. In an unprecedented and public display of his loathing for his colleague the prime minister had summoned journalists to a Downing Street press conference at which he had hijacked many of the chancellor's themes at exactly the same time as Brown was arriving for his speech in Edinburgh. It was a puerile display by the prime minister which goes some way towards illustrating the depth of hatred that exists between them. Blair had also appointed Milburn, an avowed enemy of the chancellor, to the role of election mastermind in the run-up to 5 May. It was a position Gordon Brown had previously made his own. To add to Brown's anger over the move, the prime minister brought back another of his political enemies in the shape of Alastair Campbell to work closely with Milburn on running the election.

Despite the furore over her lucrative but ill-judged Australasian jaunt Mrs Blair still confidently looked forward to playing her own upgraded part in the election. But she remained prone to attracting the worst sort of headlines. Three months before polling her long-running feud with Piers Morgan burst into the open with the publication of his diaries. Cherie was painted as vain, vengeful and 'damaged', and more importantly a political liability to her husband. Cherie was furious, insiders reveal, and determined that this attack would not pass without swift and brutal revenge. As the book hit the shelves she accidentally ran into Morgan at a party in London and was heard to mutter later, 'That bastard.' But her opportunity to exact retribution came within days. Sources reveal that Cherie was well aware of the former *Daily Mirror* editor's hopes of inheriting Michael Parkinson's role as celebrity chat-show host when he finally decides to retire; indeed Morgan and Mr Blair had discussed that very prospect at a private dinner party Cherie had invited Morgan to at Downing Street after his dismissal from the newspaper. So, when Mrs Blair met Parkinson at a party as Morgan began the rounds promoting his book, she was in no mood to put in a good word for her tabloid tormentor. 'She spent the whole time slagging Morgan off to him,' says a source. 'Parky was getting increasingly riled on her behalf. In the end he said Morgan would get his job "over my dead body".'

*

Given his many detractors, not least within his own party, it is perhaps only to be expected that Tony Blair has developed in his time at Downing Street an increasingly thick skin. It is not a characteristic with which he was naturally blessed. Despite getting used to the criticism that comes with high office, he is even now, say those close to him, wounded by the attacks on his personality which have become a feature of his recent history. For a man who retains a fundamental desire to be loved, he is stung by the realization that he inspires in some the exact opposite emotion. As a consequence, the 2005 general election campaign was, to say the very least, a bruising experience for him. Added to his problems over his recalcitrant next-door neighbour, Mr Blair was to be thrown off balance by the progressively more personal attacks on his character and honesty by Michael Howard. The Conservative leader's strategy of making the issue of trust in the prime minister a central theme of the campaign rattled Mr Blair, although he was given ample time to get used to being on the receiving end of such invective as he warmed up for the battle proper.

In a series of high-profile appearances, including a whole day spent on Channel Five in February, the prime minister was subjected to an often hostile and humiliating reception from members of the public invited to question him. The tactic was christened 'masochism strategy', a way of diffusing resentment by allowing Mr Blair to be pilloried publicly, thereby promoting new sympathy for him from those watching his ritual degradation. His staff were surprised, therefore, when after the day spent with his tormentors, the prime minister left the Five TV studios relishing his experience. 'He actually enjoyed it,' says a Downing Street source. 'It was quite astonishing, but he liked arguing his point with real people. It probably says a lot about how separated he has become from the public, particularly since his security was strengthened after 9/11, that even getting a public kicking gave him a buzz. He was talking animatedly about connecting with the electorate and wanted to do more of it.' Another source adds,

> My feeling is that he enjoyed those sparring matches with the public because not only did he actually get to meet some real people, he also got a different perspective. One of the faults about his office is that those around him have told him what they think he wants to hear. He is switched on enough to know that he needs to be challenged on issues and told when he is getting it wrong. That is one of the fundamental reasons that he has missed Alastair. He was the only one who would tell him, 'Oh, fuck off, Tony,' if he didn't agree with him.

Mr Blair was, however, distinctly less sanguine about the attacks mounted on him by his Tory opposite number as the election campaign mined new seams of the brutal and the personal. Labour had not been immune from indulging in base election tactics; the Jewish Michael Howard was famously and controversially depicted as a Fagin-like figure in a Labour poster campaign which the Tories denounced as anti-Semitic. Despite Labour identifying Howard himself as a PR problem for the Conservatives, tainted as he was by his prominent part in the previous Tory administration, he proved more than able to score points off Blair in the Commons. In March, after one particular prime minister's questions, Mr Blair's staff testify that he was 'very stressed' after a bruising encounter with the leader of the Opposition. But it was the Conservative leader's repeated assertion that Mr Blair was a liar that provoked real outrage in the prime minister. A furious Blair, on hearing Howard's accusation for the first time, repeatedly told his staff, 'How dare he? How dare he?' He was, says one, 'genuinely shocked that Howard had gone so low. The actual use of the word "liar" had a very powerful effect on him. I think he very much saw that as taboo and it shook him up. I have to say that he was incredibly angry about it.'

The Tory strategy of questioning Blair's honesty over making the argument for the war in Iraq so knocked him off his stride that it acted, in part at least, to precipitate an accommodation between the prime minister and his chancellor. Overnight, Blair and Brown moved to turn round a campaign which at times had threatened to be overshadowed by the fractured relationship at the top of government. It will long be speculated upon about what deal, if any, was struck by the two men to put 'The Tony and Gordon Show' back on the road. Brown, it is widely believed, must have secured a time-table for the handover of power before embarking on the sham that was their sudden and remarkable rapprochement. The truth, say those closest to the PM, is that Brown's decision to come out in such a startling show of solidarity with his embattled leader was a 'no-brainer'. The chancellor stood to gain nothing from a Tory victory or a Labour win with its majority cut to the bone. 'It doesn't take a genius to work out that Tony had already stated he didn't want to fight another election,' says one Downing Street insider. 'That means, barring the most unexpected accident, that within the next few years the job will be Gordon's. If Blair had won only a tiny majority, it would, in a matter of time, be Gordon's tiny majority.'

So began the formal campaign with the two architects of New Labour joined at the hip in a stage-managed display of public bonhomie. Blair called his chancellor the best for a hundred years. Brown, put on the spot, said he too would have taken the country to war in Iraq. If their love-in appeared contrived, it was then unsurprising that they decided to employ the skills of Anthony Minghella, the Oscar-winning director of *The English Patient*, to produce the four-minute election broadcast featuring the two men 'in conversation' over a bottle of mineral water. It was a sympathetically lit evocation of the political and ideological bond between the two men, full to brimming with moist-eyed reminiscences of their blood-brother partnership which had forged New Labour out of the ashes of a party thought unelectable and out of touch. 'We shared an office for what, two or three years?' recalled Mr Blair of their coming together in 1983. They had, he said, 'realized that the party had to change fundamentally'. The continuity problems that blighted the finished product – Brown in shirtsleeves, then with jacket and tie on, now in shirtsleeves again – lent more than a touch of the absurd. And who else over a drink with an old friend would say as Brown did, 'I personally believe, and you do as well, because I know we have talked about it before, I mean every child is precious, and every child is unique and every child is special and every child deserves the chance to develop their potential for moral reasons'? Given the palpable yearning of the brooding Brown to step into his rival's shoes and Minghella's involvement, the broadcast might have been released as *The Scottish Impatient*, but it nonetheless set the tone for the double-act approach to another Labour victory. In a joint interview with his chancellor in the *News of the World* Mr Blair even referred to their relationship as a 'marriage'.

The strategy appeared to work. An opinion poll conducted by Mori after the two men commenced their show of unity suggested that, among those certain to vote, a worrying five point Tory lead had been turned into a 7 per cent Labour advantage. The turnaround was christened the 'Brown bounce'. Here was a chancellor generally admired for his handling of a strong economy lending his weight to support a prime minister seriously wounded on a foreign battlefield. But if the Blair–Brown ceasefire began to settle nerves at party HQ in Victoria Street, it also precipitated a shift in the balance of power. Whereas a few short weeks earlier, when another landslide Labour victory had looked assured, Blair had refused to confirm that Brown would keep his job as chancellor, now the prime minister was glowing in his praise for his old adversary. As a quid pro quo for his loyalty, Brown would take back the reins of the Labour election strategy from his enemy Milburn. An early victim of his new authority would be Cherie Blair.

Where once she had been looking forward with excitement to her part in the campaign, even arranging for her hairdresser André Suard to take the whole month off from his Mayfair salon to accompany her around the country, with her nemesis Brown back in de facto control of the election Cherie suddenly found herself on the periphery. Relegated to touring schools in the constituencies visited by her husband and expressly forbidden from making any political statements, Mrs Blair cut a forlorn figure on the campaign trail. Overshadowed as she was by the effortlessly stylish and beautiful Sandra Howard, New Labour strategists, were, say insiders, desperate to keep her away from the media for fear she might make another public gaffe. Not content with rubbing in her obvious superiority in the style stakes, Mrs Howard was moved to take a potshot at her opposite number in her web diary of the campaign, comparing her humble blow-dries by a Tory aide in the back of the battle bus to Mrs Blair's hiring of 'arguably the best and certainly the priciest hairdresser in town'. Downing Street sources confirm that within days of the election victory they received a bill for £8,000 from Suard, passed on by Mrs Blair to the party for payment. There was, according to insiders, 'amazement' at the size of the bill. What was unknown until now is that in spite of the obvious competition between the two would-be first ladies there was an unprecedented degree of cooperation between not only the leaders' wives, but the three men fighting to get into Number Ten. For the first time lines of communication were established between the major parties and agreements reached over the style of dress for particular days of the campaign. So it was agreed, for example, that the party leaders, their wives and families would dress down in casual clothes on polling day.

Despite being pushed back into the shadows, Cherie did, however, manage to cause one flutter in the hearts of New Labour strategists. She found herself at the centre of a PR howler when, after her husband had talked about his aim to continue the work done by the government to improve the quality of school meals, she announced to parents on a visit to a Birmingham nursery that she was thinking of giving her youngest son Leo a packed lunch because the food at his state school was 'not terrific'.

Mrs Blair's low profile did not make her immune to the torrent of abuse that her husband had to endure on the campaign. The sheer venom of the verbal assaults often left those travelling around the country with the Blairs open-mouthed. Some of the most bellicose language was reserved for the prime minister's wife. 'It was actually shocking to hear some of the things people were shouting at her,' says one who shared the

battle bus. 'She would be at a school of all places and you'd
have parents shouting at her, "You rich bitch, coming up here.
Your husband has got blood on his hands. He's a murderer."
It was all shouted right into her face. These weren't one-offs
either; it happened all over the place. Cherie would just say to
them, "Well, you don't have to vote for us."' The treatment of
not only himself but his wife on the campaign trail was behind
Mr Blair's announcement on the steps of Number Ten the day
after the election that he planned to tackle the issue of respect,
or lack of it, in the nation. 'He is very serious about it,' says
one of his team. 'It was a reaction to the way he and Cherie
were abused as they travelled up and down the country.'

It was with an eye to such public outpourings against the
prime minister that New Labour apparatchiks increasingly
sought to protect him from too many spontaneous meetings
with the electorate as he toured the country. His public appearances were often handled with military precision and secrecy,
even to the extent of only inviting trusted journalists and a
rent-a-crowd of Labour supporters posing as members of the
public. Still the prime minister appeared jittery and downbeat. As the campaign progressed he seemed increasingly worn
down, say those who witnessed events at close hand, by the
relentless attacks on his character. 'It is quite usual for him to
be pessimistic during elections, but this one was different,' says
a Downing Street source. 'He seemed to get more down the
closer we got to polling day. There was a constant battle to
keep him upbeat. But whichever way he turned the subject of
Iraq kept coming up. He was finding it very hard to move the
agenda on and he started to think he could lose the election.'
Not only was his edginess on display in private; a previously
absent nervousness began to appear in his public appearances.
This symptom of the strain he was under was no more evident
than during his harassed performance a week before the election on BBC TV's *Question Time*. Mr Blair had refused a
debate with the Liberal Democrat leader Charles Kennedy and

Michael Howard, and instead each man was given thirty minutes in front of invited members of the public. For Mr Blair it was to prove an uncomfortable experience. Given a rough ride by his noisy audience, he was soon perspiring heavily. By the time his ordeal was over, the prime minister was bathed in sweat with torrents streaming from his hairline down his face and nose. Watching on the monitors, his team witnessed events unfold but were powerless to help. 'His face was soaking wet,' said one. 'But we knew he couldn't wipe the sweat away because the press would have had a field day with the picture. You can see the headlines: PRIME MINISTER FEELS THE HEAT. Instead he just had to let these rivers run down his face. It was excruciating.'

One of the few moments of cheer for Blair during a remorselessly depressing campaign came when, two weeks before polling, the *Sun* came out in support of Labour. Announcing its decision the day after the election of the new Pope with a symbolic red plume of smoke from the chimney at its Wapping HQ, the paper made plain its support was not unconditional with a front-page headline proclaiming, ONE LAST CHANCE. It would expect payback; so on the day before the election the *Sun* was granted a major exclusive with the prime minister and Mrs Blair. Were its readers to be treated to their leader's thoughts on the projected downturn in the economy over pages one, four, five and six, or the thorny issue of the vote on the EU constitution? The *Sun*, of course, had weightier issues to ponder. In what it billed as the Blairs' first ever joint interview, Britain's biggest-selling paper's splash headline read, WHY SIZE MATTERS. Inside, the couple talked about their 'twenty-five years of faithful love', the secret celebrations for their silver wedding anniversary and how they work to 'rekindle the spontaneity of their relationship while surrounded by security guards'. Tony, readers discovered, always forgets to buy a card on their anniversary and instead folds a piece of A4 in half and writes on it 'Tony loves Cherie'. 'There is a drawing of a little stick man and little stick woman and loads of kisses,' revealed Mrs Blair. 'It's not a very expensive gesture, but I think it's very romantic.'

But it was another prime ministerial revelation that drew the attention. In a first for political reporting, Mr Blair chose to reveal to the nation that he was able to have sex with his wife five times a night. When the *Sun*'s photographer cheekily suggested Mr Blair strip off for a picture to show off his physique, conveniently voted 'Torso of the Week' by a gay magazine, he asked Mr Blair how fit he was. 'Very!' chipped in an excitable Mrs Blair. Asked if he could perform five times a night, Mr Blair answered, 'At least. I can do it more depending how I feel.' The prime minister's wife was happy to confirm that he was, indeed, always 'up for it'. As a vote-winning strategy it was certainly novel. Jokey though the exchange might have been, it stretched for many the bounds of good taste. Here was a prime minister still facing angry questions about sending men to fight and die on a questionable prospectus boasting about his sexual prowess in the pages of a red-top tabloid. Moreover, the Blairs, it seemed, were once again content to invade their own privacy and that of their family in an attempt to woo voters. The couple happily talked about how their daughter Kathryn had given a reading from Shakespeare at their anniversary party, and shared with the paper how the Queen Mother had had her picture taken with Leo. But it was their admission about the nocturnal sexual athletics chez Blair that was to stir up trouble. The *Daily Express* described the interview as the 'most toe-curling of all time' while the *Daily Mail* thundered that it was 'jaw-dropping in its vulgarity'.

When they were faced with the evidence of their injudicious banter over breakfast the following morning Cherie was 'absolutely mortified', she told a friend. 'They were pretty much stitched up,' says one source willing to come to the couple's defence. 'They were just joking with the photographer as he was taking the pictures. It always looks different in black and white. It's fair to say it was not the best move they ever made.'

14

2005: THREE-TIME WINNER

As the throng of family, staff and local party workers milled around nervously downstairs at Myrobella, the prime minister's Sedgefield constituency house, Tony Blair sat alone in his bedroom on election night, watching the first results come in on a portable television. He had retreated to his room as the counts began and told all those present, including his wife, that under no circumstances was he to be disturbed. The anxiety that had kicked in at the start of this divisive campaign had left him, after a month on the election trail, jaded and exhausted. Neither he nor Cherie had slept the night before as they awaited polling day. There would be no prospect of sleep tonight either. Now a dejected Mr Blair could no longer face even those closest to him. Sitting in front of the TV, he watched friends and colleagues lose their seats. It would be a long night.

Downstairs the mood was equally sombre. Joining the Blairs and their children were Tony's brother Bill and his sister Sarah, making a rare visit with her partner. Blair's father Leo and stepmother Olwen had decided to stay at home because of their failing health, and the ongoing feud between Cherie and her sister Lyndsey meant that she was absent too. But at least one of the party was determined to lift the atmosphere. With exit polls suggesting a historic third Labour term, albeit with a substantially reduced majority, Cherie's father Tony Booth suddenly announced with admirable Scouse gusto, 'No one's celebrating. Well, I'm going to bloody well celebrate.' With that, the teetotaller proceeded to quaff several bottles of what other guests assumed was alcohol-free beer. His efforts, however, to lighten the proceedings in Sedgefield were valiant but ultimately fruitless. One who saw Mr Blair that day says, 'He looked about 110 years old. I have never seen him so deflated and down. You honestly would have thought he had lost the election. Right up to the early hours I think he still felt he could lose. There were real fears at one point that it could be a hung parliament, but the result wasn't even a relief. I just think he was totally exhausted and wrung out by the level of resentment aimed at him. It hurt him that he was seen, not as the saviour of his party, but as the biggest reason not to vote for it. You have to remember that he has always wanted to be loved.'

At the count in his constituency one candidate stood behind the prime minister on the platform with BLIAR emblazoned on her hat. Mr Blair did not even register the deliberate misspelling of his name. As the votes were read out, he and Cherie stood alongside each other staring unsmiling into the gaggle of party workers and the massed ranks of the media in front of them. When Reg Keys, who had stood as an independent candidate against the prime minister, and who blames him for the death of his soldier son in Iraq, gave a speech heavy with personal condemnation of Mr Blair, both Tony and Cherie clapped. Those close to them said husband and wife were 'shell-shocked'.

Eight years earlier on the flight from Teesside airport to London those on board had felt the crackling in the atmosphere, the feeling of anticipation, the sense of watching history being made. Tonight, somebody wished the new prime minister, who had turned fifty-two at midnight alone in his room, 'Happy birthday'. 'He'd actually forgotten it was his birthday,' they reported later. When Mr Blair arrived back at Number Ten later that 6 May morning, the only ever leader of the Labour Party to be elected to serve a third consecutive term, he told his wife he did not want any celebrations to mark his birthday. Neither would there be a repeat of the South Bank jamboree of 1997 or the hordes of well-wishers lining Downing Street.

Throughout the previous month, as he criss-crossed the country trying to shore up Labour support, Mr Blair had been in agony from a slipped disc. He had been forced to hire a new masseur to help him cope with the ceaseless pain he had been enduring during those nineteen-hour days. In the final push he had looked to his wife for reassurance as those around him witnessed the toll exacted on him by the events of the previous weeks. Once again she had advised, supported, cajoled. That afternoon, watched by his family on the steps of Number Ten, a chastened Mr Blair accepted that the nation had sent him a personal message. With his majority slashed from the 167 he won in 2001 to 66 seats he would, he promised, listen. 'I, we, the government' became the theme. For his third term he would move away from his much-derided presidential approach to government in favour of a new collegiate style. With as few as thirty-four Labour rebels now able to scupper legislation to implement his new raft of policies, including controversial plans to introduce ID cards, many on the left of the party were relishing the spirit of inclusiveness that had been forced on their leader.

But already there were calls for the man who had almost single-handedly made his party electable to go. Former ministers including Robin Cook and Frank Dobson joined the ranks of the disaffected in the parliamentary party, calling for him to hand over power to Gordon Brown sooner rather than later. There were dark mutterings that Blair could be out by the party conference in the autumn.

*

Less than a week after the end of a campaign that had exposed him to a level of vitriol unprecedented in recent British political history, Tony Blair addressed his depleted backbenchers in an attempt to quieten the clamour for his early departure. His performance in front of those demanding a change of leader would, it was widely believed, be crucially important to his hopes of remaining as premier. As his car swept out of Downing Street to take him to face his MPs, a lone demonstrator stepped forward, eyeballed the limousine and raised a placard with the solitary word MURDERER spelled out in blood-red paint. Blair faced down his critics at the meeting, but for some time his staff had noticed that the prime minister was walking with a limp. He would endure the pain in his back for another two weeks before finally being admitted to London's Royal Free Hospital for an anti-inflammatory injection. His treatment would not, his office stressed, alter his workload.

Those who know Tony Blair point to resilience as his most notable political quality. He has, they say, the ability to take the blows aimed at him, get up off the canvas and start again. It is a characteristic he shares with his wife. Two weeks after the electorate's stinging rebuke those around the prime minister witnessed a change in him. Having put on a bravura performance at the meeting of the parliamentary party, he was, say his aides, filled with a renewed vigour. Those around him talked of a refocusing on domestic issues – on the health service, on schools and public services. He was fired again with enthusiasm.

The French 'No' vote on the EU constitution later in May offered Mr Blair a get-out-of-jail-free card and the chance to scrap the proposed British referendum on the issue, due in 2006. It had been widely expected that British rejection of the constitution would signal the point at which Blair would step down in favour of his chancellor. Now there appeared to be no natural cut-off point and the potential for Mr Blair to carry on longer. Supporters of Brown sensed that once again the prime minister could go back on the 'stable and orderly transition' he had promised. There was, they said of Blair, 'a new blaze in his eyes'. The PM's rediscovered dynamism and the prospect of him actually carrying out his promise to stay the length of the parliament did of course raise issues for the party, not least the uneasy truce that existed between the PM and chancellor in the immediate aftermath of the election. Few could expect such a state of affairs to continue if Brown could not pin Blair down over the timetable for the handover. Worse was to come for Mr Brown.

But what of Mr Blair's most crucial political relationship, that with his wife? Now, as before, she remains the foundation on which he has built his life in politics. In the weeks after the election, she too, say court insiders, found new energy for the fight to come. She has not lost, however, the capacity to embarrass her husband. Before May was out, she found herself on the wrong end of more publicity. She was accused of abusing her position yet again when, on arriving at Heathrow Airport for a trip to Istanbul in her capacity as a barrister, she realized she had forgotten her passport. A police motorcyclist raced to the rescue with siren sounding and blue lights flashing while the British Airways flight was held up for her. Then Downing Street announced that she would be attending a gala dinner in Malaysia to mark the opening of a luxury shopping centre. The Starhill Gallery in Kuala Lumpur was described as 'a palace of infinite indulgence'. But there was immediate criticism of the trip and questions about Mrs Blair's involvement with the development's controversial owner Francis Yeoh. Mr Yeoh had made headlines over allegations of bribery during his conglomerate's takeover of Wessex Water in 2002. He was, however, completely cleared of claims that his company, YTL, had paid £1 million to make sure its bid was successful. Mrs Blair was reported to have arranged to stay as a guest of the Malaysian royal family and was making a speech at a legal lecture. As the clamour for her to call a halt to commercial activities increased, with senior Labour figure Clare Short joining the Tories in attacking her, Mrs Blair refused point blank.

Her behaviour, however, put her on a collision course with her husband. As it was reported that a Committee on Standards in Public Life was to investigate whether the rules which apply to ministers should be extended to their spouses, it was also claimed that Mr Blair had become increasingly uneasy about his wife's business affairs but felt unable to stop her. Indeed, sources reveal the astonishing degree to which the couple were out of tune with each other over the issue. In early June Mrs Blair was paid £30,000 to appear at an event at the John F. Kennedy Center in the US capital. She drew further fire over her use of the British ambassador to Washington Sir David Manning as her 'warm-up man' at the event. Billed as 'The First Lady of Downing Street', Cherie was interviewed by CNN anchorwoman Paula Zahn in front of a half-full auditorium of guests. She reportedly plugged her book throughout the talk and made repeated references to her children. But most embarrassing of all for the PM and his increasingly uneasy Downing Street staff was the fact that the speech coincided with Mr Blair's own trip to Washington to discuss with President Bush, among other issues, African poverty and third-world debt.

During her appearance Mrs Blair also seemed intent on digging herself further into trouble by claiming she had been the victim of sexism. Mrs Thatcher's husband Denis, Cherie told Zahn, was not criticized for his business interests. But the analogy only served to illustrate how far-reaching her self-delusion had become. Sir Denis had been a successful business-man in his own right long before his wife became PM. Nor had his wealth been achieved by cashing-in on his position as the spouse of the country's leader. The interview also high-lighted the skewed logic in Mrs Blair's persistent claims that her priority was to protect her family's privacy. As she showed a picture of her children, taken on the steps of Number Ten, she told Zahn, 'I wanted to protect the kids from the press and make sure they could walk about and have friends.' The paradox that once again she was invading the privacy of her children as she cast herself in the role of their champion appeared to have passed her by. So, too, did the contradiction in her assertion that her career had allowed her to 'keep that distance' between herself and Downing Street at the very moment she was again profiting from discussing her life inside Number Ten.

Stranger still, sources reveal, was the argument between the Blairs before Cherie flew to Washington. Insiders disclose that Mr Blair tried to persuade his wife of the potential for embarrassment over their clashing schedules, but Cherie flatly refused to cancel, telling her husband, 'My plans have been in place for ages. You rearrange your meeting.' In the event, both flew to the capital and once there Cherie was defiant when questioned about the ethics of her trip. She simply shrugged and said, 'You can't please all the people all of the time.' Blair responded wearily to the furore in the media by saying, 'I don't think there's ever anything I can say on these things that can make it better.'

Significantly, the chorus of disapproval was now joined by those in the media who had previously been supportive of the Blairs and it extended beyond the behaviour of his wife to the financial benefit Mr Blair himself accrued through her efforts on the international lecture circuit. The *Guardian* columnist Polly Toynbee wrote of them: 'Sometimes things happen to people when they spend too long in the upper stratosphere of wealth and power. They easily forget what's normal. They think they are owed equality with the richest people they meet; they soon feel poor in comparison. A sense that they "deserve" more chases away cautionary reminders of how most people live.' Downing Street officials, too, were increasingly concerned that Mr Blair was becoming the unwilling recipient of the fall-out from his wife's activities. This, finally, was the cue for Blair to act. Within days Downing Street quietly confirmed that Cherie would 'no longer be able to attend' the gala dinner in

Malaysia. Under pressure from her rattled husband Cherie had relented and scrapped the plans. She also announced that she would be donating to charity her fee for a two-hour Channel 4 documentary about the spouses of British prime ministers. Sources reveal that Cherie's decision to curtail her money-making efforts did not come without her husband arguing the case for her to scale them back. Those in the court who have become used to an admirable lack of friction between the couple, despite the uniqueness of their position, sensed increased tension between them over the issue. As ever, much of the pressure on them was due to the lack of time Blair could spare for domestic matters. So pressed was he for time that in the absence of husband and wife finding space in their diaries to sit down and discuss Cherie's schedule, the prime minister often relied on Hilary Coffman to pass on to him his wife's plans.

As Blair prepared to fly to Brussels in June for a summit with European leaders over the EU budget, there was, despite his more upbeat mood, little reason to suspect that he remained anything more than the 'lame duck' prime minister he was still being painted as. Also enfeebled, however, was Jacques Chirac who had been badly wounded by his country's rejection of the EU constitution. A battle ensued in Belgium between the two men over the EU budget, the French insistence on retaining the contentious Common Agricultural Policy and Britain's con-tinued defence of its £3 billion rebate. As the leaders failed to agree a budget, Blair emerged triumphant. Widely seen as standing firm in the face of shallow French self-interest, even France's most influential paper *Le Monde* hailed the summit as a 'double victory' for Mr Blair in burying the EU constitution and successfully drawing attention to the anomaly of how the EU, through the CAP, spends seven times more on farmers than it does on science and research. After the late-night debating in Brussels failed to secure a compromise, Blair awoke to similar headlines in the UK.

His stock was raised further by his crucial intervention when the International Olympic Committee met in Singapore to vote on the host city for the 2012 games. With Paris still favourite to win the nomination, Blair gambled his credibility on flying in to help. Once there, he and Cherie began an exhaustive round of campaigning, stating in turn the case for London to no fewer than 64 of the 100 members of the IOC. When the games were awarded to the British capital, few in the London team doubted the significance of the part played by the Blairs in the victory. It rekindled memories of how, as in Northern Ireland, Blair's personal charm and commitment to a cause could achieve impressive results. In Gleneagles for the G8 summit on poverty and climate change, a nervous Blair could not bear to watch the result on television and paced around the grounds of the hotel. When his chief of staff Jonathan Powell emerged to tell him the good news the PM threw his arms around him and 'did a little jig'. As he entered the foyer of the hotel his team ran to meet him and hugged him one by one. One of those with the PM says, 'Tony was buzzing. That sense of dynamism that he had had in the beginning was there again. You could see it in his eyes. He knew he was back.'

The Olympic victory rounded off a tumultuous seven days for Blair. He had been widely applauded by Bob Geldof and Bono for his support of the Live8 concerts the previous weekend and for his commitment to action over third-world debt and poverty.

Twenty hours later on the morning of 7 July, as he walked in the grounds of the Scottish hotel, Blair was told the news that bombs had gone off on the London Underground and on a bus in Tavistock Square. Those who were with him that morning describe the prime minister as 'emotional, but above all angry'. Aware that the bombings were most likely timed to disrupt the meeting of the world's leaders, his speech at midday, spontaneous and heartfelt, was unusually short on the theatrics that had come to characterize his appearances before the cameras. While lacking the unchecked raw emotion of London mayor Ken Livingstone's address to journalists in Singapore, Blair re-found the ability to connect completely with the mood of the nation in the way he had done following the death of Diana nearly eight years earlier. The anger and shock he displayed, underpinned by a determination that the terrorists must never win, chimed with that of the country. By comparison, Tory leader Michael Howard and his would-be replacement David Davis seemed stiff and self-conscious.

Blair addressed the nation again at 5.30 p.m. in Downing Street, this time in a tightly scripted statement. His performance had become infected with the trademark over-long pauses and hand gestures so beloved of impersonators. But his message of defiance articulated the feelings of a nation deep in shock but resolute in the face of those who would seek to destroy it.

If there was a sense that Blair's statement in London and his address, surrounded by his fellow world leaders earlier that day in Gleneagles, were forced and mannered, those with him were in no doubt of the emotion so close to the surface. When he arrived back in Scotland on a Chinook helicopter that evening, Blair was so overcome, say sources, that he asked his staff to leave him alone for a few minutes as he disappeared into his suite to compose himself. That night Blair and President Bush sat together talking and drinking coffee in the prime minister's suite until 11.15 while Dave Hill and Tom Kelly flitted about. It would be an uncomfortable night. The heightened security meant that all windows in the hotel were locked shut despite a heatwave and the leaders sweltered in Blair's airless room.

Given the mounting confidence about Blair over the previous weeks, how odd then that at a time when he was rediscovering the popularity so notably lacking at the election he should seek to revisit the mistakes of the past. Ten days before the bombing, the Blairs had been deeply embarrassed yet again by Carole Caplin. This time Caplin had fallen victim to the *News of the World*'s fake sheik, undercover journalist Mazher Mahmood, who posed as a potential client to get Caplin to spill the beans on her relationship with the couple. Over five pages the indiscreet Caplin talked about, among other things, how the prime minister had taken to drinking alcohol and coffee again since her departure and was quoted as saying, 'We had dinner last Saturday and he's in dire straits, he's put on weight . . . He's not [fit]. I can't believe the change in him since I've not been there. He's not fit in the right way. You know the job has taken its toll and as he says, you know, when you have somebody looking after him in the way I did, you're monitored, you're exercised properly, you know the massages are important.'

Nearly two years after being shown the Number Ten door, it might have appeared that Caplin was overplaying her importance to Mr Blair whom she described as being like an 'older brother'. But sources reveal that up until her latest faux pas, Blair had, indeed, been lobbying for the return of the woman who had made the couple the butt of so much derision in the past. When the *News of the World*'s exposé appeared, insiders reveal an inquest was held between Tony and Cherie. Later Cherie told friends she had said to her husband that she would not accept any responsibility for the episode. Tony had been the one, she told them, who had been calling Carole all the time.

But despite Caplin's continued potential to cause embarrassment, events, and his handling of them, restored Blair to a level of popularity he had neither expected nor dared hope for. Even those who had been most critical of him less than two months earlier now queued up to heap praise on the revitalized leader. In the Commons four days after the bombings, Michael Howard paid tribute to the 'calm, resolute and statesmanlike way' the prime minister had reacted in the wake of the attacks and how he had 'articulated the nation's sorrow'. Writing in the *Daily Telegraph*, Ferdinand Mount argued: 'One conclusion of these extraordinary up-and-down days is hard to dodge. It is that Tony Blair now occupies a status in the world enjoyed by no post-war British prime minister except Churchill and Margaret Thatcher, and in some ways his appeal is wider than either.'

In Westminster the political landscape took on a distinctly different appearance to how it had looked less than two months earlier. There was even serious talk of Blairites pressing the PM to ditch his plans to stand down before the end of a third term and carry on to the Olympics seven years hence.

EPILOGUE

2005–06: RENEWAL

The second honeymoon was never likely to last, however. The Blairs flew off on holiday to Barbados a month after the London bombings and straight into another row about freebies. This time the couple spent their longest trip yet, a full twenty-four nights, ensconced mainly at Sir Cliff Richard's Sugar Hill estate. The length of the vacation might have raised eyebrows, coming as it did at a time when nervy Londoners were again braving the Tube system back home, but in truth few begrudged the prime minister a holiday. What raised the now customary hackles in the press was a clumsy and illjudged attempt by Downing Street to keep the location a secret. While Blair's staff argued that they were merely acting on the advice of the security services in demanding a media blackout about his plans, there was an assumption in Fleet Street that the intervention of his private office had as much to do with limiting comment about the Blairs' continued preference for the hospitality of their rich friends as it did with protecting them from terrorists.

The media grudgingly accepted Dave Hill's unprecedented request but was for the most part sceptical from the outset. Why, for example, was such a demand made by the PM and his wife when the royal family and the US president asked for no such favours from the fourth estate? But the reality was that although editors were at the very least dubious about Number Ten's motives, nobody wanted to break ranks and name their choice of holiday destination for fear that if something nasty did befall the First Family, the publication that had let the cat out of the bag would find itself having to answer some very unwelcome questions. Not that it would have taken the most sophisticated or diabolical of terrorist minds to draw up a shortlist of targets given (a) the Blairs' natural reluctance to pay for anything, and (b) their annual August jaunt to Sir Cliff's Caribbean home had by now become part of the social calendar.

The British media's vow of silence became all the more absurd when Barbados radio announced the arrival of their returning VIP guests in Bridgetown on a scheduled BA flight. As pictures of their exploits, including a four-day cruise on a luxurious sixty-two-foot catamaran called *Good Vibrations*, appeared in newspapers in the UK, the press nevertheless stayed quiet about where exactly they were staying. Meanwhile, the Blairs and their entourage enjoyed the sumptuous yacht. Tony and Cherie's stateroom was equipped with a flat-screen TV and a drinks blender, it was reported, and they were tended to by a British-born chef. The highlight of the trip, Cherie told the crew, was a barbecue in a secluded bay owned by an islander. The cost to any other holidaymaker of the sailing jaunt would have been £10,000 and estimates put the whole trip close to £30,000. Once again, although the Blairs claimed they were making a donation to charity in lieu of the hospitality they had received from their hosts, they refused to say just how much they had handed over. Fleet Street, aware it was at least a principal player in the farce, began letting out clues about their whereabouts with the *Sun* launching a 'Spot the Blair' competition and its columnist Richard Littlejohn writing that the couple's host was a 'confirmed bachelor boy'.

In the end Blair outed himself when he interrupted his sunbathing to make an impromptu appearance on the island to mark the anniversary of VJ Day. With the secret out, Downing Street called an end to the charade. Mr Blair, who had – as is his wont – paid economy fares for himself and his family, was duly deposited at the back of the plane on the return flight with other holidaymakers, while their protection squad guards luxuriated in first class. It is a source of unremitting annoyance to the Blairs, say those close to them, that while it is considered appropriate for the prime minister of the country to be lumped with the masses in the World Weary Traveller compartment, members of his police protection team settle down in their fully flat beds all paid for by the taxpayer. Given the clamour over the trip, it was hardly surprising that when at Christmas the Blairs returned to the far more potentially dangerous Sharm el Sheikh, where sixty-four people had been killed in a terrorist bombing just five months earlier. Downing Street asked for no repeat of the press embargo.

Mr Blair returned to Downing Street from Barbados with renewed zeal. Keen to display to the country that his government would be tough on terrorism in the wake of 7 July, he pressed ahead with plans to extend the limit on detaining terrorist suspects from fourteen to ninety days. As he sought a consensus with the opposition parties, however, he came up against resistance from Michael Howard and Charles Kennedy and in November suffered his first ever Commons defeat when fifty Labour rebels defied the whip to throw out the ninety-day proposal. He had also found himself seemingly on the other side of the political divide from his wife. In a move that appeared to heap deep embarrassment on her husband, Cherie waited less than three weeks after the London bombings before delivering what seemed to be a coded attack on his proposals. Speaking in her capacity as a QC to a conference of 1,000 lawyers, civil servants and diplomats in Malaysia, Mrs Blair called for the judiciary to stand up to politicians in the war on terror. It would, she said, be 'all too easy for us to respond to such terror in a way which undermines commitment to our most deeply held values and convictions and which cheapens our right to call ourselves a civilized nation'.

She said courts should be 'guardians of the weakest, poorest and most marginalized members of society against the hurly-burly of majoritarian politics'. A good example of this principle in practice was, she said, the decision by the UK's highest court, the House of Lords law lords, that the British government's policy of holding foreign terrorist suspects indefinitely without charge broke human rights laws. 'What the case makes clear is that the government, even in times when there is a threat to national security, must act strictly in accordance with the law,' she said. Her comments, though perfectly reasonable for a human rights lawyer, were hugely embarrassing given that just hours after she delivered her speech, Mr Blair, at his monthly Downing Street press conference, was bemoaning the fact that the government's attempts to kick out extremists had been thwarted by judges. 'Now I am afraid occasionally what has happened is we have tried to get rid of them and we have been blocked,' he said. 'The independence of the judiciary is a principle of our democracy and we have to uphold it, but I hope that recent events have created a situation where people understand that it is important that we protect ourselves.'

Perhaps unsurprisingly, in view of the recent history of communication breakdown between husband and wife, Downing Street insiders say Mr Blair had not been shown a draft of his wife's intended speech before she left for Kuala Lumpur, and had no idea that she planned to deliver a clear rebuke to his stance. Those close to Cherie insist that there was no deliberate intent to embarrass her husband. Rather, says one who knows her, she had, for the umpteenth time, been the victim of her continued and increasingly preposterous view that it is possible to separate her role as consort to the British prime minister from her job as a lawyer in the field of human rights. That Blair should have been skewered by his own wife was an unexpected gift to their detractors; it was also an illustration of the precious little time the couple had to discuss such potential hazards, which, given Mrs Blair's propensity towards the injudicious, had become a perennial issue.

Once again, however, on her return to London, Cherie was bullish in the face of criticism over her apparent blunder.

Apparent, because it was already being floated in Westminster that her comments were part of an elaborate scheme within Number Ten to placate the large number of Labour MPs openly disquieted by Blair's plans for the detention of suspects without trial. The argument went that the more liberal elements in the party would be pacified if they believed Cherie, who they thought to be to the left of her husband, was making their case during prime ministerial pillow talk in Downing Street.

A further example of the ambiguity of Mrs Blair's position came with her decision to take on the case of Shabina Begum, the Muslim Luton teenager who took her school, Denbigh High, to court because she wanted to wear a *jilbab* to class even though it was against its uniform policy. It should be said the school's head teacher had made considerable attempts to accommodate the various religious faiths of his students within the uniform guidelines; female pupils were able to choose to wear a *shalwaar-kameez* (a tunic-and-trouser suit) as well as a navy-blue headscarf. Shabina wore the *shalwaar-kameez* for two years, but at the age of thirteen in September 2002 she told the school that the uniform no longer conformed to her religion. She was sent home and despite attempts by the school to persuade her to return, she stayed away for two years. In the absence of her father, who died when she was young, or her mother, who cannot speak English, she was represented in negotiations with the school by her brother Shuweb Rahman, who was twenty when the dispute began. His sister would not return to school, he informed them, until she was allowed to wear head-to-toe Islamic dress.

Her case was taken up by the Children's Legal Centre, which receives lottery and government grants. Controversially, she was also backed by Hizb-ut-Tahrir, an extremist Muslim organization whose website advocates the creation of a worldwide Islamic state under sharia law. Approached by the Children's Legal Centre, Mrs Blair agreed to take on the case. This was, on the face of it, a surprising move, given that Hizb-ut-Tahrir was a controversial group – so controversial that in 2005 her husband called for it to be banned. Mrs Blair's case was that her client had been the victim of prejudice. In the High Court in December 2004 Cherie said the *jilbab* was not considered an extreme form of dress code observance, but was recognized by many Muslims as a requirement of their religion. She said, 'The question of modestly dressed females is not a quirky culture thing; it is recognized as a genuine manifestation of religious belief.' Miss Begum lost the case, but won on appeal a year later. Finally, in March 2006, five law lords unanimously overturned the Appeal Court ruling and backed the school's decision.

The case was estimated to have cost taxpayers £100,000. Shabina, now seventeen, had gone through most of her secondary school life without formal education. But was the case really about school uniforms? A year earlier in an interview with the *Guardian* Miss Begum's political agenda seemed clear. 'Our belief in our faith is the one thing that makes sense of a world gone mad, a world where Muslim women, from Uzbekhistan to Turkey, are feeling the brunt of policies guided by Western governments,' she was quoted as saying. All highly political stuff. A Muslim Labour MP, Khalid Mahmood, whose constituency is in Birmingham, accused her brother and Hizb-ut-Tahrir of using the schoolgirl as a 'political football'. 'They have been working on this girl. They want an Islamic revolution,' he said.

During the final appeal the school's lawyer told the court that Miss Begum's advisers objected to the *shalwaar-kameez* because it was worn by 'non-believers'. Mrs Blair rose to disagree. 'That is not the reason why we object,' she said. 'It is because it is not modest enough.' What, then, was Mrs Blair doing taking on the case? Was this not the same Mrs Blair who in November 2001 had made an overt political intervention when she sought support for the British and American invasion of Afghanistan by inviting the media to Downing Street to 'lift the veil' on the plight of women under the Taliban? Was this not the same Mrs Blair who had posed for photographers with her thumbs and forefingers over her face to imitate the degradation of the burka? It was not surely good enough to plead the 'cab rank' defence most often wheeled out by her supporters. Would she, for example, have accepted a brief had it involved representing the BNP?

There was again speculation in the media that Mrs Blair's involvement in the case was bound up in party politics – a sophisticated 'good cop, bad cop' double act with her husband in a bid to placate Muslim voters angry with Labour over the war in Iraq. Why too was Mrs Blair granted a formal meeting with Afghan President Hamid Karzai on a solo trip to Kabul in the spring of 2006? Mrs Blair, who was in the country to chair a series of meetings on judicial reform, was neither an elected member of the British government – in which there are, of course, more than a few lawyers – or a senior member of the judiciary. Indeed, as a part-time recorder she was on the bottom rung of judges.

*

In early March 2006 the full extent of the Blairs' mortgage debt was calculated at £4 million. Public records, obtained by the *Daily Mail*, showed they took out a £3,467,500 loan on the Connaught Square house when they bought it in September 2004. On top of that, mortgages on the two Bristol flats and their Durham constituency house came to at least £472,500. This staggering debt inevitably raised questions about how they could afford repayments that, even at a conservative estimate, were at least £16,000 a month. At the same time financial experts also questioned how the prime minister and his wife had secured a 95 per cent mortgage on the £3.65 million they paid for their London townhouse when their lender, the Cheltenham and Gloucester, was offering only

75 per cent in similar cases. The sums became all the more concerning when it emerged that Michael Caton-Jones was to give up his tenancy on Connaught Square, leaving the Blairs to meet their repayments without the £2,000 a week he paid in rent. With no rental income, the huge monthly payments would swallow the whole of Mr Blair's £183,392 salary, it was estimated. A further blow to the couple was that the Bayswater house, supposed to be an investment for when the PM left office, had continued to drop in value, as had the Bristol flats, which were valued at £25,000 less than what Cherie had paid for them.

A week after this news became public Mr Blair, it can be disclosed, left Number Ten in his chauffeur-driven Jaguar and was driven the two and a half miles to Connaught Square. Emerging from his car, he bounded up the steps and went in through the front door of his house for the very first time. Arriving back at Downing Street later, he told Cherie, 'It's not bad, is it?' What is perhaps most astonishing is that few of his staff batted an eyelid about the fact that despite owning the property, which had been such a drain on his finances for eighteen months, Mr Blair had never before laid eyes on it. Even so, and despite claims that protection officers had criticised the house's position on a busy street as making it vulnerable to attack, the Blairs remained adamant that it would become their home once they left Downing Street.

Tony's decision to leave the management of the family finances to Cherie had plainly been a disaster. It was hardly surprising, therefore, that Cherie was adamant she continue her controversial efforts to keep them afloat. To this end, Martha Greene had taken on ever-increasing importance.

Greene had made herself invaluable not only to Cherie, but to Tony as well. Where once Carole Caplin had fulfilled the role of fixer and confidante to the couple, now Martha occupied that vital position. Indeed, she now became a regular visitor for one on one early-evening discussions with the PM, which would often go on for hours in the study of the Number Eleven flat. In fact, Downing Street insiders reveal that Greene's influence was such that in early 2006 she sought to cement her position at the heart of the Blair court by obtaining her own office in Number Ten from where she could oversee management of the couple. Mrs Blair, who was equally keen on the idea, argued Martha's case with the civil servants who manage the property, but to Cherie's annoyance her request was rejected. Nonetheless, friends of the Blairs say Greene has positioned herself to take over managing the lucrative career in publishing and speaking tours that awaits the prime minister when he leaves office.

Carole, meanwhile, found herself well and truly out in the cold. Her indiscretion to the *News of the World* had proved her final mistake. Before long Cherie had dispensed with her services as fitness coach and was instead receiving daily visits at Downing Street from forty-year-old Steve Agyei, who worked at the same gym as Carole and who had once appeared in a brochure for her company Lifesmart. What further angered Carole, who had trained Agyei herself, was that he had been recommended to Mrs Blair by her nemesis Martha. Carole's name was now never spoken in Downing Street. Perhaps the ultimate evidence of Caplin's fall from grace came when she celebrated her forty-fouth birthday with a party at London's Hurlingham Club. Where once Cherie would have been guest of honour on the sixty-strong guest list, which included actors Martin Shaw and Jenny Seagrove, the prime minister's wife was conspicuous by her absence.

Ever the optimist, Caplin put a brave face on being cast out by the Blairs by talking up her television series, *The Carole Caplin Treatment*, which was launched by Channel 4 in January. Heartbreakingly for Carole, however, she was informed after it ended that the station would not be recommissioning the series. Not surprisingly, the news of her dumping by Channel 4 coincided with renewed speculation she would surely seek to realize the £1 million she claimed she had been offered to write a book about her life with the Blairs. Caplin remained coy on the subject, but an alternative nightmare scenario for Tony and Cherie had emerged in the meantime: in spring 2006 Sylvia had started work on her own book with the help of a ghostwriter.

After a brief hiatus, Cherie, too, was working on improving her bank balance – by setting Martha Greene to the task of arranging yet more speaking tours. After accepting it was in the interests of all concerned for her to suspend her moneymaking activities in the short term, she was suddenly imbued in early 2006 with a renewed enthusiasm for resolving the family's financial problems. Those close to her noticed a further hardening of her attitude to the criticism she would without doubt be subjected to over her plans to take on yet more foreign lecture tours. With no need to fight another general election, Mrs Blair had decided that she must do what, as she saw it, was best for her. Once again, however, the exceptional circumstances in which the Blairs found themselves meant that there was precious little opportunity for her to discuss her plans with her husband. Indeed, following Mr Blair's third-term victory, those within the circle noticed a tension in the relationship between husband and wife that had been largely and admirably absent for the majority of his time in office. As the PM grappled with calls for his early departure and the perennial and thorny issue of Gordon Brown, their friends had noticed a new snappishness in Tony's attitude to his wife.

This was most evident in the autumn of 2005 as he became increasingly exasperated with negative headlines surrounding his wife's activities. Damaging new information about her trip to Australia and New Zealand had emerged with reports that at one event during the trip, a dinner in Melbourne at which Mrs Blair spoke, only £7,000 of the £80,000 raised went to the charity the event was supposed to be supporting. The rest, it transpired, had gone on expenses and Mrs Blair's generous fee.

At the same time the charity involved, the Children's Cancer Institute of Australia for Medical Research, found itself under investigation and threatened with closure. It had fallen foul of Victoria state laws which demand that at least 60 per cent of all proceeds from fund-raising events go to the cause concerned. Its plight led to parents of the children it helps begging Mrs Blair to return her fee to save the charity from going under, as well as calls in Britain for her to stop cashing in on her position as the wife of the PM. All of this provoked much hand-wringing in Downing Street, particularly the claim by one Australian mother that Mrs Blair had profited from 'other people's suffering'. Mr Blair was once more aware that his wife would dominate the following day's headlines as he prepared to attend a Buckingham Palace banquet celebrating the state visit of the king and queen of Norway.

Staring down the barrel of yet another imbroglio of her own making and aware she was about to come in for a renewed pounding from the press, Cherie, however, seemed impervious to the disaster unfolding before her. Indeed, her primary concern in the hours before her grand entrance to the Palace ballroom had not been the emerging scandal but how her daring off-the-shoulder gown would be received. She had made it plain to those close to her that she had no intention of paying back the money to the charity or of curtailing her career as a public speaker. In contrast, according to his Number Ten staff, Mr Blair had been in a 'foul' temper all day since being told Fleet Street was preparing to pillory her again. He was in no mood for a party.

On foreign trips Blair's team have become used to their boss's increasing frustration with his wife's habit of making them late for official functions because she takes so long to get ready or, just as likely, has found something she needs to attend to on her computer. At home, whenever they are scheduled to attend a function with the monarch, Tony's exasperated cry of 'We've got to get there before the Queen!' has become something of a mantra. Sources also reveal that Mr Blair has taken to going to Chequers on Thursday and not returning to London until Sunday, leaving his wife alone in Downing Street.

Privately, Mrs Blair remained unapologetic in the face of the fresh furore over the Australasian tour and quietly put Martha Greene on to arranging more speaking engagements in America. In preparation for the trip, Cherie also granted an interview to one of America's leading news presenters, Katie Couric, then of NBC's *Today Show*. Although Mrs Blair was nominally acting as an ambassador for the London Olympics, the interview also afforded her the opportunity to raise her profile significantly in the US.

In March 2006 she earned a reported £29,000 for addressing the Society of the Four Arts in Palm Beach, Florida, but several other US engagements were cancelled by Mrs Blair at short notice. Those close to her say she pulled out of the events after reports emerged that Special Branch officers had foiled a plot by members of the controversial pressure group Fathers 4 Justice to kidnap five-year-old Leo. It was said that some within the group had suggested taking the Blairs' youngest son hostage and releasing him unharmed to highlight the plight of fathers refused access to their children.

Mrs Blair's resumption of her speaking engagements came after the chairman of the Committee on Standards in Public Life, Sir Alistair Graham, announced he believed the ministerial code of conduct should be reviewed following complaints about the prime minister's wife. In the event, it was Blair himself who made the tacit admission that Cherie had cashed in on his position. In an unprecedented move he declared in the official register of MPs' interests the controversial series of speeches she had made in Australia and New Zealand. It was a dramatic U-turn given Downing Street's previous claims that Cherie's foreign lecture tours were unrelated to her husband's position, but in November 2005 Mr Blair confirmed that her speeches included 'some discussion of my wife's life in Number Ten Downing Street'. He also included in the register royalties she had made from her book *The Goldfish Bowl*. His admissions only led to louder complaints from the Tories that Mr Blair had broken the spirit of the ministerial code, which states that ministers should not profit from activities relating to their jobs. The Lib Dems, meanwhile, demanded she should give the proceeds of her American trip to charity.

The prime minister's declaration came as details emerged of the eighteen luxury watches, four necklaces, two bracelets, two sets of earrings, two rings, a clock and, bizarrely, a sports bag that the Blairs have received from Silvio Berlusconi in recent years. Downing Street revealed that the PM had bought two of the watches for £175 over the previous twelve months under a 'right to buy' clause with the price being set by the Cabinet Office. Given that the billionaire Berlusconi is renowned for his generosity – in 2003 he gave George Bush a £6,750 Franck Muller watch – the Tories demanded to know how the figure Mr Blair paid had been arrived at.

Meanwhile, Cherie was criticized for saying that she would have probably ended up being a shop girl if she had not had a state-funded education. Not only were her comments considered demeaning to shop workers, weren't they also politically unwise when her husband's government had been responsible for university tuition fees? Again Cherie stood accused of not learning her lesson from past gaffes, and again she appeared unmoved by the flak. If anything, the greater the barrage aimed at her, the more she has felt inclined to stick to her guns, say those close to her. 'Her ability to hang on to the belief that she is in the right, even in the face of substantial evidence to the contrary, is undiminished,' says one who has known her for many years. 'It's her method of self-preservation.'

But if Cherie had become more sanguine about attacks on her, particularly by the press, she had lost none of her propensity to anger when she believed the media was targeting her children as a way of scoring points. She was furious when it was leaked that Euan had taken a two-month work experience job in Paris bankrolled by France's richest man. During his secondment to the Louis Vuitton Moët Hennessy group, it was reported that the prime minister's son was provided with the use of a £2 million apartment in the smart avenue Montaigne, plus salary, bodyguards and a chauffeur-driven black Mercedes. In all the package was worth upwards of £40,000. Almost inevitably the Blairs were accused of exploiting their position to feather the nests of their brood, particularly as it transpired the company's fifty-six-year-old chairman Bernard Arnault had been a guest of the Blairs at Chequers. During his soujorn in Paris Euan, it seemed, had displayed a taste for the sort of high living more associated with his parents, dining at some of the city's most exclusive restaurants, including the ultra-fashionable and expensive L'Avenue, where he was seen enjoying breakfast, lunch and dinner. He was also pictured sitting in the front row of a Christian Dior fashion show with M Arnault's niece Stéphanie.

Aside from the charges of cronyism, Cherie was also angered by the publication of reports, originating in France, about Euan's trips to a lap dancing club called Le Hustler, situated close to the Champs-Elysées and part of porn baron Larry Flynt's empire. During his visit on Remembrance Sunday Euan was said to have stayed at the club until 2 a.m. in the company of two burly French minders as they watched a succession of girls undress. Other guests at the club claimed his party could be heard talking loudly in English about the 'quality' of the girls on display. The incident was yet another warning to the Blairs that they could not expect to use their celebrity to open doors with impunity. The goatee-bearded Euan had indeed posed for the paparazzi as he snagged his front-row seat at the fashion show. Sources at Dior also confirm that his attendance was viewed as such good PR for the firm that its press office tipped off photographers that the son of the British prime minister would be present.

*

On 5 May 2006 the prime minister carried out the most brutal cabinet purge of his premiership. In the face of growing demands for him to step down, he sought to circle the wagons. Into key positions in government came his most loyal lieutenants; he needed all the protection he could get. That evening, slumped in the back of his official car as he was driven to Chequers, he played absent-mindedly with a rather shabby-looking red thread that for the past ten days he had worn around his right wrist. The string bracelet, a Hindu *nada chedi*, had been given to him during a visit to a temple in Neasden, north London the previous week. The charm, he was told, would ward off harm and negativity. Mr Blair had decided it was worth a go.

Yet another 'worst week' had begun with graphic and tawdry descriptions of John Prescott's illicit sex with his diary secretary Tracey Temple. Prescott had put in a very rare appearance at the Number Eleven flat to break the news to the PM that his extra-marital dalliance was about to be splashed over the pages of the *Daily Mirror*. Blair reacted with fury, launching a high decibel rant at his deputy for close to an hour in his study. The same week also saw Home Secretary Charles Clarke's credibility destroyed by a scandal over the release from British jails into the community of foreign criminals who should have faced deportation, and ended with Labour's worst drubbing at the ballot box since the dark days of Michael Foot in 1983. Although the results fell short of the meltdown that some had predicted, Labour lost more than 300 seats in the local elections, mainly to David Cameron's Tories. Blair was determined to seize back the news agenda, which had been dominated in previous weeks by revelations that rich benefactors of the party had been promised honours in return for providing Labour with large loans. Over a Chinese takeaway in Downing Street as the results came in he finalised plans for his biggest ministerial shake-up yet. Clarke was to be sacked; Jack Straw, seen to be cosying up to Gordon Brown, paid the price by being demoted from the Foreign Office to leader of the House and key supporters were promoted. The fiercely loyal John Reid was moved from defence to the Home Office, whilst arch-Blairite Hazel Blears was promoted to party chair.

The reshuffle was designed to send out a stark message to the party – and Mr Brown – that the PM was in no mood to listen to the clamour for him to make an early exit. But this was a decision an increasing number of Labour backbenchers wanted to take out of his hands. As Brown toured the TV studios that weekend and Blair contemplated his next move amid the splendour of his country retreat, a letter calling for him to announce a timetable for his departure, said to have the support of up to seventy Labour MPs, was leaked to the *Sunday Telegraph*. At the same time a poll of 104 Labour backbenchers, conducted by Radio 4's *The World This Weekend*, found that half of them thought Mr Blair should stand down within a year. Number Ten took the unusual step of reacting to the speculation, Dave Hill sending a desperate round robin text to political journalists warning that the unrest was a plot to 'unseat the PM and reverse the Blairite reforms'. For his part the cautious Brown stuck to his latest buzzword, 'renewal', and while appealing for party unity, reissued his call for a 'stable and orderly' transition of power. Meanwhile, senior ex-ministers, including former Education Secretary Estelle Morris, joined the calls from the usual suspects on the left demanding a timetable for Blair's departure.

That weekend, with Brown's supporters sensing blood, Blair's survival instinct kicked in. Reinvigorated by the thought of the fight ahead, those who saw him that weekend were in no doubt that the last thing on his mind was submitting to the calls for his head, no matter how vocal his detractors in the party and the country had become.

Cherie, who had left her husband behind so she could attend a children's charity event in Qatar, was also adamant that Brown should not be granted his wish to lead the party and government. The very idea was, say those close to her, 'simply repellent'. The animosity between the two camps had, perhaps unsurprisingly, infected the relationship between Mrs Blair and Brown's wife Sarah. Though equally ambitious for their respective partners, they are very different women. Mrs Brown, like her husband, found Cherie's love of freebies and her cashing in distasteful and embarrassing. Privately, Sarah is said to have described Cherie as an 'oddball'. For her part, Cherie's friends mocked the sensible clothes and old banger Mrs Brown was regularly to be seen driving around Westminster. Members of Cherie's court also delighted in repeating a baseless rumour that the dour chancellor had discouraged his wife from wearing make-up. The two women could barely stand the sight of each other.

Mrs Blair had let her irritation at Brown's manoeuvring get the better of her eight months earlier at the party conference in Brighton. She was livid with his announcement that he would tour the country listening to voters over the coming twelve months – a move seen by the Blairs as an attempt to bounce them out of Number Ten within the year. As Brown's supporters like former Treasury minister Geoffrey Robinson called for the new leader to be given at least two years in the job before an election, Cherie toured the conference stalls wearing a badge which proudly boasted 'I love TB'. When a photographer chanced his arm and asked the prime minister's wife if she would miss life as first lady, Cherie responded with all the offhand condescension of the diva she had so patently become. 'Darling, that is a very long way in the future,' she replied airily. 'It is too far ahead for me to even think about.' Her response led one senior Brown ally to comment it had 'more than a hint of Imelda Marcos about it, just as the protesters are storming the barricades'. Hardly surprising then that the two teams set up rival bases, with the Blairs at the Grand Hotel and Brown, Sarah and his inner sanctum ensconced at the Metropole.

Mr Blair left his party in no doubt that he intended to see through his premiership. During his conference speech he spoke of how opportunities to improve public services had been wasted. 'Every time I've introduced a reform in government, I wish in retrospect that I had gone further,' he told the party faithful. Blair had known for some time his decision to announce he would not stand for a fourth term had been a huge mistake. Ever since, his every move had been overshadowed by the question of when he would step aside for Mr Brown. Mr Blair finally admitted his blunder in public during a bad-tempered visit to Australia at the end of March 2006. The trip had been a thoroughly unpleasant experience for the Blairs and their party. The prime minister, continually questioned by journalists about when he would announce his departure, was stressed and irritable. Cherie was tetchy and tired. She embarrassed her husband again when, jet-lagged after the long flight from London, she yawned openly during the interminable closing ceremony of the Commonwealth Games in Melbourne. Both of the Blairs were short-tempered with their staff. They had become, after nine years of staying in the finest hotels of the world, increasingly used to letting others clear up after them. Their suites were often an utter mess, with Cherie's used tights flung haphazardly on to door handles.

Another subject on which Blair and Brown disagreed was how to handle the very real threat of David Cameron, who was elected Tory leader in December 2005. Brown favoured launching an immediate attack on the new Opposition leader to paint him not as the political new blood he appeared to be but as a seasoned Tory apparatchik who, ingloriously, had been a political adviser to former Chancellor Norman Lamont at the time of Black Wednesday in 1992. Blair's preferred option was to play the long game. His instincts told him that, in the short term at least, he was best advised to play along with Cameron's early vow to end Punch and Judy politics and wait to attack him on his policies.

Even as his government became mired in sleaze and tainted with the decay inevitable at the fag end of all long administrations, Blair remained determined that he would go on his own terms and not fall victim to the assassins on his own benches. In private he told those around him he was determined not only to see out ten years in power, but to go beyond this to the end of November 2008 so he would beat Mrs Thatcher's record as the longest-serving prime minister since 1827. The Blairs, meanwhile, began taking weekly private Catholic mass, given by a Franciscan friar in Downing Street. Those close to Mr Blair are convinced he will convert to Catholicism when he leaves office. In April Mrs Blair was granted a private audience with the new pope, Benedict XVI. A month earlier her husband had appeared on ITV1's *Parkinson* to tell the chat show host he believed he would be judged not by his party or the country over taking Britain to war with Iraq, but by God himself. As his enemies circled, it seemed increasingly likely Blair's day of reckoning would come far sooner.

So what of the central relationship in Tony Blair's life, the one with his wife? As he approached a decade in power, the burdens of his position had undoubtedly put enormous pressure on it. Cherie's lingering resentment over her husband's lack of support when she has on a number of occasions found herself at the centre of a very public maelstrom, has undoubtedly

left scars. Although the memos and briefings from Cherie continue, few in their inner circle think the relationship is as close
as it once was. This might be little more than the sort of glitch
experienced in most long-term relationships. What partnership
wouldn't suffer under similar conditions? Certainly, when his
retirement comes, be it sooner or later, they can expect the sort
of moneyed lifestyle that both of them, but particularly Cherie,
has always wanted. Mr Blair will make a fortune on the American
lecture circuit and from the publishing deals that await his final
departure from Downing Street. Meanwhile, another couple,
be it the Browns or the Camerons, will take their place in
Number Ten. In all likelihood the new leader's partner will
revert to the accepted modus operandi of prime ministerial
spouses of old: posing loyally for pictures on the arm of her
husband, smiling and keeping her mouth firmly shut. How
long, I wonder, will it be before we look back on the heady
days of that building's previous flawed incumbents and allow
ourselves a nostalgic, wistful smile?

Index